D0746449

THE POSTMODERN PRINCE

The Postmodern Prince

Critical Theory, Left Strategy,
and the Making of a New Political Subject

JOHN SANBONMATSU

 MONTHLY REVIEW PRESS *New York*

Library of Congress Cataloging-in-Publication Data

Sanbonmatsu, John.
    The postmodern prince : critical theory, left strategy,
and the making of a new political subject / John Sanbonmatsu.— 1st ed.
        p. cm.
    Includes bibliographical references and index.
    ISBN 1-58367-090-4 (pbk.) — ISBN 1-58367-089-0 (cloth)
    1. Political culture. 2. Postmodernism—Political aspects.
3. New Left—History. 4. Critical theory. 5. Socialism. 6. Liberalism.
7. Social change. 8. Social movements. I. Title.
    JA75.7.S26 2003
    320.53—DC22

                        2003018734

MONTHLY REVIEW PRESS
122 West 27th Street
New York, NY 10001
www.monthlyreview.org

10 9 8 7 6 5 4 3 2 1
Printed in Canada

CONTENTS

This book is dedicated to MAUREEN and EMMANUEL, and to the memory of ANTONIO GRAMSCI.

ACKNOWLEDGMENTS

The present work, despite its many flaws, has been in progress for over ten years. There are therefore a great many people to blame.

I would first single out members of the faculty at the University of California at Santa Cruz, who taught me most of what I know, including Peter Euben (who is to be faulted for having introduced me to Machiavelli and to political theory), Bob Connell (who schooled me in the sociology of intellectuals), and Wally Goldfrank, Jim O'Connor, and Craig Reinarman. Carl Boggs was of enormous assistance and support during my thesis writing, and I am blessed to have him as a close comrade today. Above all, I want to thank Barbara Epstein, my dissertation advisor at UCSC, my confidante and cherished friend, who coaxed me through graduate school and who supported me in countless ways, professionally and personally. As Gramsci used to say: Barbara, I embrace you.

Innumerable conversations with close friends and political comrades over the years enriched my understanding of radical politics, and so helped me to clarify the ideas that took shape in this book. I want to thank especially Erin Delaney, Laurie Prendergast, Kathy Miriam, Sam Diener, Valerie Sperling, Ronald Loeffler, Nancy Zeigler, Pat Sand, Eric Begleiter, Robin Cohen, Peter Kwiek, Matt Goodman, Victoria Johnson, Santosh George, Ike Balbus, Mary Holmquist, Sandra Bartky, Al LeTops, Charles W. Mills, Jane Glaubman, Glen Mimura, Giovanna DiChiro, Sina Saidi, Ellen Scott, Bruce and Julie Samuels, Bonnie Mann, Kristen Metz, Nancy Meyer, Mujeeb Khan, Keith Topper, Eric Klinenberg, Eddie Yuen, Miki Kashtan, and Renee Lertzman. I also thank my friends Tess Oliver, Diane DeRoo, Jessie Webb, Etta Worthington, Valerie Ross, Susie Signorini, Andrea Ayvazian, Jim O'Connell, Dirk Zastrow, Lisa Webb, Sheila Peuse, Karen and Mischa Fierer, Charla Ogaz, Maurice Stevens, and my late friend, Diane Grant, for their support. My friends in the Social Movements Research Cluster at UCSC, especially Sandra Meucci,

7

also provided me with many stimulating intellectual conversations, arguments, and delicious dinners.

I would like to thank Margaret Cerullo and Carol Bengelsdorf for introducing me to the radical tradition in political thought while I was a student at Hampshire College, and also Allan Krass and my friend Michael Klare for schooling me in critical political science. Thanks too go to my wonderful colleagues in the Humanities and Arts Department at Worcester Polytechnic Institute for their support as I completed this work, especially Patrick Quinn, Ruth Smith, Tom Shannon, Michelle Ephraim, Maribel and H. J. Manzari, Gray Tuttle, and my friend and mentor, Roger Gottlieb. Numerous undergraduate students, past and present, have enlightened me, among them Inder Khalsa, Ion Meyn, Megan Holmes, and Andrew Bianchi (to name but a few). I would also like to give special thanks and recognition to Andrew Nash, my superb editor at Monthly Review Press, for his patience, editing, and faith in this project. Andrew's numerous suggestions and corrections made this a far better work than it otherwise would have been. The remaining weaknesses in this book are my fault, not his.

During the long period it took me to conceive this project and, finally, to complete it, my partner and I were sustained emotionally, and at times financially, by extended family that included Pat and Carol Sullivan, Ruth Frank, Sylvia Schroll, Akira and Joan Loveridge- Sanbonmatsu, Victor Brudney, the late Juliet Brudney, Tim Frye, Javed Rahman, Dan Brudney, and Ellen Rosendale. Thank you, everyone. We were also supported by Jane Jordan, Cathaleen Rich, and the late Madeline Zorn. Peter Tischner pulled me through the hardest parts of my dissertation writing; I thank him especially for his wisdom and encouragement.

Finally, I wish to thank my family, to whom I owe everything, including this work: my father, Yoshiro, who continues to inspire me with his artwork, protean intellect, and love of justice; my mother, Marianne, who taught me empathy and forgiveness; my sisters, Lisa and Kira, whose love and friendship sustain me year to year, and day to day; and Donna and Barbara, newest to our family, so essential to it. Our inestimable feline companions, Madeline, Percy, Frodo, Sasha, and Alfie, infused our daily lives with love and beauty, and I wish to acknowledge the blessings they bestowed upon us in difficult times. Last but not least, I wish to thank my life partner, Maureen E. Sullivan, for a quality of comradeship and existential solace that no mere words of thanks can convey.

INTRODUCTION

When the serpent sloughs off its skin, its cry goes from one end of the world to the other, but its voice is not heard.— M I D R A S H , ca. 650–900 C .E .

Perestroika, part two of Tony Kushner's epic utopian play *Angels in America*, begins with a speech by Aleksii Antediluvianovich Prelapsarionov, billed as "the World's Oldest Living Bolshevik," before the Hall of Deputies in the Kremlin in 1986, a few short years before the fall of the Berlin Wall. Prelapsarionov, an "antediluvian" socialist present at the socialist Genesis, when Marx's face moved upon the surface of the waters and the "seed words" of revolution sprouted and took root, chides those among his comrades who would abandon the security of a Beautiful Theory that could unite all through a common Word. "If the snake sheds his skin before a new skin is ready," he intones, "naked will he be in the world, prey to the forces of chaos. Without his skin he will be dismantled, lose coherence, and die."[1]

In a sense, the question posed in this work is the one left hanging in the air at the end of Prelapsarionov's speech: Can the now-dispersed forces of emancipation, having been forced by history to abandon the "skin" of socialism and the International, the Party, discover or invent a *new* form? A way to unite the many dispersed, confused, largely reactive elements struggling to right injustice and bring about a new civilization—before it is too late? And it is fast becoming too late.

World systems theorists have argued that the singular economic, social, political, and ecological crises of our time stem from the systemic crisis of capitalism as a whole—the unraveling of the modern world system put into place half a millennium ago. As they and other critics have pointed out, what makes resolving this crisis difficult is that one of its effects is the waning of the nation-state. At the very

9

moment when conscientious and concerted leadership is needed, that is, to grapple with pressing social problems on a global scale, the bases of liberal political authority and international concord are coming undone.[2] As the world system becomes more and more unstable, meanwhile, the ruling classes of America, the greatest hegemony in the history of the world, are attempting to exert control over these centrifugal forces, but in ways that are certain to provoke only more enmity and resistance abroad. In short, a violent, possibly epochal confrontation is growing between the American imperium and its tributary agencies, on the one hand, and the majority of humankind, on the other.[3]

Immanuel Wallerstein indeed predicts a "period of hell on earth" as the forces of reaction forcibly resist the initiatives of those striving for radical social change:

> We shall not witness a simple, laid-back political debate. It will be a global struggle, conducted on a life-and-death level. For we are talking about laying the bases for the historical system of the next five hundred years. And we are debating whether we want to have simply one more kind of historical system in which privilege prevails and democracy and equality are minimized, or whether we want to move in the opposite direction, for the first time in the known history of humanity.[4]

Wallerstein argues that what is at stake in this political struggle is nothing less than the terms of the global order likely to emerge at the end of what promises to be a period of upheaval and violence, the shape of a new social compact that might replace the older order wrought by European colonialism. Paradoxically, despite the strength of those who wish to prop up, indefinitely, the present order, the "chaotic situation is . . . that which is most sensitive to deliberate human intervention. It is during periods of chaos, as opposed to periods of relative order . . . that human intervention makes a significant difference."[5] It is possible, in other words, that a disciplined and focused transnational social movement, or series of movements, could play a significant role in shaping the order to come, possibly even imposing its own will on the failing status quo. What is needed, Wallerstein suggests, is "a substantive alternative to offer that is a collective creation" in place of the old system.[6]

The question is, who will pose such an alternative? Surely not the scattered forces of the powerless who, dispersed, lacking strategy or direction, are in a poor position even to preserve the democratic gains of the last two centuries, to say nothing of intervening forcefully in the global crisis in an imaginative way to lay the foundation for a new civilizational order. Despite the deepening legitimation crisis of the liberal state, forced between the Charybdis of neoliberal reform and the Scylla of rising social discontent, it is the right, not the left, with its revanchist "war of position" to preserve traditional patriarchal values and race hierarchies, and its heavy dreams of a seamless corporate world order immune to dissent, that seems to have capitalized on growing conditions of crisis. If anything, the disjuncture between the vast historical challenge before us and the ad hoc and confused response mounted by movements on the left appears to be widening. Innumerable small groups struggle, valiantly, to protect forests and estuaries from corporate pillage, or to end male violence against women, or to provide shelter or food or medical care to the billions of human beings left behind by neoliberal capitalism. Yet the sum of the disparate parts is far less than we might hope.

Observing the strivings of nations and peoples toward recognition, Hegel observed: "In world history, only those peoples that form states can come to our notice."7 Today, similarly, we might conclude that without a perceptible form or shape, existing social movements have little reality for the majority of human beings. To the extent we can still speak meaningfully of a global "left" at all, it is *gestaltlos*—"without form." But without a "body" through which to appear in the temporal world, movements are doomed to roam the earth unperceived—like spirits of the dispossessed whose rumored appearances, mysterious and fleeting, occasionally startle the living but have no effect on the course of human events.

It was not always thus. For over a century, socialism provided a shape or form for much of the world left. The power of socialism lay in its utopian imaginary, which tapped into the ancient religious vision of recuperation of the unity of humankind that had been lost at Babel. "Socialism is not merely the labor question," the narrator of *The Brothers Karamazov* observed, "it is above all things the atheistic question, the question of the form taken by atheism today, the question of the tower of Babel built without God, not to mount to Heaven from earth but to set up Heaven on earth."8 Socialism took up this question, and provided, for a time, a convincing answer to it.

The story of Babel, one of the oldest archetypes in civilization, speaks to our penchant as a species for disunity, conflict, and misunderstanding. In Genesis it is said that after the Flood, the earth was said to be of one language, one speech. All nations gathered to build a single tower of humanity, "a city and a tower, whose top may reach unto heaven." At the work site, they decided to give themselves a name, lest they "be scattered abroad upon the face of the whole earth." But God, seeing this, was displeased. "Behold, the people is one, and they have all one language . . . and now nothing will be restrained from them, which they have imagined to do." He descends to "confound their languages, that they may not understand one another's speech." Unable to understand one another, the people scatter "upon the face of all the earth." The moral of the Babel story is that unity cannot be won on this earth through human effort, that we must not imagine that we can invent whatever we can conceive in our minds. If we dream that we are capable of creation, our hubris will destroy us. Better, in short, to think locally (or tribally), not globally.

Yet we would not be human if we did not continue to rebel: the utopian image of universal harmony on earth was preserved by later generations. Ancient Jewish mystics held that the Word of God (the divine logos) was originally One. In the beginning, there was no distinction between words and things. The tragedy of human existence could be traced back to this sundering of signs from their divine essences, which has been the cause both of our alienation from God and of the perpetual conflict among the nations of humanity. The Gnostics and Kabbalists later studied the apocrypha and other obscure revealed texts in hopes of discovering the esoteric clues by which humankind could be led back to the *Ursprache*, the one, pure speech. "The stakes were very high," George Steiner observes. "If man could break down the prison walls of scattered and polluted speech [the rubble of the smashed tower], he would again have access to the penetralia of reality. He would know the truth as he spoke it. Moreover, his alienation from other peoples, his ostracism into gibberish and ambiguity, would be over."9

Christianity and, later, Islam, took up the ancient dream of a world made whole and made it the basis of their dreams of universal justice. Later still, the Enlightenment secularized the Abrahamic longing for a rebuilt Babel. In the dreams of modern reason, from the Encyclopedists and Jacobins in the eighteenth century to the socialists and anarchists of the nineteenth and twentieth, the Tower of Babel would be rebuilt, the whole restored. From the bricks and mortar of what is, human beings would construct a unified structure capable of bridging the vast difference to what ought to be: the New Jerusalem, a heavenly city on

earth. When Feuerbach wrote of the abolition of religion as the starting point of the human race, he meant that by recognizing ourselves as
the source of what we call the divine—another name for love—we might
become masters of our own self-making. Marx agreed with Feuerbach
that God was a projection of human essence, and he followed Feuerbach in holding that only an embodied, sensuous practice could lead to
the externalization of our essence as universal consciousness.[10] The
issue on which he parted company with Feuerbach concerned the kind
of practice that would lead to world transformation.

Marx's thought represented the quest for a common language of
politics, able to unite the scattered forces of the working class and create the basis for a common project of historical construction or *poeisis*.
Though capitalism had despoiled nature and broken the minds and
bodies of countless human beings, Marx believed that it was also a revolutionary force, unleashing enormous productive powers and demol-
ishing national, cultural, and other kinds of differences—creating, in
effect, the basis for a common, universal culture, a new "world-historical being." After a socialist revolution, born in the womb of history,
each would share equally in the fruits of nature, and each would fulfill
his or her own creative potential in harmony with a universal species
interest. The world would be as one, and human beings would "again"
share a common language and tongue. "The name of Esperanto has in
it, undisguised, the root for an ancient and compelling *hope*," Steiner
observes.[11] Socialism would be an Esperanto, a common language to
unite the many "nations" of the working classes, whose erstwhile differences were differences only in appearance, not in essence.

But by the end of the twentieth century, Babel had largely been abandoned. After decades of historical defeats, socialism suddenly dispersed,
like a mirage of history, as much a victim of its own burdensome dreams
as of its powerful enemies (and there were many). A whole way of living
and imagining politics seemed to have died, and with it, the notion of a
form for sustaining critical practice and carrying collective dreams of an
earthly utopia. Globalization encouraged a broad retreat from politics
and from the public sphere, a retreat into localist "enclaves."[12]

Some activists did try to reinvigorate the public sphere with a vision
of participatory democracy and universal human rights, and still others spoke urgently of the need to create a coherent, unified movement
to contain and represent the aspirations of *all* movements. Without

such a unified approach, Lydia Sargent argued, the separate movements of the left would never "exist as a collective project in anyone's
mind." Rather than "growing interactively, each benefiting from the
actions of the rest," today's scattered movements "exist at best side by
side, often surprisingly competitively. . . . Without organization and
strategy, there is nothing to work for and no way to evaluate what we've
done."[13] Similar sentiments were expressed by other movement leaders in a variety of progressive media and grassroots journals in the
United States throughout the 1980s and 90s, e.g., by leading figures in
the peace movement, in the gay and lesbian movement, among leading
feminists, environmentalists, and people of color.[14]

Yet within academic critical theory, a strong theoretical bias had
developed that was positively allergic to any discussion of the need for a
new *synthesis* of theory and practice. Postmodernists, in particular, had
taken to advocating not unity but rather the deconstruction of the *discourse* of unity, and not solidarity but "difference." Thus the joint statement issued by two well-known Western European intellectuals in 1987:

> The goal [of praxis] is not to arrive at a rough consensus on a few general statements
> covering the ensemble of current problems, but, on the contrary, to favor what we
> call a *culture of dissensus* that strives for a deepening of individual positions and a
> resingularization of individuals and human groups. What folly to claim that
> everyone—immigrants, feminists, rockers, regionalists, pacifists, ecologists, and
> hackers—should agree on a same vision of things! We should not be aiming for a
> programmatic agreement that erases their differences.[15]

Both authors of this declaration initially came to the world's attention
in connection with the extraordinary events in Paris in the month of
May 1968—Daniel Cohn-Bendit (Danny the Red) was the self-styled "anti-
Jacobin" who became the public face of the student revolt; Gilles
Deleuze, the late French philosopher, was an enthusiast of that same
revolt. Indeed, the provenance of the bias against unity in theory today
can be traced here, to the 1960s period. It was then that a "New Left"
movement came forward to challenge received wisdoms of Marxist
orthodoxy, setting in motion a sea change in the way intellectuals in
the West conceived of collective action.

The first half of the present work examines the intellectual, cultural, and economic factors that led eventually to a shift in the dominant

religious trope of Western praxis, a shift from the socialist dream of rebuilding Babel to the new, poststructuralist image of "speaking in tongues"—speaking in the expressive tongues of difference. In the first two chapters, I show how the valuation of "ecstatic" speech as the ultimate horizon of political practice can be traced back to the "structure of feeling" of the Sixties period. In a close reading of a public debate between two of the icons of the youth movement, Herbert Marcuse and Norman O. Brown, I show how the crucial debate among New Leftists about the relative value of strategy versus aesthetic expression was won by the expressivists, and how this expressivist bias eventually become a "common sense" in leading arenas of critical social thought.

Then, in chapter 3, I show how the decline of social movements and a widening gap between theory and practice left critical theory vulnerable to changes in the political economy of knowledge production in the 1980s and 1990s (the rationalization of the university). The "baroque" or superficial formal density of postmodernist texts, I suggest, represents the extension of *commodity* logics into the previously protected sphere of critical thought. I relate the emergence of "baroque" postmodernist discourse to Marx and Engels's critique of idealism in *The German Ideology* in chapter 4, arguing that the refusal of subjective experience as the basis of theoretical knowledge by French structuralists has led to the mystification of actual social relations in contemporary works like Hardt and Negri's *Empire*.

Chapter 5, "The Prince and the Archaeologist," forms a bridge between these early chapters and the rest of this work that attempts to reconstruct a basis for a theory of praxis by expanding Gramsci's strategic phenomenology of political action, leadership, and form. The Prince of this chapter, then, is Gramsci, who offered a theory of how to realize a collective socialist *virtù* and "will" in the political realm. The Archaeologist, meanwhile, is Michel Foucault—the poststructuralist critic whose broad attack on all varieties of strategic political thought, I argue, has done the most damage to the radical tradition.

Chapters 6 and 7 attempt to reclaim Gramsci's specific theory of a new form, what he called the "Modern Prince," for the present. The title of the present work, *The Postmodern Prince*, in fact echoes two earlier "princes" in modern political thought. The first is of course Machiavelli's *The Prince*, the early-sixteenth-century manual for princes on how to achieve and maintain political power. The *Prince* was the first recognizably "realist" work in Western political thought. Its appearance scandalized generations of pious readers for its unapologetic celebration of power and its seeming indifference to moral convention. Nearly five centuries later, the work retains some of its original air of controversy: scholars still quarrel over whether Machiavelli's chief motivation in writing *The Prince* was really to educate princes and rulers themselves, or whether he wanted rather to educate *il popolo*, the people, about the ruthless nature of princes. Centuries after Machiavelli's death, another Italian thinker would apply Machiavelli's principles to the problem of socialist revolution.

An obscure work, *The Modern Prince*, was written by a Marxist revolutionary, politician, and journalist named Antonio Gramsci. Imprisoned for his anti-fascist and socialist political activities in Italy in the 1920s, Gramsci spent the last decade of his life languishing in prison, where his active life ended in 1937, aged only forty-six. While in prison, Gramsci worked on what was to become his lasting legacy to the radical tradition, the *Notebooks*. It is in the *Notebooks*, a fascinating collection of Gramsci's fragmentary observations on politics, intellectuals, Marxism, Italian history, and literature, that we find the scattered "Notes on Machiavelli," the basis of a monograph he had hoped to publish on "the Modern Prince." Gramsci in fact modeled his "Modern Prince" on *The Prince*: Machiavelli's book had such chapters as, "On Avoiding Being Despised and Hated," "On Mixed Principalities," or "On the Various Kinds of Troops and Mercenary Soliders"; Gramsci's *Note sul Machiavelli* similarly isolated elements of socialist praxis under such subheadings as "Analysis of Situations," "Elements of Politics," "The Theorem of Fixed Proportions," "Number and Quality in Representative Systems of Government," "Spontaneity and Conscious Leadership," etc.

In many ways the most coherent and most theoretically original of his works, *The Modern Prince* synthesized Machiavelli's theory of a politics without illusions with Marx's theory of history. In much the same way that Machiavelli had sought to outline a politics adequate to the task of establishing a new kind of social and political order at a moment of systemic chaos and disarray—the disintegration of the feudal order—Gramsci theorized the cultivation of a "collective subject" adequate to the conditions of systemic crisis in interbellum Europe. As Benedetto Fontana observes:

> The central importance of Machiavelli for Gramsci lies in the former's profound
> sense that all traditional and accepted forms of political activity and social relations
> are disintegrating, and in the consequent search for a new and ever-elusive *topos*
> upon which to reconstitute a meaningful cultural and political order. It is this jux-
> taposition of disintegrating sociopolitical structures and institutions, and of an
> emerging "mass" or people as a new and powerful force in history, that forms the
> organizing center of the theoretical, ideological, and sociopolitical struggles of
> modern society in general.[16]

For Gramsci, as for Machiavelli, the question of unity, of how to construct a collective will, capable of leading society, was paramount. The socialist movement would have to assume form as a "modern" prince if it hoped to win the consent of the working class, and its allied classes, in leading them in the construction of a new democratic order. "The modern prince, the myth- prince," Gramsci wrote, "cannot be a real person, a concrete individual. It can only be an organism, a complex element of society in which a collective will, which has already been recognised and has to some extent asserted itself in action, begins to take concrete form."[17]

Eventually, building a political and cultural program in dialectical conversation with the people, the modern prince would gather around itself, irresistibly, the psychic and social energies of society, until its values had replaced those of the prevailing order.

In the same vein, the "postmodern prince," similarly, is the name of the new collective subject which must gather up the myriad dispersed movements of oppositional practice and culture in the *form* of a single movement whose outward expansion establishes a genuinely democratic and ethical human culture. Only in cohering into a unified identity and worldview can the dispersed remnants of the left place themselves in a position, at least potentially, to respond meaningfully to the legitimation crisis of the state and the colonization of the lifeworld by the commodity. To give this form the name of the postmodern prince is to signal that the condition of postmodernity does not require an abandonment of the struggle for such a unified identity. Rather, we must theorize and build a "concrete form" of our own, one that would be strategically adequate to our own historical condition.

My use of the term *postmodern* to describe this new prince, hence, is not to be mistaken to signal an affinity between my construction and a *postmodernist* or poststructuralist sensibility, only to describe the

transitional nature of our period.[18] The convergence of several overlap-
ping systemic crises—the breakdown of an array of institutional, cultural, semiotic, communal, and ecological systems associated with the
modern epoch—has led to the disintegration and recomposition of the
traditional basis for authority, cultural reproduction, and hence our
praxis. In David Harvey's characterization, our newly fragmented and
compressed experience of time and space—a "condition of postmodernity"— results from fundamental changes in the economic and symbolic
organization of global capitalism from the early 1970s to the present,
linked to the shift to a post-Fordist regime of capital accumulation—i.e.,
to transnational production, fragmented or "batch" production, and the
global integration of finance capital.[19] As a result of these transformations, the range of social experiences and cultural contradictions we
identify with "the postmodern" are recognizably different from those
long associated with European modernity. If modernity was long associated with, among other things, the rise of the European nation-state system, the notion of history as the expressive site of the unfolding of
reason, colonization, and the emergence of a racially homogenous world
elite, postmodernity might be said to consist of the legitimation crisis of
the liberal nation-state, the destruction of local place, technological dis-
tention, decline of Europe as the "center" or core of world economy and
culture, and the emergence and proliferation of counternarratives based
in the experiences of subalterns—among other things.

My use of the term "postmodern prince" also differs from Stephen
Gill's use of that term. Gill similarly urges the development, also after
Gramsci and Machiavelli, of a theory of a postmodern prince on the
basis of existing tendencies in collective practice. Gill argues that environmentalists, labor rights advocates, civil rights activists, and others
in the anti-globalization movement seem to be converging toward a
latent unity to challenge the "rational" structure of the neoliberal capitalist order and to define a new vision of democratic economic and
social participation. These movements are tending toward a possibly
"effective political form for giving coherence to an open-ended, plural,
inclusive and flexible form of politics" based in "innovative conceptions of social justice and solidarity, of social possibility, of knowledge,
emancipation and freedom."[20] In the "new strategic context" or *fortuna*
provided by the neoliberal global economy, Gill writes, the "postmodern prince" emerges as the sign of a corresponding *virtù* to challenge

the system—i.e., the nascent form of "new, ethical, and democratic political institutions and forms of practice."[21]

Much of this I agree with. However, I am less confident than Gill on that scattered and differentiated movements can be said to have a "form" in any meaningful sense, and more in favor of a practice that leads to the coalescence of the "different" movements. Socialists, anarchists, and academic critics alike have tended toward an "optimism of the intellect" in their assessments of the anti-globalization movement—at once overstating its accomplishments and underappreciating the degree to which these diverse movements, lacking a coherent ideology and shared strategic outlook, are unlikely to pose a significant threat to capitalism and other systems of domination and inequality. The result is that theory once again lags behind practice. Critics fail to perceive what is most extraordinary about contemporary praxis, which is not difference but a felt need for unity, while practice, unaware of its own historical overdeterminations and contradictions, stumbles courageously but blindly through the dust storms of current events. But the challenge to contemporary theory is not merely to comprehend *analytically* the movements of the present, but to identify the deepest needs and desires that drive them, and to help them flower. Theory must, in a sense, water the germinal truths buried in the loam of practice.

Thus, while I agree with Gill that one of the material and historical bases of the postmodern prince is the anti-globalization movement, then, I do not think that such a prince either can or should be conflated with that movement. As I argue in chapters 6 and 7, the *totality* of claims made by contemporary movements for liberation goes beyond a critique of global capitalism, per se, to pose a deeper challenge to existing human civilization. Moreover, while the emergence of a postmodern prince is importantly related to conditions and trends in the capitalist economy, its emergence cannot be predicated on the existence of macrostructural contradictions alone; it must find its basis in the psychic and material life needs of animal existence. While the contradictions of capitalism generate points of friction and opposition, counter-identities and counter-discourses, the "resistance identities" that emerge can take any of a variety of forms, not all of them progressive. It is therefore of utmost importance that we specify the *normative* as well as ontological bases of the unity of the postmodern prince. To this end, I conclude with a sketch of what I call *metahumanism*, a general ontology and ethics to serve as the philosophical basis of the unity and *telos* of the postmodern prince. Metahumanism is the life-philosophy through which the postmodern prince would strive to achieve what Gramsci called "the realization of a superior, total form of modern civilization."[22]

1 Romancing the Left

Fascism sees its salvation in giving [the] masses not their right,
but instead a chance to express themselves. The masses have a right
to change property relations; Fascism seeks to give them
an expression while preserving property. —WALTER BENJAMIN

Let us begin by returning to that key moment in our recent past when Marxist socialism came into crisis and a new "common sense" about the proper means and ends of practice began to take shape in radical political thought. The New Left and the counterculture movements of the 1960s and early 1970s represented a passionate, deeply romantic cry against the alienation, hypocrisy, and violence of modern technocratic society—in short, a rebellion against modernity itself.

What we now simply call "the Sixties" represented an imaginative cultural and political rebellion against systematic and deeply entrenched structures of power. The advent of the New Left, Black Power, and antiwar movements represented a visceral impulse to tear down the remaining structures of the colonial world system, capitalism, and bourgeois propriety. The claims of the New Left were as much cultural and existential as political. This was indeed, as Herbert Marcuse called it, a "great refusal" of the technocratic rationalization and domination of the lifeworld.

But it was also, at least initially, a refusal of the verities of Marxism. For several generations of workers and intellectuals who hoped to change the world, Marxism had the appearance of a *paradigm* in Thomas Kuhn's sense of that word. Sheldon Wolin rightly describes Marxism as "one of the most extraordinary paradigms in the history of Western

political thought."[1] Although there were other important forms of political practice, feminism and anarchism among them, Marxism remained
for many years *primus inter pares* almost everywhere that oppositional
movements and critical philosophies flourished. No other theory or
practice offered such tools for making revolution, for grasping the features of real social relations, and none provided such a compelling language of social critique and collective action, or seemed to proffer such a
promising vision of hope for the oppressed.

But to many observers, the experimental social movements of the
1960s seemed to forge a whole new form of theory and practice. Writing in 1971, Massimo Teodori listed five core themes at the heart of this
new "political-organizational praxis."[2] First, the New Left emphasized a
"moral revolt" against society, a revolt rooted in individual self-expression. Second, it encompassed a wider and deeper critique than Marxism, seeming to take into detailed account the entire cultural and
psychic fabric of society. Third, it eschewed more traditional spheres of
political participation, emphasizing instead the tactics of direct action.
Fourth, its adherents generally affirmed a commitment to grassroots
or "participatory" democracy. Finally, the movement was committed to
the general "decentralization and multiplicity of structures and
actions."[3] This latter element was perhaps the most striking point of
departure between Old Left and New.

While Teodori was in broad sympathy with the movement, he wor-
ried that its utopian vitality was not yet translating into an effective
politics. The New Left had thus far failed "to resolve the problem of the
general strategy the new forces are to follow." This was "not a minor
problem, and the American New Left has not yet solved it."[4] What the
New Left lacked was a "new theoretical synthesis," one capable of providing "an analysis of the structures of American society, a vision of
future society, and the ways and means of bringing about the transformation which will lead from one to another." Teodori concluded:

> The New Left is not . . . lacking in ideals, partial analyses, and proposals for a
> method of political action, [but] rather a unifying frame of reference, the priorities
> for the various points of struggle, and the internal consciousness of building a polit-
> ical force as an alternative to the existing order. Many attempts have been made to
> fulfill this need for theoretical reflection on the direction the political struggle
> must take, but so far none of them is comprehensive enough to be considered the

theory of the New Left. The process of building a theory is historical. . . . It will probably be a long process, requiring the contribution of at least one generation, and
strictly bound to the praxis of the struggles that take place now and in the future.
A few signs, although they are still very weak, can already be seen.[5]

But such a synthesis never came. There was to be no "unifying frame of
reference" to help prioritize action, nor to lend the New Left's "partial
analyses" a greater coherence and effectiveness. Nor was there to be a
general strategy. Instead, over the next few years, the New Left and civil
rights movements—politically isolated and strained internally by ideological and social contradictions—shattered into a dozen competing
factions, movements, and identities. Yet the Sixties had nonetheless
effected a shift in tone or "style" in Western praxis, one that decisively
privileged emotive and aesthetic expression of an inner, "radical"
nature over considerations of strategy, theoretical coherence, or the
patient construction of a counter-hegemonic movement. In subsequent
decades, the "structure of feeling" of the Sixties—its characteristic
elements of impulse, restraint, and tone—later settled in the practices
of the social movements and became sediment in the "baroque" discourses of the academic intelligentsia.

A ROMANTIC STRUCTURE OF FEELING

That the Sixties indeed had a particular structure of feeling will be self-
evident to anyone who lived through them—a structure that set certain
limits on experience, action, and modes of inquiry.[6] Participants and
critics at the time observed that what seemed to matter more than
developing a vision of the future, effective forms of action, political
strategy, theoretical coherence, or even a majoritarian politics, was the
ur-moment of political and cultural expression. "This was a mood," Nigel
Young later observed, "militating against academic pomposity or theoretical prolixity; regarding detached analysis with skepticism, prefer-
ring participation and experiential recollection; trusting the
spontaneous and expressive as against the calculated and measured.
The 1960s were a time, not for 'reflection,' but for 'evocation.'"[7]

Charles Taylor uses expressivism (after Isaiah Berlin's similar "expres-
sionism") to describe the sea change in European civilization at the end
of the eighteenth century with the advent of Romanticism as a literary,

cultural, and political movement. Romanticism was in many ways the West's *cri de coeur* against its own project of modernity and industrialization. Holbach and Helvetius had portrayed "Man" as a rational, self-interested subject—and manipulable object. This rationalist view sharply separated culture and nature, subject and object, thought and feeling, and so on. Against this scientistic view which tended to view the human subject as simply another object in the universe, the outcome of mechanical, natural laws, Kant had developed a philosophy that would rescue the subject by restoring to it an unconditional or absolute freedom. The freedom of the subject owed to its capacity for reason and self-autonomy—its ability to act in accordance with truth, independently of nature, inclination, and desire. With the Romantics, however, the nature of the self was recast: first, as a feeling self, and second, as the source or originating font of knowledge and values. The German Romantics sought to rescue feeling from the tyranny of reason. The Romantics emphasized human existence as "a unity rather analogous to that of a work of art, where every part or aspect only found its proper meaning in relation to all the others. Human life unfolded from some central core."[8] Against the pre-Enlightenment view, which placed value in the harmony between our intentions and our actions in the world, but also in contradistinction to Kant's emphasis on the unity of individual will and an absolute moral law, the Romantics tied action to inner nature. They saw the subject's inner nature as ontologically prior, the source of all value. Sentiment, rather than reason, was the surer guide to the self.

The premodern, Aristotelean outlook had ascribed virtue to our acts in the world, by linking thought and deed. But the Romantics seated virtue in the subject's own feelings about the world.[9] "Attend to yourself," Fichte wrote in *The Science of Knowledge*. "Turn your attention away from everything that surrounds you and toward your inner life; this is the first demand that philosophy makes of its disciple. Our concern is not with anything that lies outside you, but only you yourself."[10]

But it was not enough to be in touch with one's inner truth and experiences: one must also express that nature. Only through expressing our inner nature could we become, could we define ourselves. Since "our access to nature is through an inner voice or impulse," as Taylor puts it, "we can only fully know this nature through articulating what we find within us."[11] Human beings "reached their highest fulfillment in expressive activity."[12]

Taylor describes a conflict between instrumental reason, on one side, and a more holistic, spiritual conception of life, on the other—a tension between, say, Francis Bacon's scientism and William Blake's antinomianism. And he suggests that this conflict has periodically surfaced in the West over the last century, most recently in the counterculture of the 1960s and 1970s. The counterculture, Taylor suggests, shows that people still "live by . . . forms of Romantic expressivism." For the "goals which inspired the revolt of May 1968 in Paris were closer to Schiller than to any other twentieth-century writer. The picture of a restored harmony within the person and between people, as a result of *décloisonnement*, the breaking down of barriers between art and life, work and love, class and class, and the image of this harmony as a fuller freedom: all this fits well within the original Romantic aspirations."[13]

As in the Romantic period, the political and cultural expressions of the movements of the Sixties were lit with a great inner warmth and passion. Feeling was seen as superior to reason, and praxis was viewed in emotive and often aesthetic terms, as a creative and spontaneous project of *poeisis* or "making."[14] New Left leader Tom Hayden advised activists to "depend more on feel than theory," because "action produces its own evidence which theory alone can never do."[15] What mattered was "living the revolution" in the present.[16] Daniel Guerin, in his popular manual on anarchism, summed up the ethos when he approvingly cited Max Stirner's aphorism that the individual should turn inward as a source of power and inspiration: "Do not seek in self-renunciation a freedom which denies your very selves, but seek your own selves. . . . Let each of you be an all-powerful I."[17] In short, the expressivist structure of feeling was rooted in a chain of equivalence between speech, subjective inner truth, and action or praxis.

Many Sixties observers explicitly drew an analogy between the counterculture and a Romantic sensibility. On the one hand, critics of the youth generation and New Left were wont to dismiss the New Left and antiwar movements as dreamy, immature, and unrealistic. Yet sympathetic observers also noticed an affinity between what was simply called, by the late 1960s, "the Movement" and Romanticism. For example, Theodore Roszak observed in a series of essays published in 1968 that just as the earlier romantics had challenged the spiritual emptiness of early capitalist modernity, the latter-day romantics of the New Left and counterculture similarly opposed the alienation and inhumanity of

modern society—the reduction of life, experience, and nature to rationalized procedures, bureaucracy, and the quest for profit. Comparing the
writings of New Left icons Herbert Marcuse and Norman O. Brown,
Roszak noted that "we return to the mainstream of the rich German
Romantic tradition that Marx abandoned in favor of a so-called 'scientific' socialism. It is as if, with the benefit of hindsight, [Marcuse and
Brown] have been able to see that the stormy Romantic sensibility,
obsessed from first to last with madness, ecstasy and spiritual striving,
had far greater insights to yield than Marx suspected. In particular, the
tradition was to issue forth in the work of Freud and Nietzsche, the
major psychologists of the Faustian soul."[18]

Probably few would dispute the notion that by the late 1960s, an
expressivist emphasis could be seen in, say, the violence of the Weather
Underground, the theatrical politics of Abbie Hoffman and the Yippies,
or the movement's romantic identification with charismatic revolutionaries domestically and in the third world. Yet a proto-expressivist
element had arguably attended the very earliest stirrings of the New
Left, with the founding of Students for a Democratic Society (SDS) and
the Free Speech Movement. The Port Huron Statement, the document
that launched SDS, was virtually a negative image of the typical public
policy paper. In contrast to the passionless, bureaucratic prose of the
state or a Rand Corporation planning document, these were young people speaking earnestly and from the heart about their experiences
growing up in America, combining sophisticated sociological analysis
of American society with humanist references to "loneliness, estrangement, and isolation."[19] This same humanist impulse infused all the student protests throughout the world, including the fierce idealism of
the Free Speech Movement in Berkeley in 1964. Fearful of "any speech
with consequences," Savio argued, university bureaucrats acted to
"suppress the most creative impulses" of the students.[20]

Four years later, the same expressivist sentiment reappeared, but on
the other side of the Atlantic. Like the Free Speech Movement, the
explosion on the streets of Paris in May '68 grew directly out of the
deepening contradictions within the French university system and
within postwar Western political economy and culture. The sudden
and surprising explosion of social protest in the 1960s was seen on
practically all sides as a result of mass disaffection with the postwar
political, social, and cultural order: that is, with modern society as

such. In Sartre's famous interview with Daniel Cohn-Bendit, the brilliant, precocious spokesperson for the May Movement, "Danny the Red" explained that the movement's strength lay "precisely" in its "'uncontrollable' spontaneity." Cohn-Bendit and others sought to spur this spontaneity to new heights, not to channel it into programs or demands: the movement "must avoid building an organization immediately, or defining a program; that would inevitably paralyze us." The short- term goal would be to disrupt the normalcy of society through speech acts—"Liberate expression!" someone scrawled in Paris. "The movement's only chance," Cohn-Bendit told Sartre, "is the disorder that lets men speak freely, and that can result in a form of self-organization." And "now that speech has suddenly been freed in Paris, it is essential first of all that people should express themselves."[21]

The eventual failure of the May revolt to yield more than slight reforms in the system, however, soon became apparent. President Charles de Gaulle skillfully defused the situation, and before many months had passed the workers went back to work, and the students back to school, having won some reforms and freed "the imagination," but leaving the apparatus of the French state and capitalist ownership unchanged. In his analysis at the time, the sociologist Alain Touraine drily remarked: "The May Movement, after a few weeks of mass actions, had not yet succeeded in transforming political life or unleashing a social revolution. It began to consume a major part of its energy in violence or self-expression—words. Many consider this self-expression the great event of the month of May; this is not my point of view."[22]

May 1968 represented a turning point in the radical tradition. The French Communist Party opposed the youthful protestors, denounced them as "adventurist," and indeed sided with the federal authorities in calling for the restoration of order. Hence, from the point of view of the rebels in the streets of Paris, their uprising was not only against alienation, consumerism, imperialism, and technocracy, but also against the status quo in Marxist thought and practice. "The socialist 'system'. . . has now collapsed," Willener observed a year later. "The historical evolution that has taken place within socialism in the last fifteen years has brought the whole edifice toppling down in ruins."[23] As one sympathetic French academic observed at the time, the May events represented "a critique of what a revolutionary party should not be,"[24] while another remarked that in Paris, the individual "who had to be liquidated, and really was liquidated in May, was Lenin. I don't mean Lenin as a historical personage, of course, but Lenin as a model. Leninism is dead, and this may enable us to re-read Marx with different eyes."[25] The "anti-Jacobinist" Daniel Cohn-Bendit defended the essential spontaneism of the movement in his interview with Sartre, by casting the uprising as a revolt against the Leninist tradition. "What has happened in the last fortnight is to my mind a refutation of the famous theory of the 'revolutionary vanguard' as the force leading a popular movement. . . . It was more conscious theoretically and better prepared, the active minority was able to light the fuse and make the breach. But that is all. . . . We must abandon the theory of the 'leading vanguard' and replace it by a much simpler and more honest one of the active minority functioning as a permanent leaven, pushing for action without ever leading it. In fact, though no one will admit it, the Bolshevik Party did not 'lead' the Russian Revolution. It was borne along by the masses."[26] Indeed, by the 1960s, many intellectuals and young radicals throughout the developed world had concluded that an "opportunity for retooling" the dominant paradigm of critical praxis had arrived—a "Reformation," so to speak, to unseat the "Catholicism" of Marx.

As early as the 1950s, long-standing anomalies within the Marxist tradition seemed to loom larger than before; and by the late 1950s the paradigm had been pushed to a breaking point in Western theory and practice. Following the Soviet invasion of Hungary in 1956 and the Prague Spring (itself an experiment with a new form of socialism) it was clear to many European intellectuals that socialist theory desperately needed revision. At the same time, the initiative for praxis began to shift from Europe to the periphery—the third world, where the indigenous anticolonial movements for national liberation came to the fore. Even in the United States, where socialism had long since ceased to be a real influence in the national political culture, there were signs that socialist thought needed to be revisited and revised. In 1957 A. J. Muste called for a new democratic American socialism.[27] More important, the American civil rights movement had begun to demonstrate that a wholly novel form of political struggle was possible, one based not on class identity but on an ideal of racial equality.

For many, the rise of SDS and the antiwar movement in the United States seemed to bring with it the promise of a new conception of agency. In 1969, reflecting on the experience of the previous several years, Teodori observed:

The adjective "new" is . . . used to designate the contrast between the political phenomena that developed during the 1960s and the political movements of the 1930s
(which continued until 1948, the symbolic date of the traditional left's collapse)
whose forms were communist, socialist of various kinds and, to a lesser extent,
anarcho-syndicalist and whose organized expression took place essentially through
the labor movement. But what the adjective "new" designates above all is not a temporal or generational fact so much as a political tradition of the past. The emergence of a New Left position (not yet a force or an organized movement) related to
the development—more in praxis than in theory—of a series of original themes,
varying in quality, which cross the boundaries between specific projects and constitute a common nucleus of experiences between the different movements.[28]

For many activists, neither capitalists nor capitalism per se, but rather
"the system" was the main obstacle thwarting human freedom. Even
liberalism and liberal institutions were identified with a "fascist" logic.
The logical solution to the problem of the "system"—whether authoritarian socialist or technocratic liberal capitalism—was therefore that
the movement itself would "be antisystematic and antitotalist."[29] In
the United States, what united the Free Speech Movement, SNCC, SDS's
Economic Research and Action Project (ERAP), and other groups was a
skepticism toward centralized authority and any form of a party apparatus. Instead, most New Left activists championed direct democracy,
collective decision making, and spontaneous—and often theatrical—
actions. In theory, at least, participating in the New Left did not
demand adherence to any particular ideology. All beliefs, tactics, and
modes of self and group expression were welcomed. In contrast to the
"rational" strategic planning of the elites, the movement reveled in
improvised actions and the proliferation of ad hoc committees focused
on particular issues.

An ocean and continent away, meanwhile, in France, autogestion,
or autonomous self-management, became the ideal of the young rebels.
"What is their strategy?" asked Hervé Bourges rhetorically in a book of
interviews with the youthful leaders of the May revolt. "To be present
everywhere, to invent forms of action adapted to the circumstances: a
flexible formula suitable for a small number, and ensuring the success
of particular interventions."[30]

In the United States, critical philosopher Herbert Marcuse spoke of a
"libertarian socialism"—what to earlier generations of radicals would

surely have seemed an oxymoron. This libertarian socialism would be a struggle in which erotic and aesthetic dimensions of human freedom would be constitutive of practice, not deferred to a moment "after the revolution." Among other things, socialist ideals of organizational unity and strategic leadership would have to be thrown out. The "old model" of a praxis centered on "the notion of the seizure of power" would have to give way to "some kind of diffuse and dispersed disintegration of the system, in which interest, emphasis and activity is shifted to local and regional areas." Instead of a "large centralized and coordinated movement," the left should embrace "local and regional political action against specific grievances—riots, ghetto rebellions and so on."[31] As Marcuse boldly declared at a political rally, to cheers from the audience:

> As against these [traditional political] forms, what seems to be shaping up is an entirely overt organization, diffused, concentrated in small groups and around local activities, small groups which are highly flexible and autonomous.

> I want to add one thing here that may almost appear heretical—no primitive unification of strategy. The left is split! The left has always been split! Only the right, which has no ideas to fight for, is united! (Much laughter.)

> Now the strength of the New Left may well reside in precisely these small contesting and competing groups, active at many points at the same time, a kind of political guerilla force in peace or so-called peace, but, and this is, I think, the most important point, small groups, concentrated on the level of local activities, thereby foreshadowing what may in all likelihood be the basic organization of libertarian socialism, namely councils of manual and intellectual workers.[32]

As many critics observed, Andre Gorz's "autogestion" and Marcuse's call for a "libertarian socialism" had clear affinities with earlier anarchist and anarcho-syndicalist practices and theories. Paul Goodman, Albert Camus, Ignazio Silone, and other anarchist or vaguely anarchist thinkers were indeed in vogue throughout the 1960s and '70s. Slim tracts like Daniel Guerin's *Anarchism* and Regis Debray's *Revolution in the Revolution* helped popularize anarchistic and guerilla ideologies. The New Left often exhibited such qualities as anti-intellectualism, identification with the most marginalized and oppressed sectors of society, and an implicit faith in the "propaganda of the deed."[33] Authenticity— the sincerity of one's inner motivation—plus knowledge gained from personal experience became a governing ideal of behavior.

In this regard, there was one further similarity between the New Left culture and the anarchism of old: an increasingly marked indifference, as the protests unfolded, to the consequences of one's actions. Proof of one's worthiness came to be measured not in particular outcomes, but in ceaseless activity and in direct, personal involvement in the world. This distinctive sensibility emerged, however, less out of an ideological commitment to anarchist teachings than out of a Protestant, specifically antinomian, cultural norm.

FAITH VS. WORKS

The challenge posed by the social movements of the 1960s was as much spiritual as "political," a response to a perceived "failure of a particular form of civilization"—the modern, scientific-technocratic order as such.[34] The New Left represented something far beyond sheer negation or nihilism, it was the ecstatic, if disheveled, dream of a new civilization. To those caught up in it, the movement, which provided a new existential and spiritual model of self and other, seemed at times to prefigure a New Jerusalem, an "imagined community" or collectively shared identity. Many contemporary observers in fact compared the New Left, favorably or unfavorably, to the Protestant Reformation.[35] Paul Goodman argued that, like the Protestant sects of the seventeenth century, the new spiritual rebels sought "liberation from the Whore of Babylon and return to the pure faith." To the young rebels, even worse than the "imperialism, economic injustice or racism" of the "affluent societies" was their "nauseating phoniness, triviality, and wastefulness, the [kind of] cultural and moral scandal that Luther found when he went to Rome in 1510"— that is, on the eve of the first Reformation, before Luther famously nailed his ninety-five theses to the church door in 1517. The youthful leaders of the New Left rebellion thus resembled the youthful figures of the first Reformation—Luther, Müntzer, Melanchthon, Jonas, all of whom had been in their twenties. They, too, squared off against a university system inhabited by "monks" resistant to any change in the status quo:[36]

Viewed as incidents of a Reformation, as attempts by young people to purge themselves and recover lost integrity, the various movements are easily recognizable as characteristic protestant sects. . . . The dissenting seminarians of the Pacific School of Religion or of the Jewish Theological Seminary in New York . . . are Congrega-

tionalists. Shaggy hippies are not nature children, as they claim, but self-conscious
Adamites. . . . Heads are Pentecostals. Those who spindle IBM cards and throw the
dean downstairs are Iconoclasts. The critique of the Organization is . . . Jansenist.
Those who want a say in the rules and curriculum mean to deny Infant Baptism,
like Petrobrusians. . . . The support of the black revolt is desperately like Anabap-
tism, but God grant that we can do better than the Peasants' War. The statement of
Cohn-Bendit . . . that the reason to be a revolutionary is that it is the best way of life
at present, is unthinkable from either a political revolutionary or a man imbued
with primitive religious faith, but it is a hard-core self-conscious protestantism.[37]

Like the earlier sects, the New Left and counterculture had a distinctly
millenarian flavor. Its hope for a "New Age" and its occasional anti-intellectualism and skepticism toward reason brought the New Left within
the ideological orbit of antinomianism—the religious movement of the
radical English sects of the early 1600s. The very word *antinomian*, from
anti and *nomos*, meant going against the Law of Moses—i.e., developing a
New Covenant with Christ in which the individual would achieve grace
through faith, rather than in adhering to the rigid moral Law of Moses.
"Jesus was all virtue, and acted from impulse, not from rules," as
William Blake wrote.[38] The ideology of the antinomians was "anti-hegemonic" insofar as they posed a challenge to "general 'common sense' as
to what is possible and what is not, a limited horizon of moral norms
and practical probabilities . . . a structure which serves to consolidate
the existent social order, enforce its priorities, and which is itself
enforced by rewards and penalties."[39] Indeed, the explicitly political
radicalism of the antinomians posed a serious enough threat to the
established forms of authority—above all, the religious authority of the
state—that they were violently repressed after the Restoration.

Blake's denunciation of reason and scientific empiricism as "'the
Satanic principle,'"[40] his hostility to "polite" society and bourgeois
norms, and his highlighting of the virtues of "ecstatic" speech and
"faith" over and against works in the world, would reemerge in the
antinomians of the late twentieth century. Modern science had brought
the polio vaccine, but it had also brought racist eugenics and the Man-
hattan Project, yielding great destructive forces that were brutalizing
human and animal life. As Marcuse put it, the youth culture was "a
moral rebellion, against the hypocritical, aggressive values and goals,
against the blasphemous religion of this society."[41] Countercultural and

New Left elements in the United States and Western Europe but also in Eastern Europe, Japan, Mexico, and other Latin American countries, thus articulated a "Great Refusal" of the existing society. And like earlier antinomians, the new libertarian socialists viewed the state itself as the most menacing threat to freedom, as Antichrist. "The anarchist regards the State as the most deadly of the preconceptions which have blinded men through the ages," as Guerin put it.[42]

One effect of the movement's antinomianism was to privilege expression over strategy and practical outcome. Purity of action, and the demonstration or exteriorization of one's faith, became privileged over the achievement of consequences in the world. "In the new culture envisaged, and, for a time, lived," Alfred Willener, a Swiss scholar, observed at the time, "the act of creating is as important as, in fact more important than, the product that results. It is...the inversion of the instrumentalism that is to be observed in the thinking of many modern specialists...the aim here is to give preeminence to any...attempt to express creativity, independently...of the (external) objectives actually achieved."[43]

This existentialist-inflected idiom of "actionism" clearly paralleled Protestant culture in its obsession with inner faith. The nineteenth-century German Romantics drank heavily from the ecstatic and emotive strain in Protestant culture, a strain that privileged outward expressions of faith over the patient creation of "works" in the world. For Martin Luther, let us recall, inner faith counted above all else. Yet faith could only be manifested externally. True, one's external works could not change one's already predetermined fate. Yet, as Erich Fromm observed, "the very fact that [the believer] is able to make the effort is one sign of his belonging to the saved."[44] This emphasis on faith over works became insinuated into the marrow of eighteenth- and nineteenth-century Romantics. As Berlin observes, this sea change in outlook represented a sharp turn away from a concern with consequences in the external world, for once "we alone are the authors of the values, then what matters is our inner state—motive, not consequence. For we cannot guarantee consequences: they are part of the natural world, the world of cause and effect, of necessity, not of the world of freedom. . . . What matters now is motive, integrity, sincerity, fidelity in principle, purity of heart, spontaneity; not happiness or strength or wisdom or success, or natural beauty, or other natural values, which are outside the realm of moral freedom."[45]

Just as the Calvinist's ceaseless activity was seen as a token of his faith in God, so too did the counterculture activist see in her ceaseless revolt against society evidence of being among the saved. Calvin took up Luther's conception of an externally manifested faith and combined it with the spirit of capitalism. In Calvin, Luther's rejection of Catholic "works" in the world for the primacy of inner "faith"—the basis of religiosity as nothing but faith itself—was taken up in the doctrine of predestination. "Salvation or damnation are not results of anything good or bad a man does in his life, but are predetermined by God before man ever comes to life."[46] One of the consequences of this doctrine of predestination was to generate a certain anxiety and feeling of powerlessness in the Protestant subject. The attempt to escape from this anxiety and self-doubt over the purity of one's own faith leads, as Erich Fromm observed in his study of the authoritarian personality, to "development of a frantic activity and a striving to do something."[47]

> Calvinism emphasized the necessity of unceasing human effort. Man must constantly try to live according to God's word and never lapse in his effort to do so. . . . The fact that one did not tire in that unceasing effort and that one succeeded in one's moral as well as one's secular work was a more or less distinct sign of being one of the chosen ones. The irrationality of such compulsive effort is that the activity is not meant to create a desired end but serves to indicate whether or not something will occur which has been determined beforehand, independent of one's own activity or control.[48]

Since the subject could effectively do nothing to change her predestined status before God, she therefore had to sublimate all external "irrational" doubts in the worth of her actions. In this manner, action was not to be evaluated based on its actual effects in the world, but on the basis of its coincidence with an internal faith. Doubt was sublated—it "remained in the background and had to be silenced again and again by an ever-growing fanatic belief that the religious community to which one belonged represented that part of mankind which had been chosen by God."[49]

While the Sixties' structure of feeling shaped the choices of those who participated in the movement, it would be a profound mistake to conclude that antinomianism and expressivism somehow *determined* the behavior and outcome of the social movements of the period. An expressivist cultural element did come to dominate New Left discourse, but only after the expressivists won a series of internal debates and struggles within the movement about whether a general strategy or coherent ideology was needed to bind the opposition together.[50]

If a moment could be singled out when expressivism became the dominant "spirit" of the movement, it would have to be 1965, the year that President Johnson radically escalated the war in Vietnam, and the Student Nonviolent Coordinating Committee (SNCC) began to emphasize Black Power rather than the Southern Christian Leadership Council's (SCLC) liberal ideal of racial equality and universal "brotherhood." It was in this year that a key debate about the ends and means of the movement was won by those who favored spontaneism and decentralization over strategy and formal political involvement. In fact, for years a debate had been growing within the movement, over questions of strategy and the virtues of building "autonomous" movements and institutions rather than a more coherent approach. By the mid-1960s, some within the movement had begun openly to question the efficacy of direct action. Civil rights veteran Bayard Rustin famously called for a shift from "protest to politics," which would have channeled the radical opposition into the Democratic Party apparatus. He was attacked by Staughton Lynd and others as politically naive. However, in the spring of 1965 the editors of *Studies on the Left* conducted a debate in the journal's pages over whether the movement should continue to focus on local, decentralized, and largely spontaneous grassroots actions, or whether to move to a new stage of ideological and organizational unity. Younger activists like Tom Hayden advocated the former course, while older ones, like Stanley Aronowitz and James Weinstein, argued that a "radical center" and a more general strategy were needed.[51] Teodori concluded that after this debate, "the autonomist and anti-coalitionist position gained the upper hand" within the movement.[52] By this time, SDS's ambitious Economic Research and Action Project (ERAP), which had tried to organize the urban poor in the northern states, had largely dissolved into separate, local projects. Although "many members of the organization had hoped to form a national union of local programs into a kind of superorganization of poor people," this never happened.[53]

By the time of the national convention of SDS in June 1965, many members of SDS were dismissive of questions of strategy and organization, which they feared stank of "'elitism,' hierarchy, structure—almost anything that anyone might perceive as an obstacle to free will."

Concerns about the clear drift within the movement toward a symbolic and expressive politics were raised by some participants, including Paul Potter and Dick Flacks. But no consensus was reached.[54] In November, activists led by Arthur Waskow began to organize the National Conference for New Politics, in the hopes of counterbalancing the growing centrifugal tendencies within the movement with a unified national structure, and possibly launching a third party. While the conference brought together five thousand radical and liberal activists and intellectuals from across the spectrum of the New Left, from local SDS and civil rights organizers to left-leaning Democrats,[55] when the conference was convened in the fall of 1967 the autonomist impulse was too strong to resist. The different factions and movements walked away afterward, each planning "to carry on its own particular political activity, without national involvements."[56]

The decline of the discourse of strategy can be seen in the devolution of the civil rights movement. The New Left, from its inception, had of course been indebted to the tactics and strategies of the struggle for civil rights by African Americans against segregation. Free Speech activists like Mario Savio had witnessed the poverty and racism of the South first-hand while participating in the SNCC-organized Freedom Rides. Although the early civil rights movement had been anchored in Protestant Christian spirituality—the far-flung network of black Baptist churches—the movement had been as strategic as it was expressivist. On the one hand, the movement relied heavily on the charismatic authority of its leaders and on the spontaneism, faith, and "authentic" experiences of its constituents. On the other hand, though action originated in and was sustained by feeling, movement leaders never made the mistake of conflating action with self-expression—or with revelation of an inner identity. Strategicism prevailed simply because the facts of institutionalized racism in the South mandated it. Racism, codified in the law, took shape in the segregation of space. And it was backed up by arbitrary force: systematic, state-sanctioned terrorism. The life-and-death stakes of the struggle required sober economy of thought, planning, and a strategic sensibility. Action was thus subordinate to campaigns carefully devised by the movement's "organic" intellectuals. Direct action was the weapon, the tool, for achieving specific political objectives. In short, praxis had as much a strategic as a moral telos.[57] Notwithstanding the movement's rootedness in spirituality and a truly vital religious culture, faith never took precedence over "works." From bus boycotts and sit-ins to behind-the-scenes contacts with federal authorities, the movement brought instrumental, critical thought, strategic leadership, and spontaneous action together with a Christian, humanist ethics.

By the mid-1960s, however, the civil rights struggle had entered a more difficult period, shifting from a frontal "war of maneuver" against segregationist institutions to a "war of position" against racism as an economic and ideological structure. Meanwhile, the U.S. state (through COINTELPRO and other mechanisms) became more repressive, assassinating movement leaders and fomenting miscommunication or violence within the movement. As a result of internal and external pressures, the movement shifted from the charismatic (patriarchal) strategicism of the Southern Christian Leadership Council to the more expressivist style of the Student Nonviolent Coordinating Committee (SNCC). Instead of appealing to white conscience and trying to extract concessions from the state, SNCC began organizing the poor, trying to build parallel or counter-institutions at the grass roots. By 1965, the rhetoric of the civil rights struggle had shifted toward separatism and expression of a militant, "organic" black identity. By 1966, Stokely Carmichael, the leading exponent of the new Black Power movement, saw SNCC's role chiefly as one of helping "'to express the feeling of the black community in the tone of the black community,'" as he put it.[58] Later, Marion Barry was to praise SNCC's role in this "awakening [of] the simmering feelings of blackness that black people had but had not expressed."[59] By 1967, notwithstanding the success of SNCC and the Black Panthers in raising consciousness at the grassroots level, it had become clear even to SNCC founder and organizer Ella Baker (who had earlier walked away from SCLC because of its sexism and elitist leadership style) that awakening communal feeling was no substitute for an effective strategy. SNCC's "greatest difficulty," Baker later told an interviewer, "has been in reconciling its genius for individual expression with the political necessity for organizational discipline." SNCC, she said, had broadly failed to develop "basic leadership" in key regions of the South.[60]

THE PENTECOSTAL MYSTICISM OF NORMAN O. BROWN

The tension between strategy and expressivism played itself out in a public debate between Norman O. Brown and Herbert Marcuse over Brown's *Love's Body*. Both critics cast their intellectual lot with the youthful opposition. In their spirited exchange, we can see how closely contested such terms as "politics" and "strategy" were at the time, and how Marcuse's position eventually shifted from an expressivist toward a strategic outlook.

Roszak later described *Love's Body* as "Dionysus with footnotes," an "oracular outpouring" containing "no effort to prove or persuade, but to try out, to play with, to invoke portentous illuminations."[61] Playful, elusive, intentionally ambiguous, the book's amorphous form seemed to underscore its explicitly antinomian message. Brown took up a variety of archetypical themes in human civilization, under chapter headings such as "Liberty," "Unity," "Freedom," and so on, in the form of aphorisms which themselves were all paraphrases of classical and modern literature.

Brown's main argument was that Logos, or reason, was the enemy of love, Eros—a cruel weapon used to stave off the subject's true, unmediated experience of the life principle itself. Only by dissolving Logos, then, and merging with the oneness of the world, could the subject overcome its estrangement from itself, and from the object-other. Brown argued that at the infant stage, the subject senses no differentiation between self and other, self and world. Society then destroys and occludes this primary ontological state. Society's "reality principle" was in fact nothing but Thanatos or the death principle in disguise.

One of the book's central conclusions was that politics was founded on a patriarchal myth, a myth that was founded in fratricidal violence. Drawing on Hobbes and Locke, Brown suggested that politics, as well as "normal" society, represented the repression of "reality." The old language of politics and state founding was the language of deception and lies. Politics was the phallus, hatred of Eros made manifest. As Brown wrote later in his response to Marcuse, the language of politics would have to be abandoned in its entirety. "The next generation needs to be told that the real fight is not the political fight, but to put an end to politics. From politics to metapolitics."[62]

What Brown mean by "metapolitics" was a return to the primordial fusion experienced at Pentecost. He wrote:

> Pentecostal freedom, Pentecostal fusion. Speaking with tongues: many tongues, many meanings. The Babylonian confusion of tongues redeemed in the Pentecostal fusion....Pentecostal spirit is a principle of unspoken, unconscious unity, behind

the diversity of conscious tongues; a unity which is supra-personal, a unity in which personality is dissolved. Literal meaning is conscious meaning, a possession of the ego...contentious, divisive; opinion, dogma. To seek unity through univocation is to assure disunity. The blessing of multiplicity rejected returns as a curse....Instead of the Pentecostal fusion, the Babylonian confusion, the battle of books.[63]

According to Genesis, humankind was originally undifferentiated, one, able to experience a "true Esperanto or speaking with tongues; the primordial language from before the Flood or the Tower of Babel; lost yet ready to hand, perfect for all time; present in all our words, unspoken. To hear again the primordial language is to restore to words their full significance."[64] To experience this again, we would need to return to the "old gnosis" which would take us back to the Word of God—the one speech. As George Steiner wrote of Jakob Böhme (1575–1624), the great alchemist who also sought the key to the *Ursprache*:

Being erratic blocs, all languages share in a common myopia; none can articulate the whole truth of God or give its speakers a key to the meaning of existence. Translators are men groping toward each other in a common mist. Religious wars and the persecution of supposed heresies arise inevitably from the babel of tongues: men misconstrue and pervert each other's meanings. But there is a way out of darkness: what Böhme calls "sensualistic speech"—the speech of instinctual, untutored immediacy, the language of Nature and natural man as it was bestowed on the Apostles, themselves simple folk, at Pentecost. God's grammar sounds through echoing Nature, if only we will listen.[65]

The way "back" to this primordial unity, the new alchemist Norman O. Brown urged, was to abolish the cruel logos itself. Paradoxically, the unity lost at Babel was only to be recuperated through a fissioning of logos, i.e., destruction of intelligibility, razing the prison house of meaning. Only by unleashing the symbolic against the literal, the freedom of the psychic and spiritual against the tyranny of the real, could Eros—love's body, the whole body of the human spirit—be won. Seek "in the rough ground, the anomalies; not in the explanations. . . . The truth is in the error. We slip out from under the reality-principle, into the truth; when the control breaks down. By great fortune, gratis, by grace; and not by our own work or will" (p. 244). Letting go of our will, of attachments to outcomes and projects, we destroy the false bases of intelligibility that bind self to society. We "break down the boundaries, the walls. Down with the defense mechanisms, character-armor; disarmament" (p. 149).

In Brown's metaphysical view, "the iridescence [of meaning] is flux, is fusion, subverting the boundaries between things; all things flow" (p. 247). To reexperience this oneness with Nature, the unconscious must be released and given free rein, or rather, "the goal can only be conscious magic, or conscious madness," or "dreaming while awake" (p. 254): "Free speech; free associations, random thoughts; spontaneous movements" (p. 243). As Roszak notes, Brown sought "to discover a language beyond language, unrestricted by such conventional disciplines as logicality, continuity, or even normal sentence structure."[66] "Empty words," Brown urged, "dissolve the solid meanings" (p. 260). Poetry must therefore replace politics. "Freedom is poetry, taking liberties with words, break-ing the rules of normal speech, violating common sense. Freedom is vio-lence" (p.244). True freedom could only be won through the act, the praxis, of speaking in tongues—the sheer multiplication and fragmenta-tion of human expressive activity. "A vast pun, a free play, with unlimit-ed substitutions. A symbol is never a symbol but always polysymbolic, overdetermined, polymorphous. Freedom is fertility; a proliferation of images, in excess. The seed must be sown wastefully, extravagantly. . . . Too much meaning is meaning and absurdity reconciled" (pp. 248–49).

To vanquish the reality-principle, speech must be "resexualized." "The tongue was the first unruly member" (p. 251). "Sexual potency, lin-guistic power, abolished at Babel and restored at Pentecost. At Pente-cost, tongues of fire, a flame in the shape of a male member. Speaking with tongues is fiery speech, speech as a sexual act, a firebird or phoenix" (p. 251). Language would have to be "carried to the extreme, to the end" (p. 257); we would have to "reduce [words] to nonsense, to get the nonsense or silence back into words" (p. 259).

Marcuse found Brown's view to be morally repugnant and politically irresponsible. On the one hand, Marcuse welcomed Brown's attempt as a bid for the complete liberation of the human imagination. "But," he wrote, "then comes the hangover; the imagination falters, and the new language looks for support in the old. Support in quotations and refer-ences, which are to demonstrate or at least to illustrate the points made; support in returning to the primordial, elemental, subrational; to the infantile stages in the development of the individual and of the species. . . . The grand leap into the realm of freedom and light is thus arrested and becomes a leap backward, into darkness."[67] What disturbed Marcuse was Brown's refusal of reason. Brown argued that "fusion" or "mystical participation" (p. 254)—erasure of all distinctions between subject and object, mind and body, male and female, spirit and void, meaning and nonsense, person and mask—would require that the idolatry of reason be overthrown.[68] According to Marcuse, this was an idealism even more radical than Hegel's, for the latter had at least retained some meaningful notion of mediation. Brown's "fusion," however, "would be the end of human life, in its instinctual as well as rational, unsublimated as well as sublimated, expressions."[69] From Marcuse's perspective what was at issue was the very possibility of preserving a historical mode of consciousness. Was it really necessary, as Brown suggested, to destroy history in order to save Eros? Marcuse didn't think so. Brown "obliterates the decisive difference between real and artificial, natural and political, fulfilling and repressive, boundaries and divisions. . . . Fulfillment becomes meaningless if everything is one, and one is everything."

Notwithstanding Marcuse's sharp criticisms of *Love's Body*, however, the two theorists shared a similar antinomian sensibility. "Apocalypse," Brown had averred, "is the dissolution of the group as numerical series, as in representative democracy, and its replacement by the group as fusion, as communion" (p. 255). Marcuse too spoke of resisting any channeling of the "Great Refusal" into the traditional mechanism of liberal democracy, which "would divert energy to snail-paced movements." Marcuse was impatient: "Electioneering with the aim of significantly changing the composition of the U.S. Congress might take a hundred years," he argued, and this was too long to wait when the peoples of Southeast Asia were being carpet-bombed.[70] A genuine democracy would require "abolition of the existing pseudo-democracy" itself.[71]

As these sentiments suggest, Marcuse's reading of the New Left and counterculture, like Brown's, was itself strongly expressivist. As he saw it, the movement was both an expression of the contradictions of capitalist society and of the phenomenal form of a future, universal freedom. The very militancy of the protesters—their willingness to refuse the dominant mores of society while inventing novel forms of life—prefigured the new order that would need to come into being. The new praxis "emerges in the struggle against violence and exploitation where this struggle is waged for essentially new ways and forms of life: negation of the entire Establishment, its morality, culture; affirmation of the right to build a society in which the abolition of poverty and toil terminates in a universe where the sensuous, the playful, the calm, and the beautiful become forms of existence and thereby the form of the society itself."[72]

In emphasizing form in this way, Marcuse was reclaiming Marx's and Hegel's earlier expressivist conception of historical activity as the coming to appearance of a hidden logic of freedom. Marcuse, however, recast praxis through the prisms, first, of Kant's aesthetics of the sublime, and second, Freud's concept of desublimation. Total "reconstruction" was to be conceived not narrowly, as a change in economic production alone. Rather, Eros would be constitutive of praxis, and vice versa. Aesthetic-socialist practice would free the libidinal energies of human beings through an ever-widening dialectic. This "aesthetic dimension," which had been repressed by earlier Marxists, was the true motor of freedom. It was the process through which subjectivity and feeling would be transmuted "into form, into reality" (p. 32), the portal through which "reality . . . would assume a Form expressive of the new goal." In short, "art would be an integral factor in shaping the quality and the 'appearance' of things, in shaping the reality, the way of life"; and the struggle to create the new Form would manifest through the "existential quality" of this revolutionary life, the "authenticity" of the activists would "show forth" in the course of struggle (pp. 90–91).

Finally, in his *Essay on Liberation*, Marcuse admired the movement's "strong element of spontaneity, even anarchism," its "expression of the new sensibility, sensitivity against domination," and the shift in "initiative . . . to small groups, widely diffused, with a high degree of autonomy, mobility, flexibility" (p. 91). The "radical protest tends to become antinomian, anarchistic, and even non-political," he wrote. The "weird and clownish forms" of the movement, its "satire, irony, and laughing provocation" when confronted with "the gruesomely serious totality of institutionalized politics," represented "a necessary dimension of the new politics" (p. 68). Marcuse did note that "spontaneity by itself cannot possibly be a radical and revolutionary force" in the face of the entrenched repressive power of the totally administered society; some "organization" was needed (p. 91). He wrote: "The radical transformation of society implies the union of the new sensibility with a new rationality"; the "imagination becomes productive [only] if it becomes the mediator between sensibility on the one hand, and theoretical as well as practical reason on the other, and in this harmony of faculties . . .

guides the reconstruction of society" (p. 44). Nevertheless, in the *Essay*, Marcuse failed to specify what this "organization" might be. And the tenor of his remarks shows him to be on the whole sanguine about the movement's lack of a strategy or effective form.

Notwithstanding Marcuse's criticism of Brown for the latter's willingness in *Love's Body* to thrown historical intelligibility and reason overboard, then, Marcuse's own view of praxis was at the time not altogether different from Brown's. Both theorists held stubbornly to an expressivist conception of subjectivity, history, and political praxis—poetic "fusion" in Brown's terms, an "aesthetic dimension" in Marcuse's. It is therefore not hard to see how Nigel Young might conclude that, in 1967, Marcuse and Stokely Carmichael, the two reigning figures on the New Left at the time, together "helped to undermine" what remained of the movement's frail "strategic orientation."[73]

Soon, however, it became clear to all that the movement had begun to spin out of control. As a result, Marcuse became less sanguine about its ongoing failure to resolve properly the tension between expressivism and strategicism, sense and sensibility. With the publication, in 1972, of Marcuse's *Counter-Revolution and Revolt*, a crucial shift of emphasis in fact occurs in Marcuse's thought, a back-pedaling away from his earlier expressivism.[74] At first, the Marcuse of *Counter- Revolution and Revolt* seems close in spirit to the Marcuse of the *Essay*. He writes that the New Left's very "separation from the masses" is "factual," its "isolation" from society "well founded" due to its ontologically privileged status as a phenomenon that is inherently "expressive of the social structure of advanced capitalism" (pp. 32–33). The movement, he argues, is in fact, in actuality, an anti-majoritarian movement. "'Power to the people' does not mean the (anything but 'silent') majority of the population as it exists today; it means a minority—the victims of the majority."[75] He also suggests that the movement's fragmentation is "natural," owing to the lack of any real "tangible common goal" uniting the opposition (p. 36).

Yet for the first time, Marcuse also acknowledges the possibility that the advanced "one-dimensional" capitalist system might "express" itself in terms of pathological degeneration, producing "divergent and dispersed nuclei of disintegration." In other words, the centrifugal tendencies of the system itself could lead to "decentralized, diffuse, largely 'spontaneous'" elements of the radical opposition. This meant that "such points of local dysfunctioning and disruption can become nuclei

of social change only if they are given political direction and organization" (p. 42). We must distinguish, Marcuse writes, between situations
in which a social movement has successfully "taken root in a popular
base," and one in which the movement is isolated. If a movement is isolated, there must be a "'suspension' of premature (or obsolete) ideological conflicts in favor of the more urgent task of building up numerical
strength." Quality, in short, would have to be supplemented with
"quantity" (p. 37). Marcuse blames the "weakened" state of the movement in part on the movement itself: on "(1) ideological conflicts within the militant opposition and (2) the lack of organization" (p. 36).
Evincing frustration with the "ritualization" of the movement and its
regression to a shrill Marxist-Leninist rhetoric (p. 33), Marcuse now
acknowledges that communicating with the masses is an "acute" problem. "The 'people' speak a language which is all but closed to the concepts and propositions of Marxian theory" (p. 37).

For the first time, Marcuse also now distances himself from one of
the most characteristic aspects of antinomianism, its *anti*-evangelical-
ism. As E. P. Thompson observed, the antinomians of the seventeenth
century were not interested in universalizing their ideology, but "to
preserve and to hand down the divine vision."[76] Antinomianism, past
or present, is not so much counter- hegemonic—in the Gramscian sense
of a movement which works to widen the circle of believers until it
extends to all of society—as *anti*-hegemonic. Gramsci credited the
Protestant Reformation with having created the possibility of the socie-
tal-wide democratization of knowledge: Martin Luther had translated
Christian scripture from high Latin into the language of the people—
the "vernacular" (the term derives from "slave"). In making the scripture available in a "common" tongue in this manner, rendering it
intelligible to ordinary people, Luther and others not only ended the
monopoly of the Catholic church, but created the preconditions for
modern social movements. In contrast, the antinomians sought not to
extend their community outward, but to maintain their purity in the
teeth of corruption. Norman O. Brown had admired the purity of the
"fringe" and had seemed to evince indifference to the *political* question
of how his peculiar brand of neo-Pentecostal mysticism would—or
indeed could—be taken up by the mainstream.

The Marcuse of the earlier *Essay* had spoken, like Brown, of the need
to destabilize meaning. To negate the negation of freedom, the move-

ment would have to develop its own language in order to subvert dominant discourses. "Today," Marcuse wrote, "the rupture with the linguistic universe of the Establishment is . . . radical: in the most militant areas
of protest, it amounts to a methodical reversal of meaning" (p. 41). The
counterculture had come to "develop their own language, taking the
harmless words of everyday communication out of their context and
using them for designating objects or activities tabooed by the Establishment" (p. 41). Marcuse praised the "anti-art" movement for its "destruction of syntax, fragmentation of words and sentences, explosive use of
ordinary language, compositions without score, sonatas for anything"
(p. 48). He was especially impressed by the "language of black militants"—"a systematic linguistic rebellion, which smashes the ideological
context in which the words are employed and defined, and places them
into the opposite context—negation of the established one" (p. 42).

But in *Counter-Revolution and Revolt*, Marcuse for the first time sees the
danger in an expressivism that intentionally renders itself unintelligible. The opposition, he now sees, speaks in a language—that of socialism—which common people can neither hear, nor understand, while
"the radical difference between a free society and the existing one
remains obscured" (p. 31). "The primary liberation," he writes, "cannot
be 'spontaneous' because such spontaneity would only express the values and goals derived from the established system. Self-liberation is
self-education but as such it presupposes education by others." Marcuse now began to sound a great deal like Antonio Gramsci, who had
emphasized the importance of radical pedagogy in widening the public sphere and constructing the counter-hegemonic bloc:

> In a society where the unequal access to knowledge and information is part of
> the social structure, the distinction and the antagonism between the educators
> and those to be educated are inevitable. Those who are educated have a commit-
> ment to use their knowledge to help men and women realize and enjoy their
> truly human capabilities. All authentic education is political education, and in a
> class society, political education is unthinkable without leadership, educated
> and tested in the theory and practice of radical opposition. The function of this
> leadership is to "translate" spontaneous protest into organized action which has
> the chance to develop and to transcend immediate needs and aspirations toward
> the radical reconstruction of society: transformation of immediate into organ-
> ized spontaneity. (p. 47)

As a "counterforce" to the system, it would thus be necessary to develop "an effectively organized Left," one capable of "dispelling," through education, "the false and mutilated consciousness of the people so that they themselves experience their condition, and its abolition, as vital need, and apprehend [for themselves] the ways and means of their liberation" (p. 28).

MORBID SYMPTOMS APPEAR

Refusing both Leninism and spontaneism, Marcuse eventually sought a middle ground, one in which the aesthetic dimension, with its erotic, Dionysian energy, could be harnessed alongside reason. But by that time the die had been cast—an antinomian, anti-hegemonic ethos led activists to privilege their own expressive identification with the most marginalized elements of society over a political praxis that might have actually transformed the wider society.

By the early 1970s, the question of strategy became moot, as the movement unraveled. SNCC began ousting whites from their organization, while the Maoist sectarianism of the Progressive Labor Party (created in 1964) began to poison SDS from within. Progressive Labor (PL), though predominantly a white, middle-class student movement, allied itself with the most militant black nationalist elements, and fetishized violent action. From the PL perspective, the logical answer to revolution in the third world was a revolution of black Americans led by a disciplined "cadre."[77] After the assassination of Martin Luther King, Jr., the millenarianism of the New Left and Black Power movements became even more pronounced. SDS finally imploded, giving way to the delusional revolutionary fantasies and terrorist violence of the Weather Underground.

As the movement became more and more desperate, it became correspondingly more protective of its boundaries, and more neurotic. Activist doubts became sublated both in frenetic, ill-thought-out protest activity, and in the disciplinization of behavior and norms within the movement. The nineteenth-century anarchist Max Stirner once "declared that the anarchist frees himself of all that is sacred, and carries out a vast operation of deconsecration."[78] In the late 1960s and early 1970s, freedom from the sacred seemed to legislate new forms and spaces of the "sacred," a shelter in which the community of believers could protect themselves from an uncomprehending, profane world.

The habit within the women's movement of subjecting women as well as men to the discomfort of examining, through a feminist microscope, their most intimate relationships, grew organically out of a deeply ethical worldview that required brutal self-honesty and cultivation of a collective "goodwill." However, this focus on individual ethics had its costs, too. Freedom at times became conflated with a moralistic disciplining of self and other. To the extent that authenticity required self-purification, cleansing the self of corrupt thoughts and feelings, it segued easily into antinomian sectarianism. In Ernst Troeltsch's distinction between a church and a sect, the latter is characterized by a deep ambivalence toward involvement with the outside world. In the sect, once the inner circle of true believers has purified itself, those who remain on the outside—dupes of the false idols of the corrupted world—are viewed with condescension. A movement that had begun as an experience of anger, but an anger that took joy in solidarity and mutual affection, progressively turned chialistic. Paranoia choked the movement at the margins. Certainly such paranoia was not without its basis in reality: by the late 1960s, state repression and infiltration of the movement was well-known (although the true extent of government efforts to destroy the movement would not be known until later). However, as pressures in the movement mounted, a milieu of self-suspicion—an internally directed rage and surveillance, identification and vilification of external and internal enemies within the movement and within the self—settled in.

The early New Left's existentialist emphasis on self-transformation, under the spell of the anarchist credo of "propaganda of the deed," melded into the aesthetic project of refashioning and expressing the inner self—whether the Yippie's childlike revolt against authority or Che's "New Socialist Man" or underground militants like members of the Symbionese Liberation Army. The revolution would be lived in the present. As Marcuse commented, "Our goals, our values, our own and new morality, our OWN morality, must be visible in our actions. The new human beings whom we want to create—we must already strive to be these human beings right here and now."[79] For the counterculture, "the personal is political" meant holding up all aspects of private life to close public scrutiny—everything "from the way we brushed our teeth to the way we fucked."[80] Self-scrutiny and group scrutiny of the self—constant measuring of the self's fit with the radical ideal—was expressivist. Even as the (corporate, state, white, pig, square, etc.) "enemy" was condemned, the price of moral purity was constant vigilance directed toward any sign of the "enemy within." The movement's "Protestant existentialism" (as one critic called it) became indistinguishable from a generalized anxiety over one's authenticity. The result was a gnawing sense of abjection. "The student is shit. He is the privileged person in an underprivileged world of suffering. . . . We begin by killing the enemy within us," read one leaflet distributed at the University of California at Berkeley in 1968.[81] The French historian and social critic Michel Foucault wrote that "the major enemy, the strategic adversary is fascism. . . . And not only historical fascism . . . but also the fascism in us all, in our heads and in our everyday behavior, the fascism that causes us to love power, to desire the very thing that dominates and exploits us."[82]

In the most militant sectors of the movement, an authoritarian, masculinist personality structure developed. The Black Panthers' misogynistic rage, the growth of Progressive Labor, the exuberantly antisocial acts of groups like the Motherfuckers—all were evidence that the movement was spiraling out of control.[83]

THE EXPRESSIVIST LEGACY

By the early 1970s, the expressivist ethos of the New Left also got channeled into nationalism and assertions of identity. For African-American activists, praxis came to mean getting in touch with and expressing the black or African inner soul, manifested in nationalism. The objective of the black arts movement, for example, was said to lie in "expressing through various art forms, the Soul of the Black Nation": "blues and the people who create them are the Soul Force of the race, the emotional current of the Nation."[84] Herder's thought also echoed in the Brown Power movement—for example, Rendon's Chicano Manifesto, which declared, "I am a Chicano because of a unique fusion of bloods and history and culture"; "To be Chicano is to find out something about one's self which has lain dormant, subverted, and nearly destroyed"; "There is a mystique among us Chicanos"; "To be Chicano is nothing new; it is as old as our people. . . . To be Chicano means that a person has looked deeper into his being and sought unique ties to his brothers in la raza."[85]

By the mid-1970s, feminists too had taken up the expressivist charge. Women in the antiwar movement, grown tired of their contemptuous and misogynistic treatment at the hands of their male counterparts, had left to found a movement of their own. While many radical feminists adopted highly politicized forms of action, others took to defining praxis as finding and unleashing the inner woman or inner lesbian. "What is a lesbian?" began "The Woman Identified Woman," manifesto of the Radicalesbians. "A lesbian is the rage of all women condensed to the point of explosion. She is the woman who, often beginning at an extremely early age, acts in accordance with her inner compulsion to be a more complete and freer human being than her society . . . cares to allow."[86]

The expressivist cultural habitus of the 1960s and 1970s thus settled, like a fine but choking silt, over the political practices and assumptions of the decades that followed. On the one hand, expression helped free up the imagination and libidinal energies of millions of people who had correctly perceived the injustice and spiritual vacuum at the heart of modern capitalist culture, and the creativity manifest on the streets of Paris in May 1968, and elsewhere, had the salutary effect of throwing new light on entrenched systems of repressive power and domination, from imperialism and racism to state terror and patriarchy. Expressivism also helped smash, once and for all, the stranglehold that Communist parties held over social movements in Europe and elsewhere.

But expressivism also had its costs. Expressivism left capitalism unbound by smashing bourgeois cultural norms that had previously placed subjective limits on consumerism and thus stifled capitalist expansion. What developed as a counter-logic within advanced capitalist culture became constitutive of the new logic of post-Fordism.[87] In *The Whole World Is Watching*, his study of the symbiotic relationship between the mass media and Students for a Democratic Society, Todd Gitlin notes that by the mid-Sixties, the accelerating pace of historical events amplified what Debord called the "society of the spectacle" and led him and others within the movement to experience disorientation or Dionysian ecstasy (or both). "Inside the movement," Gitlin writes, "one had the sense of being hurled through a time tunnel, of hurtling from event to event without the time to learn from experience."[88] In retrospect, this subjective sense of space–time compression corresponded to a wider transition in Western economy and culture toward a new regime of commodity production (what Harvey has termed a "condition of postmodernity").[89] The expressivist aesthetic enabled a qualitative deepening of commodity logics in the lifeworld. Foucault's call for an ethic of "care of the self" would become the rallying cry of global capitalism, which was happy to oblige by engineering new desires and products for individuals in multiple niche markets. The Yippie cry "Do it!" had been transformed by the Nike Corporation's *detournement* into "Just do it!" while banks put up expressivist billboard ads like "Use Your American Express Card. Win Prizes. Scream Uncontrollably."

The second effect of the expressivist structure of feeling was to prevent the New Left from clarifying its ideology and constituting a viable form for itself. Like a storm drawing warm moisture and energy from the open waters of history, the movement's fury swept up much of the United States and the European continent in its rage. This new energy in turn produced irresistible, centrifugal forces within the movement. The influx of new recruits into SDS from 1965 to 1968, young people lacking in political experience or indeed any real basis for historical comprehension, made it increasingly difficult for the center to hold. And the "heightened metabolism" of the movement, as Bookchin calls it, had the effect of assuring that no coherent social theory of praxis would be left behind in the New Left's wake.[90] But this lack of a clear strategic vision would later haunt social movements, which would soon have to struggle with all their resources against the determined onslaught of the political right from 1980 on.

Gitlin describes his experience of the Sixties as a loss of intelligibility, the breakdown of historical "syntax" that occurs at moments of organic crisis or revolution. "Life came to seem a sequence of tenuously linked exclamation points," Gitlin writes, those within the movement experiencing "discontinuity and a loss of a sense of political reality, a loss of context."[91] For some, like the Motherfuckers and Norman O. Brown, this breakdown in the intelligibility of history seemed inevitable and, in a certain sense, desirable. The destruction of historical intelligibility—the fragmentation of meaning and social experience (which Lukács at an earlier juncture in history had described as "reification") came to be seen as the ultimate goal and the everyday "method" of collective agency. If the loss of syntax was a fact, however, it took the discourses of postmodernism and identity politics of subsequent decades to turn "speaking in tongues" into an intellectual virtue and a common sense.

2 Speaking in Tongues

Feet off the ground. Freedom is instability;
the destruction of attachments; the ropes, the fixtures, fixations,
that tie us down.—NORMAN O. BROWN, *Love's Body*

In the aftermath of the upheavals of the 1960s, Norman O. Brown's Dionysian and Pentecostalist vision wended its way deep into the marrow of Anglo-American critical theory. Subversion of language and speech, rather than transformation of consciousness or material institutions, came to be seen as the proper method and proving ground of praxis. Those who hoped to change society were told not to concentrate on vying for power or engaging in a "positive" struggle to institute new meanings and beliefs, but rather to focus on deconstructing and disrupting signs and discourses. By destroying syntax, breaking down conceptual categories, encouraging the proliferation of "different" identities and discourses, and fragmenting the subject, subaltern classes could move from "margin" to "center." How the expressivist discourse of "speaking in tongues" became consolidated within one particular school of critical thought, feminism, is the subject of this chapter.

When Mary Daly published her pathbreaking book, *Gyn/Ecology*, in 1978, the U.S. women's movement had already lost much of its earlier momentum. Grassroots feminist "consciousness-raising" and creative, free experimentation in novel forms of women's culture and practice had begun to be replaced both by women's community organizations and professional lobbying groups like the National Organization for Women and the National Abortion Rights Action League. A general shift was also well under way from movement protest activity toward development and refinement of feminist theory. *Gyn/Ecology* was a bellwether of this transi-

tion. Daly consolidated the experiences of the early second wave movement into something resembling a coherent feminist philosophy.

As an original philosophical contribution to radical feminist critique
and historiography, *Gyn/Ecology* was as significant for Daly's generation as
The Second Sex had been for de Beauvoir's. Rich in historical analysis and
critique of patriarchal institutions, norms, and ideologies, *Gyn/Ecology*
ranged widely through history and across world culture to expose an
array of misogynistic practices, from witch-burning in Europe and foot-
binding in China to ritual genital mutilation in Africa. At the center of
the book was a brilliant ideology-critique of Judeo-Christian mythology,
whose patriarchal premises and linguistic conventions Daly skewered
with her characteristic mix of outrage and subversive glee. To a totalizing
patriarchal project, Daly counterpoised her own positive, reconstructive
project—a "metaethics" of radical feminism. This metaethics was firmly
planted in an expressivist—and essentialist—foundation.

Daly argued that centuries of patriarchal oppression had resulted in
the silencing of women, and that the dominant system of language itself
colluded in and produced this silence. Overcoming patriarchy would
therefore require the invention of a wholly new language of female resistance. It was "a practical, tactical" matter for women to begin "using new
words and transforming/recalling meanings of old words."[1] And *Gyn/Ecolo-
gy* was itself the showcase of the author's own linguistic pyrotechnics.
Daly spun out new words and tropes to explode the "phallocracy" of civilization. Drawing upon elemental pagan images from radical feminist
culture and premodern witchery, Daly ingeniously combined a Romantic
sensibility with a dizzying linguistic prolixity. "Speaking with tongues of
fire," was how Daly described this process of ontological awakening (p.
340). Women's resistance to oppression would be a "Sparking," an effort
at "igniting the divine Spark in women.... Sparking is creating a room of
one's own, a moving time/spaceship of one's own, in which the Self can
join with other Self- centering Selves" (p. 319). Feminist practice was to be
conceived as "enspiriting"—an "expressive active verb, an Active Voice
uttering the Self utterly, in a movement/Journey that spirals outward,
inward" (p. 340). Drawing deeply on Heideggerian ontology, Daly sought
to reverse the polarity between silence and speech in Genesis. "In the
beginning was not the word," Daly wrote. "In the beginning is the hearing. Spinsters spin deeper into the listening deep.... Gyn/Ecology is Un-
Creation; Gyn/Ecology is Creation" (p. 424).

Gyn/Ecology was striking for the manner in which it appropriated and intensified the expressivist poetics of *Love's Body*, even though Daly explicitly distanced herself from Norman O. Brown, arguing that Brown presented a false, idealized femininity that tacitly recuperated patriarchy (p. 67). But as in *Love's Body*, *Gyn/Ecology* named "ecstasy" as the central practice in the unmaking of the master. As Josephine Donovan observes of Daly's epic ontology myth, Daly "structures her otherworldly journey upon the Gnostic myth of the soul's redemptive passage. In this myth the soul must say the correct or magical words at each stage of the journey in order to pass the hostile gatekeepers."[2] Women must voyage through the "Passages of the Labyrinthine Way of Ecstasy" (p. 32). But would the walls of Patriarchy come tumbling down at the sound of women uttering incantatory words like "A-Mazing," "Voyaging," and "Spinning"? Daly seemed to think so; that through "spiraling" and "spinning" out "magic words" and webs, feminists would spontaneously disentangle patriarchy's web. "We have learned that Hags break through to the Background of language, breaking dead silence and breaking the deadening babble" (p. 402).

Daly's thought had a significant impact on the American women's movement at the time. In particular, *Gyn/Ecology* provided theoretical legitimation for lesbian separatism, which was seen by some women as the only or best available form of praxis. Separatist groups like Lesbian Nation offered politically radicalized lesbians an escape from Babylon—the oppressive, universal corruption of patriarchy—through a retreat into the self-confirming space of the community of believers. Unfortunately, the utopian turn in feminist thought and practice ultimately failed to translate radical feminism into a politics of social change.[3] Separatism was less a strategy than an antinomian form of revolt, insofar as living the prefigurative community took priority over changing the norms of the wider society.

Whereas for Hegel intersubjective struggle with the Other is part of a dialectic of history that expands "outward" in a wider and wider dialectic, Daly's "dialectic" was turned resolutely inward, toward the female Self. It was as though Daly had decided to leap back in time, past Hegel, to the thought of the earlier Romantics whose thought Hegel had himself appropriated but surpassed.

For Fichte and Herder, linguistic differentiation of human beings had resulted in cultural and ontic distinctions between peoples. Thus Fichte, defending the sui generis nature of the German *volk*, suggested that language develops "continuously out of the actual common life of [a] people" while Fichte argued that foreigners living among a people find that they do not transform the wider organic culture, but rather find themselves transformed. As Fichte put it: "Hence they do not form the language; *it is the language which forms them.*"[4] Language, in short, constitutes human reality.[5] Daly took this notion and based her feminist metaethics on it. "As she becomes dispossessed, enspirited," she wrote, the Female Self "moves out of range of the passive voices and begins her own Active Voice, speaking her Self in successive acts of creation. As she creates her Self she creates new space" (p. 340). Hence the Munchausen subject, so characteristic of all expressivist ideologies: the subject who pulls herself out of the muck of a corrupted world by her own hair. A recurring theme in Romantic thought was the idea of creating the self *ex nihilo*.[6] "Woman Gives Birth to Herself" a lesbian poster declared in the 1970s, a sentiment captured by Daly in *Gyn/Ecology* when she wrote, "We transmute the base metals of our man-made myth by becoming unmute, calling forth from our Selves and each other the courage to name the unnameable."[7]

This expressivist ethos, of an ecstatic speech at once capable, magically, of subverting the hegemonic order and fashioning a new self, was taken up by later feminists. Chicana writer Gloria Anzuldua's "Speaking in Tongues: A Letter to Third World Women Writers," composed only two years after *Gyn/Ecology*, marked an especially important turn on the feminist expressivist road. Language was to be the crucible of an authentic identity. "Ethnic identity is twin skin to linguistic identity—I am my language."[8] Women of color, Anzuldua observed, had been rendered silent and invisible. The lesbian of color indeed "does not even exist." Phenomenal nonexistence stemmed from the fact that women's "speech, too, is inaudible. We speak in tongues like the outcast and the insane."[9] The solution: do not adopt the sterile, disembodied voice of white, male society, but rather "speak in tongues." Through linguistic effusion and confusion, the Chicana Self would smash through the corrupt and stifling language of the hegemonic order. "Audre [Lorde] said we need to speak up," Kathy Kendall wrote in a letter to Anzuldua, reprinted in "Speaking in Tongues." But as in Daly's discourse, Anzuldua seemed to reduce political praxis to the unearthing of a preexisting essence or inner self.[10] Identity, through expression, arises out of the "center" of a self, as an artistic creation, *ex nihilo*. "Why should I try to justify why I write? Do I need to justify being a Chicana, being woman? You might as well ask me to try to justify why I'm alive.... The act of writing is the act of making soul, alchemy. It is the quest for the self, for the center of the self."[11]

This "return" to the inner soul required a studied naïveté. The Romantics and antinomians placed privileged myth-making and art over science and empirical knowledge, suspicious of reason.[12] In identity politics discourse, history is similarly invoked for mythic or mythopoetic purposes. Self-creation means valuing sensibility over sense, aesthetic expression over reason.[13]

THE CYBORG SPEAKS IN TONGUES

In the identity politics discourses of the late-1970s and early '80s, one still sees a residue of the existential passion of the Sixties era, such as an unabashed celebration of authenticity, revolt against convention, and organic nature as the basis of an inner essence. Yet within the space of a few years, critical theorists had carefully excised from their texts any last vestigial traces of the humanistic warmth that had animated earlier New Left and early second wave feminist practice. As if embarrassed by the effusive Romanticism of the hippies and radical feminists, postmodernists were to retain only the formal aspects of the earlier expressivist moment, while jettisoning precisely those cultural aspects that had infused the earlier movements with such irresistible vitality and power—e.g., rejection of consumer materialism and professionalism, critique of technology, and faith in consciousness-raising. And no longer would Nature be seen as the proper source of subversive values.

Donna Haraway's "A Cyborg Manifesto: Science, Technology, and Socialist-Feminism in the Late Twentieth Century" is one of the most important documents marking this transition. Perhaps the single most widely read feminist tract of the 1980s and 90s, the Cyborg Manifesto was to launch not one but several minor industries in cultural studies.[14] Haraway's essay represented the moment when postmodernism successfully exorcised the demons of essentialism, while nonetheless preserving the expressivist ethos *formally*, at a new level of abstraction.

The wider political context of the Manifesto was the U.S. religious right's success in making its vaunted "family values" platform into national policy. But Haraway's more immediate political purpose was to consolidate the gains of poststructuralist feminism over the earlier "vanguard" of second wave feminists. She began her work with a mock confession. The Manifesto, she said, was a "blasphemy," a heretic's "ironic" attack on accepted truths. What she had in mind were the received wisdoms of radical feminists like Mary Daly and Catherine MacKinnon, on the one hand, and critics of modern science like Herbert Marcuse and Carolyn Merchant, on the other—Haraway cited all four critics by name in her essay.

The Manifesto worked through two broad problematics. The first of these was the status of the subject in theory. Feminist women of color had sharply questioned the supposed unity of the subject of feminism—"woman"—arguing that the conceit of a single subject served to occlude actual differences in women's experiences, e.g., differences of race and sexuality. Meanwhile, successive poststructuralist theorists had reduced "the subject" as such to the status of a mere epiphenomenon of discourse. This was a complete about-face from the earlier organicism of radical feminism, which had sought a foundation for feminist praxis in ontology. Haraway and others, emboldened by the emergence of "ludic" feminists and queer activists who rejected essentialism and thronged to more optimistic portrayals of women's condition in society, thus criticized antipornography feminists like Andrea Dworkin and Catherine MacKinnon on grounds that they had succumbed to a simplistic account of power and had naively adopted women's experience as the leaping-off point of a feminist epistemology.[15] In place of the older model of the stable, self-identical subject of feminism, poststructuralists now emphasized a disintegrated, diffused "subject" that was itself an effect of power, or discourse.

The second broad problematic explored in the Manifesto was the relationship between academic feminism and techno-science. Drawing equally upon narratives of women of color as well as feminist science fiction, Haraway fashioned a new trope and myth, what she called the "Cyborg," to capture the creative flux of a new posthumanistic "subject." As the sign of this new non-subject, the Cyborg represented a break with the traditional fetish of "the unity of women" (p. 159). Instead of trying to overcome the multiple, "unassimilable" or irreducible play of identity and discourse that constitute so-called woman, the Cyborg would mark the coordinates of a new politics of difference and "affinity" (p. 155). The Cyborg thus represented postmodernity itself. It symbolized the multiple displacements of the postmodern condition, the constant unsettling and transpositions of identity and culture.

In this regard, the "Cyborg Manifesto" served as a further refinement of Norman O. Brown's expressivist mysticism. On the one hand, Haraway explicitly criticized *Love's Body* on grounds that Brown's "only escape from . . . domination . . . was through fantasy and ecstasy, leaving the body politic unchallenged in its fundamental male supremacy." Brown had "betrayed" socialist feminism by turning "nature into a fetish worshiped by a total return to it."[16] Certainly, Haraway's rejection of nature as the basis of oppositional consciousness marked a striking departure from Brown's framework. On the other hand, Haraway's debt in the Manifesto to Brown's expressivism was substantial. Haraway echoed Brown's fetish of linguistic disruption and the destruction of fixed meaning and literalism, writing that "cyborg politics insist [sic] on noise and advocate pollution" (176). And while critical of Brown's mystical conception of fusion, Haraway enjoined her reader to take "pleasure in . . . potent and taboo fusions" (173). More impressively, Haraway reiterated Brown's Pentecostalist theme calling for "an imagination of a feminist speaking in tongues to strike fear into the circuits of the super-savers of the new right " (p. 181).

The Cyborg Manifesto was a frontal theoretical attack on the unity "lost" at Babel—i.e., Marxist socialism. "Cyborg politics is the struggle . . . against perfect communication, against the one code that translates all meaning perfectly," Haraway intoned (p. 176). For the earlier "feminist dream of a common language, of perfectly faithful naming of experience, [was] a totalizing and imperialist one" (p. 173). Against the universal code that might translate different dialects of identity and practice, rendering them intelligible to one another, feminists ought to "resist representation, resist literal figuration," while "still erupt[ing] in powerful new tropes, new figures of speech, new turns of historical possibility. For this process, at the inflection point of crisis, where all tropes turn again, we need ecstatic speakers."[17] This insistent metaphor, of continual irruption of "difference," was clearly intended by Haraway to serve a proscriptive normative function. Social movements "must never again . . . connect as parts to wholes, as marked beings incorporated into unmarked ones, as unitary and complementary subjects serving one Subject of monotheism and its secular heresies."[18] "Speaking in tongues" becomes a kind of "categorical imperative" of praxis, a way to distinguish between legitimate and illegitimate forms of discourse.

Haraway's Manifesto was in fact a calculated blow aimed at Mary Daly. Haraway appropriated Daly's ecstatic imagery of a "spiral dance"[19] —Daly's love of discursive play and neologism. But she was serious about purifying professionalized feminist discourse of any residue of the messy organicism of Daly's feminism. The Manifesto thus sought to deconstruct cultural feminism at its very "heart," by detaching human culture from nature.

For Daly, the solution to women's oppression lay in setting boundaries between women and the masculinist culture that had enslaved and degraded them for millennia. Daly took particular offense at Norman O. Brown for glorifying Dionysus as a "boundary-violator, as the one who drives women mad." In reality, talk of boundlessness served to obscure the fundamental power differences between women and men.[20] Dionysus, in short, was only Apollo in drag.[21] Rejecting Brown's "invitation to incorporation/assimilation," Daly countered with a "radical feminist ecstasy" through which women would construct boundaries of their own.[22] Daly was especially concerned to critique the subordination of the lifeworld to the death-fetish of the machine. Ironically, Daly reserved her angriest words for cyborgs—which she saw as a final apocalypse of women's subjectivity. "Male-mothered genetic engineering is an attempt to 'create' without women. The projected manufacture by men of artificial wombs, of cyborgs which will be part flesh, part robot, of clones—all are manifestations of phallocentric boundary violation."[23]

But Haraway sought to negate this negation: to overturn Daly's every effort to patrol the borders between women's lives and the probes of instrumental reason and techno-science. Echoing Brown's call for "subverting the boundaries between things,"[24] Haraway wrote that her "cyborg myth is about transgressed boundaries, potent fusions, and dangerous possibilities which progressive people might explore as one part of political work" (p. 154). Boundaries, far from being the promising basis of women's subjectivity and freedom, were enemies to be rooted out and destroyed. Hence the Manifesto's recurring hymn to the flux of identity. The figure of the cyborg invoked earlier mythic hybrid figures like the Centaur and Amazon, who signified "boundary pollutions" (p. 180). Like Marx and Engels in their manifesto, Haraway argued that capitalism was constantly reshifting and re-creating identity. But while Marx and Engels understood capitalism's process of decomposition and upheaval dialectically, Haraway seemed to treat the core dynamic of modernity—namely, that "all that is solid melts into air"—as a good in itself. In her framework, instability becomes the deus ex machina of revolutionary social change.[25]

The Manifesto sees capitalist technoscience as the most potent agent of history. Haraway in a sense thus gives the cyborg artificial legs so that it can walk, tongues so that it might erupt into ecstatic speech, and so on. Technoscience, by breaking down barriers and boundaries and muddying ontological and epistemological certainties—"dualisms"—generates new "pleasures" and "radical" political possibilities. In poststructuralist thought, it will be recalled, the need to transgress boundaries arises out of the need to deconstruct the dualisms at the heart of the Western tradition, which are typically identified as the malicious culprits behind normalization and the subjugation of the oppressed. "High-tech culture," she writes, "challenges these dualisms in intriguing ways. It is not clear who makes and who is made in the relation between human and machine" (p. 177). "The machine is not an it to be animated, worshipped, dominated," Haraway tells us. "The machine is us, our processes, an aspect of our embodiment. . . . We are responsible for boundaries; we are they" (p. 180).

How extraordinary a statement is this last: we cannot usefully distinguish between a living being and a thing. *"There is no fundamental, ontological separation in our formal knowledge of machine and organism, of technical and organic,"* she writes (p. 178). Such an assertion, which would have shocked even a Bacon or Descartes (both of whom had the peculiar penchant of seeing animate creation in mechanistic terms), rushes beyond mere epistemological critique to the very edge of a positivist metaphysics. According to Haraway, it is no longer we subjects who make the world: our own artifacts now create us. "The cyborg," Haraway wrote, "is our ontology; it gives us our politics."[26] Machines are our "friendly selves" (p. 178).

It is of interest to note that at the same time Haraway was writing the "Cyborg Manifesto," corporations were pouring billions of dollars into research and advertising campaigns to subvert the traditional distinction between machines and people. High-tech mavens and corporate entrepreneurs like Nicholas Negroponte (head of MIT's Media Lab) were finding new ways to change popular thinking about machines, often by erasing the conceptual machine/person distinction. "Little by little," Negroponte wrote, "computers are taking on personalities. . . . The persona of a machine makes it fun, relaxing, usable, friendly, and less 'mechanical' in spirit. Breaking in a new personal computer will become more like house-training a puppy."[27] Hence, the Apple computer company's very successful "Say Hello to iMac" campaign, in 1997. Other companies similarly marketed mechanical, computerized "pets" that eerily mimicked animal behavior.

Haraway describes the following conceptual pairings as "troubling dualisms": "self/other, mind/body, culture/nature, male/female, civilized/primitive, reality/appearance, whole/part, agent/resource, maker/made, active/passive, right/wrong, truth/illusion, total/partial, God/man" (p. 177). Yet the theorist's sleight of hand conceals a singular fallacy—a conflation of ontological facts and social ones. Is the distinction between "maker" and "made" really the same as that between male and female, or between God and human? Is the difference between right and wrong a "dualism"? How about the attempt to draw a distinction between truth and illusion (or even truth and lie)? Is the distinction (not a "dualism") between whole and parts, or reality and appearance, comparable to such socially constructed distinctions as gender (or race)? What about the most elemental ontological distinction of all—between persons and things?

Haraway's cyborg is neither male nor female, neither human nor animal, neither human nor machine, neither subject nor object—rather, it is precisely that entity that crosses all boundaries. Haraway thus takes reification—the treatment of people as things, and machines as people—and perversely enshrines it as the central productive process of feminist praxis.

With the Manifesto, thus, the expressivist impulse, which had developed in the Sixties as a humanistic revolt against alienation and reification, cast off the remnants of its earlier spiritual dimensions. A telling contrast can be seen when we juxtapose Haraway's poststructuralist recuperation of technology and Theodore Roszak's *Making of a Counter-Culture*.

In the latter, Roszak vividly expressed his sympathy with the countercultural critique of technoscience. To Roszak, the careless brutality of scientific experiments on animals were as morally indefensible as the "rational" discourse of waging thermonuclear war. "To spare a sigh for the fate of animals undergoing laboratory experimentation," he wrote, "is generally considered cranky in the extreme."[28] Years later, in *Modest Witness @ Second Millennium*—an improvisatory snapshot of the

transmogrifications of tropes in the commodified culture of technosci-
entific research—Haraway would turn her back against both Daly's outrage at the instrumentalization of life and Roszak's empathy for
animal suffering.[29] Adopting a breezy, Nietzschean tone, she now
wrote: "The mice at Charles River [Laboratories] . . . and in laboratories
everywhere, are . . . sentient beings who have all the biological equipment, from neuronal organization to hormones, that suggest rodent
feelings and mousy cognition, which, in scientific narratives, are kin to
our own hominid versions."[30] Here, Haraway deploys irony to distance
herself, and us, from any affective approach to the animal subject.
Meanwhile, the poststructuralist discomfort with empirical claims
leads Haraway to refer to animal cognition as a quality consistent only
with "scientific narratives"—as though to acquit herself, and us, of having to weigh in on the ontological and moral status of mice. She writes:

> I do not think that fact makes using the mice as research organisms morally
> impossible, but I believe we must take noninnocent responsibility for using living
> beings in these ways and not to talk, write, and act as if OncoMouse™, or other
> kinds of laboratory animals, were simply test systems, tools, means to brainier
> mammals' ends, and commodities. Like other family members in Western biocul-
> tural taxonomic systems, these sister mammals are both us and not-us; that is
> why we employ them. . . . Technoscience as cultural practice and practical culture
> . . . requires attention to all the meanings, identities, materialities, and account-
> abilities of the subjects and objects in play.[31]

This is all Haraway can muster about the ethical or political implications of the commodification of the "natural" world and the grotesque
atrocities visited upon hapless animals, who are brought into the
world infected with AIDS or diabetes, or made to grow human ears out
of their backs, or to produce drugs for Big Pharma. Absent is anything
remotely resembling an ethical framework.

Even worse, however, the overwhelming impression left by the narrative of *Modest-Witness* is that genetic engineering is itself a mode of transformative, perhaps even "critical" practice. In one last appropriation—and
reversal—of a concept of Mary Daly's, Haraway describes the OncoMouse
as a "vampire." Daly used that trope to describe the parasitical exploitation of women's culture by Judeo-Christianity. But here, Haraway finds in
the vampire the figure of a redeemer, one who smashes boundaries:

> The existence of vampires tropes the purity of lineage, certainty of kind, boundary of community, order of sex, closure of race, inertness of objects, liveliness of subjects, and clarity of gender. . . . Figures of violation as well as possibility and of escape from the organic-sacred walls of European Christian community, vampires make categories travel. . . . [V]ampires are ambiguous—like capital, genes, viruses, transsexuals, Jews, gypsies, prostitutes, or anybody else who can figure corporate mixing in a rapidly changing culture that remains obsessed with purity (p. 80).

Here again, Haraway conflates social categories with ontological ones—the "inertness of objects" rendered equivalent to the "order of sex, closure of race." Genetic engineering, in blurring the putatively "ontological" boundaries between species is thus essentially progressive. As a "vampire" who unsettles boundaries, OncoMouse is an antiracist, antisexist revolutionary agent. "Whether s/he proves to be otherwise productive or not, OncoMouse™ has already done major semiotic work" (p. 80). Expressivism had come a long way.

Contemporary poststructuralist critics persist in making use of Haraway's "cyborgs" and vampires, and still celebrate "boundary crossings" between persons and things. Michael Hardt and Antonio Negri, for example, in their best-selling *Empire*, affirm the inherent power of "the hybridization of humans and machines."[32]

> Bodies themselves transform and mutate to create new posthuman bodies. The first condition of this corporeal transformation is the recognition that human nature is in no way separate from nature as a whole, that there are no fixed and necessary boundaries between the human and the animal, the human and the machine, the male and the female, and so forth; it is the recognition that nature itself is an artificial terrain open to ever new mutations, mixtures, and hybridizations. Not only do we consciously subvert the traditional boundaries, dressing in drag . . . but we also move in a creative, indeterminate zone . . . in between and without regard for those boundaries.[33]

The authors seem unaware of how closely their discourse resembles that of the corporate bioengineers, the scientist- entrepreneurs busy smashing the boundary between subjects and objects by creating so-called "biological machines" or "hybrots"—hybrid entities that use the living brains of animals to control robotic devices.

"BREAKING THE SILENCE":
POSTMODERNIST IDENTITY POLITICS

In the 1990s two erstwhile intellectual antithetical intellectual cur-
rents—poststructuralist French philosophy and identity politics—con-
verged. This may seem surprising. Postmodernism, after all, takes as its
starting point the disruption of stable forms of identity.[34] Postmodernism is often seen as esoteric and elitist, while identity politics arises
out of the almost folk idea that claiming one's unique cultural heritage
can provide a secure foundation both for understanding power and constructing a political project. Postmodernists, moreover, are hostile to
"essentialism" in all its iterations, while identity politics seems most
characteristic when taking essentialist form—e.g., in the quest for the
"black soul" or an "inner lesbian." Nonetheless, by the 1990s, these erstwhile strange bedfellows had found common ground in the discourses of
high theory. Now, women of color could struggle for justice not through
expressing an inner identity, but serving as a *transit* point or vector for
discourse: "As gendered and racial subjects, black women speak/write in
multiple voices.... It is this subjective plurality ... that, finally, allows the
black woman to become an expressive site for a dialectics/dialogics of
identity and difference."[35] The author of course entitled this particular
essay, "Speaking in Tongues."

The transformation in theory that made it possible to have one's
identity politics and one's anti-essentialism, too, occurred gradually,
indeed, almost imperceptibly. In the 1980s, praxis had become identified in many circles of praxis with "breaking the silence"—a phrase
popularized in a paper given by Audre Lorde at the Modern Language
Association in 1977, in which she had spoken eloquently of the need of
marginalized, historically silenced and invisible subjects to transform
silence into speech and action.[36] Other feminist critics, most notably
bell hooks, took Lorde's call to heart and made it the center of their
own theorizing. "When we dare to speak in a liberatory voice," hooks
wrote in *Talking Back*, "we threaten even those who may initially claim
to want our words. In the act of overcoming our fear of speech ... in the
process of learning to speak as subjects, we participate in the global
struggle to end domination. When we end our silence, when we speak
in a liberated voice, our words connect us with anyone, anywhere who
lives in silence."[37] "Talking back," therefore, was "the expression of our
movement from object to subject—the liberated voice."[38] Speaking "is

not solely an expression of creative power," but "an act of resistance, a political gesture"—"a gesture of defiance that heals."[39] Here hooks collapses praxis into an "act" or "gesture" of speech. Strategy, meanwhile, appears only as a moment within speech: reflecting on the obstacles faced by women of color seeking to create their own forms of representation, hooks concludes that it "is difficult to maintain a sense of direction, a strategy for liberated speaking."[40]

By the 1990s, the metaphor of "breaking the silence" had become a tired but inescapable cliché for the utterance of many an oppositional or radical sentiment. "The subaltern are [sic] screaming. / Achieving their voice-consciousness. / The subaltern are screaming, affirming our lives. . . . / I refuse to be silenced, I refuse to be swallowed up. I will act so my voice does not get lost in the wilderness. . . . I shall speak against elitism, racism, colonialism. . . . / I have made my call. I await a response, a confirmation that I have been heard . . . ".[41] Alas, the expressivist's call and response always begs the question of who it is we expect to be the listening and responding. And what is expected to happen after the subaltern has been "heard"? Will speech alone ("speaking truth to power") effect the desired changes? It is almost as though what happens next doesn't matter. In this regard, one of the disappointing aspects of Mary Daly's otherwise brilliant materialist critique of patriarchy in *Gyn/Ecology* is the impression she gives that it is irrelevant whether feminist gestures and signs are perceived by others. "Whether or not we will 'be heard' is not the central question," she wrote. "What matters is that Hags ourselves hear, and hear our Selves" (p. 401).

In contemporary theory, lack of interest in the *dialogical* and pedagogical dimensions of critical practice undoubtedly derives from the post-structuralist's antipathy toward phenomenological accounts of human being. As I show in later chapters, the rejection of experience as the basis of knowledge has had the effect of rendering critical thought indifferent to any and all questions concerning ideology, consciousness, and meaning—what Ferry and Renault, in their study of the relation of French post-structuralism to the New Left, term the "formidable destruction of the very idea of humanity as intersubjectivity."[42] The shrinking of praxis to an essentially "one-dimensional" temporality—to an ephemeral utterance of speech—may reflect the loss of historicity under postmodernity.

Whatever its roots, it seems fair to ask how a theory of politics that cannot explain how subaltern groups might go beyond merely breaking the silence to actually being heard (that is, establishing a discourse based in mutual recognition and a common tongue) can be politically advantageous in the long run. But such a question cannot be raised within the framework of poststructuralism and identity politics, which continue to construe praxis as the unveiling of a hidden voice. Theorists continue to construct the same set pieces, to repeat the same thematic patterns of the expressivist common sense. Thus Trinh T. Minh-Hah, in phrases that could have been written by Anzuldua, or Haraway, or Norman O. Brown, or any of the Futurists: "Finding a voice, searching for words and sentences: say some thing, one thing, or no thing; tie/untie, read/unread, discard their forms; scrutinize the grammatical habits of your writing and decide for yourself whether they free or repress. . . . Shake syntax, smash the myths, and if you lose, slide on, unearth some new linguistic paths. Do you surprise? Do you shock? Do you have a choice?"[43] By 1989, when Minh-Hah jots down these words, she and other critics have successfully detached writing not only from mimesis and meaning, but also from the notion of a subject able to express anything at all. No longer can we distinguish between self and other, between one subject and multiple subjects. "No primary core of irradiation can be caught hold of"; "'I' is, itself, infinite layers. . . . Despite our desperate, eternal attempt to separate, contain, and mend, categories always leak."[44]

Alluquere Rosanne Stone, an apprentice of Donna Haraway, took praise of the disintegrated subject to new extremes in *The War of Desire and Technology at the Close of the Mechanical Age* (1995), a work "about emergent technologies, shifting boundaries between the living and nonliving, optional embodiments . . . in other words, about the everyday world as cyborg habitat."[45] In *The War of Desire*, Stone unveiled a new model of radical politics—mental illness. Multiple personality disorder, Stone argued, is a promising model for new "architectures of multiple embodiments and multiple selves"; a model for "multiplicity as resistance by other means" (pp. 43–44):

> Some forms of multiple personality are useful examples of such a social mode ready to hand. Further, in the language of the programmers who already inhabit the frontiers of the technosocial, multiple personality is a mode that is already in place, fairly debugged in the current release. Multiples exist around us here and now, and regardless of the bad press accorded to multiple personality "disorder," some remain invisible, living their lives quietly and gracefully. . . .

The cyborg, the multiple personality, the technosocial subject . . . all suggest a
radical rewriting, in the technosocial space . . . of the bounded individual as the
standard social unit and validated social actant.

As undoubtedly "radical" and "transgressive" as this conceit is, it is not,
for all that, original. It was Norman O. Brown, writing in 1964, who
excitedly observed that "schizophrenics pass beyond the reality-principle into a world of symbolic connections. . . . Schizophrenics pass
beyond ordinary language . . . into a truer, more symbolic language: 'I'm
thousands. I'm an in-divide-you-all.'"[46] Stone merely appropriated
Brown's benedictory "blessing of multiplicity" and retooled it as a new
commodity concept for the academic market.[47]

LA LINGUA CONTINUA?

Ironically, the appropriation by identity politics and postmodernist
theorists of Pentecostal mysticism in the 1980s and 1990s obscured the
moral of that story. In Acts of the Apostles, after the intervention of the
Spirit at Pentecost, people from the many nations come to dwell com-
munistically with one another ("And all that believed were together,
and had all things common"). In dividing property according to need,
and in "continuing daily with one accord" in communion with Christ,
the believers develop a "singleness of heart." The blessed community
grows, sweeping up the peoples of other kingdoms with its divine
vision of unity. Now, neither a metaphysical Holy Ghost nor even the
chosen prophets are needed as translators. Communication is enabled
by the bonds of love and mutuality. The Word of God becomes flesh, set
in motion through mystical intervention, but realized concretely
through the material practice of the spiritual community.

   The difference between the story of the Tower of Babel and the story
of Pentecostal fusion in Acts, then, is that the utopianism of the former
is initiated by human agents, and ended by divine intervention, whereas in Pentecost, fusion is initiated metaphysically, then carried out by
grassroots organization. The fable of Pentecost in this manner recuper-
ates the unity lost at Babel. Yet contemporary critical theorists choose
to forget this moral—the founding of the unified spiritual community
through evangelical expansion—in order to perseverate on an inciden-
tal moment in the narrative, that of "speaking in tongues."

In 2000, Hardt and Negri's *Empire* successfully repackaged nearly half a century's worth of "just so" stories from the lengthy chronicles of poststructuralist thought. Heralding the "nomadism" of a "multitude" of new political subjects generated by global capital, the authors excitedly describe "the transgression of customs and boundaries."[48] The rise of the "multitude" suggests "a secular Pentecost" in which "the bodies are mixed and the nomads speak a common tongue."[49] This mildly revised version of the Pentecost trope, though welcome for its new emphasis on unity (a "common tongue"), is nonetheless another discouraging sign that the structure of feeling of the Sixties continues to define—and constrain—the critical theoretical imagination.

With the decline of the left and the continued erosion of the public sphere, critical intellectuals took to the sheltering confines of the Western academy, where they now construed the struggle for social justice chiefly as a struggle over syntax, rather than over meaning and the actual institutions of power—a fervent war not against capitalism, patriarchy, or the state, but largely against convenient demons like essentialism or phallologocentrism. Women and men who had been New Left activists became academics, where they consolidated a "common sense" of praxis as speaking in tongues. Yet to make this transition, many of the values of the New Left and second wave feminism—e.g., their suspicion of professionalization and the values of the middle class, their humanistic critique of commodification and technology, their faith in experience and consciousness-raising—had to be suppressed. The Sixties optimism of the will had become an optimism of the intellect.

In recent years, "expressivism" has come under critical scrutiny for the first time by social theorists. So far the critique has not gone deep enough into the origins, or full scope, of the problem. This critique is often limited to expressivism's epistemological form—"essentialism."[50] But the postmodernist war against essentialism is almost comically misplaced. It misconstrues the "problem" of identity insofar as it reduces "essentialism" to an epistemological fallacy, rather than seeing it as it is, viz., a sign for the "structure of feeling" of a bygone era—a constellation of habits, styles, and affects that placed inner expression above or beyond consequences during the Sixties. Ironically, postmodernists expunge the best features of expressivism, such as rooting politics in passion and experience, critiquing instrumental reason, and distinguishing between authentic and inauthentic modes of being, while preserving its least convincing and indeed most debilitating aspects: a shallow temporality, the shrinking of praxis to enunciation, self-righteous self-certainty, contempt for reason, and a cavalier disinterest in questions of strategy. As Teresa Ebert observes: "Difference, it is now clear, is not simply an epistemological practice to unfound universalist foundations, it is a political apparatus to perpetuate the regime of nomadic, molecular subjects, and in so doing to keep the existing social structure intact."[51]

EXPRESSIVISM AS REIFICATION

Like the young New Leftists in the streets of Berkeley and Paris who had little patience for "academic prolixity," Gloria Anzuldua evinced disdain for "the esoteric bullshit," as she called it, of academic theory:

> Throw away abstraction and the academic learning, the rules, the map and compass. Feel your way without blinders. To touch more people, the personal realities and the social must be evoked. . . . Write with your tongues of fire. Don't let the pen banish you from yourself. . . . Don't let the censor snuff out the spark, nor the gags muffle your voice. Put your shit on paper. . . . Find the muse within you. The voice that lies buried under you, dig it up. . . . Shock yourself into new ways of perceiving the world, shock your readers to do the same.[52]

This belief, that for spontaneous speech to remake the world it would have to "shock," was a signature element not so much of the Romantics, but of the Futurists, who in the early twentieth century sought a mode of expression to describe the dizzying pace of modern urban life and the age of the machine. The Futurist movement was an important precursor to and model for what soon became the aesthetics of fascist militarism. Expressivism delinked knowledge and truth from nature— in a move Charles Taylor describes as a shift from mimesis to expression. But where the Romantics embraced nature as the horizon of being, the Futurists de-linked reason from expression and purged culture of nature. The Futurists turned not to nature as the source of truth and beauty, but human artifice: the machine and the metropolis, the exhilarating rush of modern events. Against "scientific or photographic," i.e., naturalistic, representation, Marinetti instead championed "words-in-freedom"—an "imagination without strings": "Our lyric intoxication should freely deform, reflesh the words, cutting them short, stretching them out, reinforcing the center of the extremities....Thus we will have the new orthography that I call free expressive."[53]

Futurists like the Russian artist Alexei Kruchenyk put Marinetti's call for an "instinctive deformation" into experimental aesthetic practice, disrupting the intelligibility of texts and images through neologisms, nonsense phrases, reversal of meaning, and so on, all with the goal of rupturing experience and culture by "freeing" words through sheer speed.[54] Other Futurists, e.g., Gino Severini, Giacomo Balla, and Guillaume Apollinaire, held academic learning in contempt. Marinetti wrote:

> Casting aside every stupid formula and all the confused verbalisms of the professors, I now declare that lyricism is the exquisite faculty of intoxicating oneself with life, of filling life with the inebriation of oneself. . . . The ability to color the world with the unique colors of our changeable selves.[55]

If this bold statement sounds as though it could have been published last month in some prestigious cultural studies journal, it is because another iconoclastic thinker, the French historian Michel Foucault, writing nearly three quarters of a century after the Futurist Manifesto, made similar sentiments popular in Anglo-American theory. For example, in his extravagant praise for what he called "heterotopias"—the creating of difference through the heterogeneity or fragmentation of space—Foucault invoked the same tone of giddy wonder and millenarian hope that Marinetti had to describe the "revolutionary" impact of, literally, *non-sense*. "Heterotopias are disturbing," Foucault wrote,

> probably because they secretly undermine language, because they make it impossible to name this and that, because they shatter or tangle common names, because they destroy "syntax" in advance, and not only the syntax with which we construct sentences but also that less apparent syntax that causes words and things (next to and also opposite one another) to "hold together"....[H]eterotopias...dessicate speech, stop words in their tracks, contest the very possibility of grammar at its source; they dissolve our myths and sterilize the lyricism of our sentences.[56]

The question these and similar pronouncements by Foucault obviously provoke is whether the similarity between postmodernism and Futurism is mere accident, or whether there might not be something more interesting afoot—e.g., parallel historical conditions that led to a privileging of fragmentation, smashing of linguistic convention, and contempt for nature, in both discourses. Although more work would have to be done to make this a convincing argument, it appears that the striking *formal* similarities between Futurism, on the one hand, and poststructuralism and identity politics, on the other, may have something to do with what David Harvey identifies as the two major "sea changes" in the capitalist organization of space-time in the twentieth century. What both the revolt against bourgeois sentimentality at the dawn of that century and the radical critique of feminists of color, at its dusk, appear to have in common is that both represent key moments of transition from one regime of capital accumulation to another in the West—a shift to Taylorist Fordism, in the early 1900s, and a shift to post-Fordist accumulation, in the 1980s.[57]

Seen in this light, Marinetti's call to destroy syntax and intelligibility echoed capitalism itself, as it busily furnished the materials for a potent new round of "creative destruction," which was to include global depression and two world wars. Similarly, the postmodernist aesthetics of the 1980s, which celebrated the play of superficiality and which privileged fragmentation and loss of intelligibility over meaning (and irony), correspond formally to the "logics" of late capitalism.[58] But if such an "elective affinity," to use Weber's expression, can be observed in the postmodernist aesthetic vanguard's synergistic mimicry of the new modality of commodity fetishism, perhaps we can also see an affinity between post-Fordism and the reified language of "speaking in tongues," "boundary crossings," and the fetish of the "diaspora" of critical theory of the same era. "Critical" social practice may be mimicking, and indeed codifying, the logic of a new regime of capital, as well as the social pathologies—like mental illness and mass murder—that have accompanied it. Hence, the confluence of material and intellectual factors, which have come to a head in "baroque" theory—or the mediocritization and standardization of thought and its overdetermination by the commodity—is the subject of my next chapter.

3 Baroque Theory

Modern critical philosophy springs from the reified structure
of consciousness.—GEORG LUKÁCS

During the 1980s and 1990s the lifeworld of the advanced capitalist
countries was colonized and penetrated by capital and commodity
fetishism more rapidly, and at a more profound psychic and anthropological level, than in any comparable period in the history of capitalism. A *risorgimento* of monopoly capitalism, encouraged by a
rampaging stock market and permissive federal regulators, led to new
concentrations of wealth, a rollback of the social welfare state, and the
privatization of public goods. Coterminous with these macroeconom-
ic policies, which arose in direct response to profitability crises in capitalism, a "postmodern" culture took shape in which the commodity
came to stand in for every possibility of historical, lived human experience. Suffice it to say, in such a pervasive context of cultural corruption, it would indeed have been remarkable had critical knowledge
escaped unscathed, retaining its integrity in the face of the power of
the market. In the event, it did not.

The general decline and disarray of left social movements in the
West after the 1970s led to a decoupling of theory from practice. This in
turn made Western critical thought vulnerable to the new institutional and political milieu in which it found itself inside the academy,
where it had largely retreated. As critical social thought became
increasingly estranged from actual practice, and more enmeshed within an increasingly rationalized Western university system, theory
became caught in the orbit of that massive sun whose gravity irresistibly distorts the trajectory of all bodies—the market.

As theory became vulnerable to the spatio-temporal rhythms and relations of the new regime of global capital, less and less directly engaged in the problems of human society, it became more heteronomous in its determinations and correspondingly less *truthful*. In content, theory became idealist; in form, meanwhile, it became *baroque*. Following is an artifact from what might be called the late-twentieth-century baroque period in cultural studies:

> The installation of the phallic Damoclean sword as a Social Ideal evokes an ambivalent social identification embodied in the muscular tension of the borderline native. His "disincorporation" in paranoia and melancholia are attempts to break the marginality of the social and political limits of space; to redraw the boundaries in a psychic, fantasmatic space. The Damoclean sword installs an ambivalence in the symbolic order, where it is itself the immobile Sign of an authority whose meaning is continually contested by the fantasmatic, fragmented, motility of the signifiers of revolt. . . .
>
> Let us call the melancholic revolt the "projective disincorporation" by the marginal of the Master. This narrative speaks from the elision between the synchronous symbol of loss and its non-referential, fragmented, phantasmatic narratives. . . . My revolt is to face the Life of literature and history with the scraps and fragments that constitute its double, which is living as surviving, meaning as melancholia.[1]

By the early 1990s, it had become difficult to wander far through the miasma of cultural studies without encountering texts of similar opacity as in this excerpt from "Postcolonial Authority and Postmodern Guilt," by Homi K. Bhabha. Aesthetically, texts such as this call to mind the "transitoriness and mutability" of expression common to the baroque period in European art and architecture. For, like the late Baroque period in art and architecture in the court of Louis XIV, which saw costly materials lavished in the service of an immensely decorative aesthetic, one which often gestured emptily toward function and utility, such baroque theories are distinguished by an extravagant ornateness, a redundancy of form, that is all the more striking for the exceedingly slight idea at the center of the artist's conception.

A baroque aesthetic, characterized by density of expression and frenetic rhythms has suffused Western capitalist culture in recent decades, infecting everything from popular culture and science to literature and video games.[2] Bhabha's erstwhile "critical" discourse is therefore analogous, in a weird way, to the general privileging of superficial form over content throughout our commodified culture. The graphic information analyst Edward Tufte's observation that PowerPoint (the Microsoft Corporation's ubiquitous business presentation program) "is entirely *presenter-oriented*, and not *content-oriented, not audience-oriented*," applies equally to Bhabha's style.

In "Postcolonial Authority and Postmodern Guilt" and in his *The Location of Culture* (in which a later version of the essay appears) Bhabha presents a series of meditations on the representation of "the native" as a figure in postcolonial literary fiction. His ostensible focus is on the importance of the "time lag," or moment of contingency, in postcolonial narratives—the temporal break, that is, between the moment of experience and the representation of that experience. On Bhabha's usage, the "time lag" disrupts fixed meanings, hence undermining liberal, rational, and humanist conceptions of historical agency and meaning. But the exact meaning of Bhabha's essay is obscure, buried as it is beneath layers of playful erudition, self- referential allusion, and theoretical "dappling." The essay is structureless and even *atemporal*: an idea is not so much developed here as spatialized. Freud, Barthes, Foucault, Mohanty, Lacan, Stuart Hall, the subaltern studies group—all the canonical figures of postcolonial studies are breathlessly invoked, then quickly dispatched, with that familiar mix of facility and indifference characteristic of Bhabha's cosmopolitan style. The author's prose, florid, clever, suggestive of boundless, depthless play—a striking rhetorical virtuosity coupled with a density of expression bordering on opacity—suggests an *aestheticized* conception of knowledge. For what seems to count as theoretical "success" here is the ability of the work in question to invoke an experience of the Kantian sublime—a sense of transcendental awe, vertigo, or "exhilaration" in the viewer at the sheer intricacy of it all.[3]

Typical of the baroque period is the late-seventeenth-century bronze ewer by Massimiliano Soldani, described by one art historian as a work "so ebullient and so openly expansive that the characteristic slender form of the prototype is almost totally forgotten. Here we cannot really speak of relief decoration on the body of the vase, for *the very shape of the ewer is determined by the rhythmic flow of the ornament.*"[4] Like Soldani's ewer, baroque theory is technically ingenious, formally inventive, aesthetically protean. Yet with every added ornamental layer its "usefulness" in

Bronze Ewer with Amphitrite and a Nereid, MASSIMILIANO SOLDANI (c. 1710–15)

understanding society, and illuminating paths to overcoming it, seems to diminish. Following Jameson, who suggests that under the present regime of commodity fetishism "exchange value has been generalized to the point at which the very memory of use value is effaced,"[5] we may conclude that *baroque* theory is in fact a form of "critical" knowledge that has *lost the memory of its original use value*. Or, to put it another way, baroque theory is theory in which the polarity between its use value as a mode of normative historical critique and strategic insight, on the one hand, and its exchange value as a commodity to be traded in the academic market, on the other, has flipped.

The notion that philosophy, which has always prided itself on remaining aloof from temporal interests, might simply "give in" to market forces has haunted the tradition ever since Socrates labored to distinguish his own "love of wisdom" from other Sophists' teaching of rhetoric and dialectic purely for monetary gain. However, it was only with the advent of the modern capitalist era, as the commodification of labor became both compulsory and universal, that market pressures on knowledge became correspondingly acute. By the mid-nineteenth century, Marx and Engels believed they could discern within the conceptual structures and aporias of German idealism the values and divisions of bourgeois society as such. In the 1920s, Georg Lukács elaborated Marx and Engels' critique in his brilliant work, *History and Class Consciousness*, with his famous description of *reification*—the cultural process in capitalism by which subjects are turned into objects, and objects into seeming "subjects," under the twin pressures of commodification and rationalization. Lukács extended Marx's critique of speculative thought to show how philosophy had been overdetermined by commodity relations.[6] In later years, members of the Frankfurt School sharply criticized Enlightenment thought for having mistaken efficiency and instrumentalism for truth. Horkheimer commented in 1947: "Industrialism puts pressure even upon the philosophers to conceive their work in terms of the processes of producing standardized cutlery. Some of them seem to feel that concepts and categories should leave workshops clean-cut and looking brand-new."[7]

Even Horkheimer could not have foreseen that by century's end, "critical" theory itself—an emancipatory discourse rooted in the French Revolution—would come to mimic the logic of the commodity. Yet by the 1990s critical knowledge was being marketed, packaged, and sold much like any other commodity. Academic presses, some pushed to the margins of publishing existence, were under growing pressure to compete for and "sign" the latest up-and- coming theorists. Editors from academic presses visited colleges and universities where "brilliant" theories had emerged before. Like athletics scouts, they aggressively sought out new works and rising academic stars with likely marketability. Once acquired, each book is anointed with its own marketing plan to maximize its visibility and placement among other knowledge commodities in the crowded "marketplace of ideas."[8]

Critical theory, a discourse that originally evolved out of urgent human needs, came to be overdetermined by commodity relations. Its use value was supplanted by its exchange value. As we will see, confronted with new conditions of knowledge production, critical producers of knowledge adapted to the new conditions. Theory assumed new guises, new camouflages, in order to survive the brutal selection process of the market.

"USE VALUE" AND THE BAROQUE ARSENAL OF THEORY

I have borrowed the metaphor of a baroque tendency in critical thought from Mary Kaldor's The Baroque Arsenal, her now classic study of the evolution and devolution of the modern weapons system.[9] Despite the obvious differences between strategic weapons and critical theory, in both cases we find a highly trained intelligentsia, drawn from a similar institutional base (the capitalist university system of the West), producing commodified artifacts on the basis of a highly specialized division of labor. Kaldor's study is therefore suggestive in showing what happens when a form of knowledge intended for application is forced to develop in the absence of an organic connection between theory and practice—i.e., a meaningful link between the criteria determining the formal qualities of the produced object, on one side, and its practical application or use in the field, on the other.

The subject of Kaldor's study is the complex institutional and decision-making environment in which the design and production of highly advanced, capital-intensive weapons systems like strategic bombers, nuclear submarines, ICBMs, and so on, took place during the postwar period. Kaldor was struck by a signal paradox at the heart of the weapons system design process: an inverse ratio seemed to inhere between the enormous capital and labor investments needed to produce new, high-tech weapons, and the diminishing *utility* of the weapons themselves at the far end of the production process. The arsenals of the United States and its allies had become "immensely sophisticated and elaborate," but also "less and less functional" from an economic and military perspective. As "feats of tremendous ingenuity, talent, and organisation," Kaldor wrote, the "baroque" weapons system "achieved a certain grandeur, a certain ability to instill social awe, that is often to be found in the baroque, whether art, architecture, or technology." Yet this very "grandeur" seems "to portend degeneration" rather than dynamism or innovation. Paradoxically, then, the more complex and densely layered these weapons systems become in form, the more "reliability declines and operational costs increase at an exponential rate."[10] Today's baroque weapons systems now require tens of thousands of spare parts and thousands of highly specialized personnel to be maintained. They are more prone to accident and breakdown than the older systems, and they are more difficult and costly to service. Their price tags, meanwhile, have increased exponentially. By the late 1970s, the production cost of the average fighter plane was one hundred times what it had been during World War II; a new bomber, two hundred times more expensive.[11] Since Kaldor's book was first published, subsequent developments in U.S. weapons design and deployment patterns only seem to have confirmed her conclusions.[12]

The question is, what caused the reification of the modern weapons system? Kaldor finds a link between the baroque weapons system and the context in which the systems emerged. Politically and militarily, that context was one of "peace." To be sure, between 1945 and 1975 the United States fought two major wars in Southeast Asia and often intervened militarily in third world countries. Yet America's overall strategic doctrine and procurement policies, especially vis-à-vis the major weapons systems, were shaped by deterrence theory and planning for a global thermonuclear war with the Soviet Union. Because of the Cold War stalemate, however, doctrine and hardware were forced to develop along speculative lines, through threat assessment and gaming models. But as strategic weapons design developed independently of the exigencies of actual warfare—that is, outside of a context of use in combat—procurement decisions and war theory became more and more vulnerable to the play of arbitrary forces and competing institutional interests. "In the absence of trial by battle, the quantity and nature of the armaments we acquire is determined as much by the environment in which we take decisions as it is by the posture of a potential adversary."[13]

Two institutional processes or forces seem to have shaped procurement outcomes. First, the bureaucratic conservatism of the liberal capitalist state. Political and military leaders generally favored continued refinement of already existing systems—the submarine, strategic bomber, fighter, and so on—which, they believed, had already been "proven" during World War II. Rather than develop entirely new kinds of armaments to meet changing mission needs, state and military leaders thus favored "follow-on" weapons systems. That is, at the end of a production cycle, monies were directed toward developing a more advanced version of the same basic design: the F-80 fighter was replaced directly by the F-104, which was eventually replaced by the F-16, then the F-117, and so on.[14] Exacerbated by interservice rivalry (competition for scarce state resources), bureaucratic inertia seeped into the design process.

The second institutional force was the technological dynamism of leading corporate defense contractors themselves. Throughout the postwar period, the U.S. Department of Defense favored keeping a competitive procurement environment, which ensured that the prime military contractors would remain few in number and huge in scale. (In the 1990s, consolidations within the military industry became more frequent and larger in scale, increasing competitive pressures.) In response to this tight market, they were forced to turn to small-scale technological advances to increase the value-added component of their commodities. In this manner, the bureaucratic conservatism of the state dovetailed with the technological dynamism of corporate capital in a way that severely distorted the design process. The enormous productive capacities of the primes increasingly focused on "trend innovation"—perpetual, micro-incremental enhancements of already existing technical "performance characteristics." That is, planes were made to fly farther, submarines to operate more quietly, bombers to carry more (or better) munitions, and so on.[15] The net result of this "contradictory process in which technology was simultaneously promoted and restrained" was that increased inputs yielded dwindling returns in terms of weapons readiness and potency, even as the weapons systems themselves achieved spectacular *aesthetic* effects (the "shock and awe" of the 2003 invasion of Iraq).

Kaldor's exemplary empirical analysis demonstrates how a form of knowledge intended originally for "use," when developed outside a context of direct practice, fell victim to exogenous forces, forces that shaped them in ways unintended by their designers or producers. To see the relevance of Kaldor's account for the plight of critical theory today, we first need to consider the "use value" of critical theory. We must then carefully attend to the specific constellation of institutional and cultural forces that have shaped theory over the past quarter-century. Only then will we be in a position to see whether and how closely critical forms of theoretical reflection have indeed taken on baroque distortions.

For earlier generations of radical intellectuals, theory was closely tied to its usefulness both in illuminating structures of power and in providing a theory of how actually to change society. In the nineteenth and twentieth centuries, revolutionaries treated "critical" knowledge both as a good in itself and also for its strategic properties, as an organic fund for collective appropriation by a cadre of activists committed to social change. Knowledge for many earlier radicals, whether Gandhi, Lenin, or Ella Baker, had an "existential" import. In order to change social conditions, revolutionary intellectuals struggled to survive in the face of brute state repression. One produced knowledge so that others literally might live, and often one did so at great personal risk. To those in power, the radicalized intellectual was an even more potent threat than the violent militant. Hence the solemn comment by the fascist prosecutor at Gramsci's trial in Rome in 1928: "We must prevent this brain from functioning for twenty years."[16]

For Marxists and anarchists, practice was the proving ground of theory. Theoretical knowledge, as a dialectical guide to practice, could be taken back into the shop, retooled, then set out into the world again.[17] Only through a "process of testing and developing theory," as Mao Tse-tung put it, might the revolutionary achieve a truthful and accurate—which is to say, useful—knowledge. "Discover the truth through practice, and again through practice verify and develop the truth."[18] Of course, contra this declaration by Mao, by no means did a dialectic between theory and practice guarantee the truth value of either. Yet the assumption of a necessary relation between theory and practice did serve as a kind of structural "surety" that theory would not mirror the interests of a particular class or state.

Earlier Marxists had warned that knowledge produced outside a context of direct use risked what Gramsci called "speculative" and "scholastic" distortions. The history of Western Marxism after World War I, however, is in some respects the history of a declension from a politically engaged theory to a more scholastic one. While third world revolutionaries put radical knowledge to direct use in their struggles against colonialism, in the advanced capitalist countries, particularly in the United States, the critical intelligentsia, faced with the decline of working- class and revolutionary movements in the West, retreated into the relative sanctuary of the academy. The result, Perry Anderson argued in *Considerations in Western Marxism*, has been a "formal shift" away from concrete economic and political analysis toward a more esoteric and theoreticist discourse characterized by, among other things, the privileging of form over content, an impenetrable and self-enclosed style, a tendency toward specialization, and a shift in attention away from the problem of totality. In short, theory in the developed capitalist countries came to adopt "an increasingly specialized and inaccessible cast," becoming "a prolonged and intricate Discourse on Method."[19] Anderson's analysis misses the historical significance of the civil rights and the second wave feminist movements, both of which forged a novel conception of praxis, and for a time brought theory and practice into harmony. However, he is correct when he observes an overall trend toward formalism in theory. What remains to be seen is how the lack of an organic link between theory and practice may have made theory vulnerable to exogenous forces that encouraged the most speculative trends to run amok.

Rapid expansion of university education after 1945 had two main consequences for the production of knowledge. The first was to upend many of the protected traditions and professional protocols of the academic field itself. The mass influx of students signaled the beginning of the end of the special, guildlike status enjoyed by the professoriate for centuries. The second consequence of the rapid growth of the universities was to heighten the importance of higher education from the perspective of the state. As the Cold War escalated, the university became vastly more integrated both with the state and capitalist production. In the United States, state elites' appreciation for the university's ability to sustain a highly differentiated economy was matched by its function in providing a measure of social control and legitimation and serving as the preeminent knowledge base for maintaining military hegemony.[20] Corporate links to the university were also strengthened. Such arrangements, while enthusiastically supported by university administrators like Clark Kerr at the University of California, came under sharp criticism from students and some faculty in the extraordinary upheavals of the 1960s. In retrospect, however, despite students' success in breaking the domestic consensus on the Vietnam War, establishing ethnic studies programs, and securing basic civil liberties on campus, the student protests of the 1960s had little long-term effect on the corporatization of the university.

As Sheila Slaughter and Larry Leslie show, from the mid-1960s to the present the university system has been subject to an intensive and extensive rationalization process in order to meet the demands of a post-Fordist, globalized world economy.[21] To find a precedent for this massive qualitative shift in the basic organization and mission of the Western university system, they argue, one would have to go back to nineteenth-century industrialization. Globalization today "is destabilizing patterns of university professional work developed over the past hundred years."[22] Beginning in the late 1970s, as intercapitalist competition began to take its toll in inflation and declining productivity rates in the United States, the state began to scale back its funding for education and other discretionary programs in order to spur economic growth. To streamline production and reform the economy to better enable the expanded consumer sphere, production was organized along post-Fordist lines. Vertical production controls were abandoned for more flexible, horizontal arrangements, and batch production began to be tied in earnest to micro-niche marketing. As the state turned sharply against social Keynesianism and the welfare state, cutting social services, selling off public institutions, and introducing market norms into every conceivable area of society, the university system became ground zero of the rationalization process.

Beginning in the 1980s, in the wake of sharp cutbacks in public support for higher education, universities began a profound redefinition of their basic educational missions. We now see a shift of resources from the humanities, social sciences, and natural sciences to the applied sciences and professional schools. Universities have increased spending on administration—public relations, legal departments, and technical support—while decreasing spending on instruction and physical plant.

Whole departments and programs deemed "redundant" or inessential (particularly traditionally female-dominated fields like education and foreign languages) have been sharply cut back or even eliminated. Meanwhile, universities have also quietly effected a transfer of teaching responsibilities from tenured faculty to casual, part-time labor—graduate students, itinerant readers, and lecturers. Between 1975 and 1993, the number of part-time adjuncts employed in the United States went up nearly 100 percent, while adjuncts as a whole counted for 46 percent of the American professoriate (up from 22 percent in 1970).[23]

Closely imbricated with the rationalization of the university was the commodification of knowledge as such. In *The Postmodern Condition*, Jean-François Lyotard had linked the decline of the "universal" intellectual to the transformation of knowledge in the dawning information age.[24] The information revolution and with it the spread of computer technologies is destroying the nominal values that historically served to legitimate Western knowledge and the institution of the university. Formalizing critiques first popularized by radical students during the upheavals of the 1960s in France and the United States, Lyotard argued that the function of knowledge is essentially "to supply the system with players capable of acceptably fulfilling their roles at the pragmatic posts required by its institutions."[25] Now that the state is concerned almost exclusively with reproducing technical competencies, the qualitative aspect of knowledge is being negated and replaced by a quantitative aspect. "The relationship of the suppliers and users of knowledge to the knowledge they supply and use," Lyotard wrote, "is now tending, and will increasingly tend, to assume the form of commodity producers and consumers to the commodities they produce and consume— that is, the form of value. Knowledge is and will be produced in order to be sold, it is and will be consumed in order to be valorized in a new production: in both cases, the goal is exchange. *Knowledge ceases to be an end in itself, it loses its 'use-value.'* "[26]

Lyotard's prognosis proved to be prescient. So central has the commodification of academic knowledge been to the new economic order that Slaughter and Leslie aptly describe the overall transformation of the university today in terms of a shift "from a liberal arts core to an entrepreneurial periphery." Federally enacted laws have encouraged outside corporate entities to commodify the products of academic research and give the state's blessing to the privatization of knowledge.

Facing historic declines in state funding for higher education, public research institutions have been among the most eager to get on board with the new philosophy. At first, university administrators turned to corporations chiefly as a way to replace public funds. But now it is clear that the instrumentalization of knowledge serves a *political* function as well. "Technology transfer" arrangements between academia and private corporations are leading to the consolidation of a new "common sense" philosophy about knowledge, based on naked instrumentalism. The commodification of knowledge has indeed already become so normalized that universities no longer make any effort to hide it.

The question, however, is how the shift to an entrepreneurial culture in the university may have affected, or even distorted, critical discourse. An important clue is provided by sociological studies showing what typically occurs when less successful, peripheral players in an organizational hierarchy must somehow cope with their own marginalization within a given institutional field. Paul J. DiMaggio and Walter W. Powell, for example, have found that such players tend to adopt the same, or homologous, habits and strategies as those employed by the hegemonic players; they tend to adopt *isomorphically* to the dominant regime.[27] The baroque genre is perhaps best grasped as an *adaptive* measure by intellectuals to survive in the face of "forced obsolescence" (the declining fortunes of popular social movements) as well as the rationalization of the knowledge industry. Baroque theorists have responded to a changed institutional climate marked by dwindling university resources and corporatization with essentially three specific isomorphic adaptations. The first is outright identification or collusion with corporate capital. The second is *commodity aesthetics* or "trend innovation"—the adoption of formal or rhetorical strategies (repetition of set patterns, use of reified language, and so on, all in mimicry of the dominant commodity regime) to shore up declining use and exchange values. The third, finally, is the "anthropological" metamorphosis of the intellectual's own person into an object of erotic power.

First, with competitive pressures increased at all points in the university system, some academics along the "periphery" have adapted to the new entrepreneurial culture with what can only be called a vulgar careerism. One anthropologist, for example, who in the 1960s received his academic training in "community, social organization, Latin America, ethnohistory, and culture change," describes in *American Anthropolo-*

gist his own personally successful "transition from academic, research-oriented anthropologist to practical, results-oriented business consultant."[28] No doubt striking a chord with his audience—mainstream academics who have not been blind to their own envelopment by the new corporate ethos—the author is reassuring. "Anthropology does have unique gifts to bring to business," he says. Corporate networking, which has largely replaced live "face-to-face" contacts, has generated "another opportunity for the application of anthropology." The key to realizing these opportunities lies in the facts of post-Fordist, entrepreneurial knowledge. "The new emphasis is on flexible, open production groups...and an extension of networks. . . . Also desired are collaborative relations of production, distribution, and sales, relationships that are meant to benefit everyone's self-interest." And lest we forget, the former grassroots organizer reminds us, "Enlightened self-interest is the engine of change."[29] Enlightened self-interest appears to have been on the mind of Harvard professor Henry Louis Gates, Jr., similarly, when he appeared in 2002 in a two-page color advertisement in *The New York Times Magazine* for IBM's ThinkPad computer.[30]

The literal commodification of theory can be observed in academic feminist theory, where one sees the use value of feminism diminished by corporatization, on the one side, and poststructuralism, on the other. If we had to limn the overall arc of Franco-Anglo-American academic feminism in the last quarter-century, we could probably do no better than to place Adrienne Rich's dream of a "woman-centered university" at its start, and Lucy Suchman's subordination of feminist poststructuralism to the needs of the modern corporate research park at its end. In 1979, when Adrienne Rich wrote "Toward a Woman-Centered University," many feminists agreed with her about the need for a revolution in higher education.[31] Written at a time when feminist scholars were just beginning to gain a toehold in the academy, Rich's essay sounded a presciently cautionary note. The university, she noted, was an elitist system whose norms and power structures had reproduced fundamental hierarchies between men and women, teachers and students, academy and community for centuries. Academic feminists therefore faced a double burden. Not only would they have to invent a non-masculinist curriculum, they would also have to dislodge an obstinately patriarchal culture that was actively hostile to the democratization of knowledge and the meeting of social needs. Transforming the university would therefore mean challenging "the hierarchical image, the structure of relationships, even the style of discourse, including assumptions about theory and practice, ends and means, process and goal" of university education.[32] Rich proposed a radically democratic alternative—an "androcentric" university—where hierarchy, professionalization, and elitism would be overthrown, and feminists would challenge the specialization of knowledge and the reduction of truth to quantitative measures.

But what happened was the opposite. The shift toward market-based criteria of knowledge, along with increased competition for academic positions, took their toll on women in the university, leading some feminist theorists to respond to the rationalization and commodification of knowledge by following suit.[33] Some feminists sought to beat men at their own game, by abandoning grassroots, activist publications for rigorous peer-reviewed journals intended to legitimate feminist knowledges. A turning point came with the founding of the journal *Signs* in 1975.[34] The creators of *Signs* consciously modeled it on "rigorous" academic journals. Based at a prestigious campus (the University of Chicago) the new journal favored, in McDermott's words, "detached, intricately argued, specialized rational analysis"—in marked contrast with the impassioned discourse of *Frontiers* and similar grassroots journals.[35] As the women's movement declined throughout the 1980s, grassroots feminist journals underwent successive, increasingly severe financial crises. Some, to survive, adapted by striking up formal institutional arrangements with university presses. By the 1990s, McDermott finds, "feminist academic journals [had] been drawn completely inside the university and [had] only tenuous connections to the splintered and withered community movement."[36]

Having lost its ties to organic movements and practices, Anglo-American feminist thought also became more and more drawn to poststructuralism. Second wave feminists like Adrienne Rich had sought to tear down the hierarchies between the academy and the community, student and teacher. They had sought to create new, potent social use values in knowledge. The new generation of feminist theorists, however, assimilated to the masculine culture, and at times seemed even to amplify the system's cult of professionalization. Rather than seeking to found a vital feminist theory capable of improving women's lives, feminist academics now became mired in scholastic debates about "essentialism" versus "anti-essentialism."[37] By the 1990s, Adrienne Rich's plea for a true community of feminist scholars and activists—for the creation of a university that "would serve the needs of the human, visible community in which it sits—the neighborhood, the city, the rural county"—had been left by the wayside.[38]

Enter Lucy Suchman. In the late 1990s, Suchman, a feminist ethnographic researcher and science studies scholar, was an employee at Xerox PARC, a private research center based in Palo Alto, California. PARC brought together scientists, design engineers, and social scientists in a "culture of collaboration" to facilitate the technology transfer process—i.e., the creation of "new and innovative products." PARC's mission statement described it as "a tremendous strategic resource for Xerox," one that "delivers devices, subsystems and modules of technology that enable Xerox products and product concepts." PARC "creates new Xerox business opportunities" and "generates revenues for Xerox"; and many "mechanisms, both formal and informal, ensure that PARC research is closely linked to the market."[39] In this technology-transfer environment, Suchman found a seemingly unlikely niche for her brand of poststructuralist feminism.

Suchman successfully parlayed her expertise in postmodernist discourses into a capitalist tool. In one PARC paper ("Working Relations of Technology Production and Use") Suchman applied feminist epistemology to the problem of corporate product design. Drawing on the works of such figures as Donna Haraway and Gloria Anzuldua, Suchman sketched "what a feminist politics and associated practices of system development" would look like if applied to the technology transfer process at companies like Xerox.[40] The style and content of Suchman's prose resounded with the familiar catchphrases of technoscience studies, from "detached engagement," "border crossings," to "the view from nowhere" and "partial knowledges." For example: "The movement is from [sic] a single, asituated, master perspective that bases its claims to objectivity in the closure of debate, to multiple, located, partial perspectives that find their objective character through ongoing dialogue. . . . The feminist move in particular reframes the locus of objectivity from an established body of knowledge . . . to knowledges in dynamic production, reproduction and transformation."[41]

Suchman's ostensible aim in this and other papers was to show "that feminism offers a way to begin to replace the designer/user opposition— an opposition that closes off our possibilities for recognizing the subtle and profound boundaries that actually divide us—with a rich, densely structured landscape of identities and working relations."[42] To put the matter more plainly, however, Suchman argued that technology design- ers should work more closely and collaboratively on site with users to determine their actual needs in the workplace. Here, for a time, baroque feminist theory, which had previously shown itself to be quite useless in terms of serving the social needs of actual women, appeared to have dis- covered something like its métier—viz., as a "useful" tool for making commodities and technological processes more responsive to the needs of multiple users, and hence more productive for capital. In 2000, how- ever, Xerox unceremoniously closed PARC permanently, saying that the research there had proved unprofitable. Apparently, the rhetoric of "border crossings" proved as worthless for the generation of surplus value as it had for feminist praxis.

COMMODITY AESTHETICS

Such examples of "selling out," though the exception rather than the rule, indicate the degree to which a form of knowledge once grounded in critique has systematically been corrupted by power. However, isomor- phic adaptation by the critical intelligentsia to new pressures toward forced obsolescence have typically taken more subtle form—commodity aesthetics and the "follow- on" system in theory (trend innovation).

In an effort to shore up the appearance of use value in a saturated market, the producer engages in a series of ingenious improvisations at the level of aesthetic form. To sell, the commodity must now achieve what Wolfgang Haug calls "aesthetic innovation"—i.e., "the subordina- tion of use value to brand name."[43] It is for this reason that baroque theorists are concerned less with persuasiveness of argument or coher- ence of thought than with the successful presentation of an *original style*. Homi Bhabha, for instance, has successfully positioned his work as a superior "good" within the niche market of theory, where his eru- dition signals a distinctive "brand name" of theoretical competence: no one can "riff" on postcolonial semiotics the way Bhabha can.[44]

Virtuosity of aesthetic expression first became indispensable in the accumulation of "academic capital" in postwar France. The reasons were, again, structural. In the postwar period, the relative autonomy of academics, their frankly anachronistic status as independent commodi- ty producers, was progressively eroded by the state and the market.[45]

The modern technocratic state no longer requires the traditional "services" of intellectuals in legitimating social norms because capitalism essentially legislates values for them. In France, for example, Niilo Kauppi shows that after World War II, French intellectuals underwent a transformation from "state-centered" to "market-centered" intellectuals, as the rise of the mass media effectively undermined the traditional intellectual field.[46] For previous generations of French establishment intellectuals, academic prestige had been acquired only through long years of largely anonymous scholarly research. The massive economic restructuring of the educational system in the 1950s and 1960s, however, diminished the influence of older fields and strengthened newer ones, opening the way for interdisciplinary research and also making possible the rise of new stars. The result was a profound rupture in the older French intellectual field, as "media and cultural journalism made possible accumulation of economic income and cultural fame with less investment."[47] By the 1970s, scholarly ideas and debates began to be taken up in the mainstream press, and young, chic professors were glamorized in the media as stars or celebrities.[48]

Kauppi shows how the breakdown of the blood-brain barrier between academia and popular culture made possible "the rapid ascension of certain groups to high academic and literary positions."[49] The avant-garde French journal, *Tel Quel*, home to Foucault, Barthes, Sollers, Kristeva, and others, was the nexus for the expansion of the new French "style" in theory. Structuralism and poststructuralism encouraged a "strategy of innovation," allowing theorists like Kristeva and Derrida "to present new products and research areas by adopting dangerous and daring profiles."[50] With the help of journalists like Didier Eribon, the critics at *Tel Quel* were able to popularize their discourses while crafting a careful "self-image."[51] From about the 1970s, Michelle Lamont shows, a "sophisticated rhetoric" became "a structural requirement for intellectual legitimation" within the French intellectual field.[52] Lamont specifically shows how Jacques Derrida's impressive ascension within the French and American academic fields, at a time of otherwise declining interest in philosophy as a discipline, lay partly in Derrida's canny ability to diversify his intellectual portfolio, as it were, by appealing to literary scholars and anthropologists. Derrida's "theoretical trademark" as a prestigious cultural good, Lamont writes, "is so clearly packaged and labeled that it can readily circulate in the intellectual community."[53]

Ironically, while the principals of the structuralist and poststructuralist movements—Derrida, Foucault, Althusser, Lacan, Lyotard, Kristeva, Deleuze, Guattari—were all French, the aesthetic elements of both
only fully flourished when they had made their way to the United States.
Marx and Engels once noted the ease with which ideas "evolved on
another soil" (France) were later imported wholesale "to the conquered
country" (Germany). However, they observed, "whereas in its home it
was still encumbered with interests and relationships left over from earlier periods, here it can and must be established completely and without
hindrances."[54] In the late twentieth century, poststructuralism proved
unable to overcome certain hindrances in France, especially a native and
entrenched humanism, the state meritocracy, and the persistence of
labor and socialist movements that never accepted many postmodernist
claims. No such encumberments, however, stood in the way of the postmodern turn on this side of the Atlantic, where the "French ideology"
found a most hospitable climate for its febrile and chaotic growth: an
open academic field, advanced commodity fetishism, and stark class
inequalities favoring the cultivation of a star system.

The rise of the so-called star system in the American humanities, a
direct result of the corporatization of the Western university, maps
more or less exactly onto the moment when French theory was imported into the United States in the early 1970s.[55] Postmodernist critics, as
a group, are among the few academics in the humanities to have
profited from this system—and the only ones thus far to have received
sustained, even glamorous, media attention.[56] Encouraged by university administrators hoping to enhance the prestige, hence competitive-
ness, of their institutions, the star system has only further skewed the
maldistribution of limited university resources, and exacerbated class
and gender inequalities at all points of the academic system.[57] By the
1980s, the top humanities departments in the United States had begun
to vie with one another nationally for the leading stars, the way universities compete for athletes. "We're hot now and everyone knows that," a
professor at Duke University remarked in the late 1980s. "I don't think
any other English department in the country can boast of the lineup of
home-run hitters we've got here."[58] But what must be emphasized is
that the emergence of the star system in U.S. universities coincided
with an "anthropological" strategy of innovation organized around the
body of the critical theorist as such.

With the advent of the star system, a good theory, even a "true" theory, came to be conflated with a theory produced by a charismatic intellectual; revelation of truth, meanwhile, became indistinguishable from revelation of the person or body of the intellectual himself. As Haug relates, human sensuality itself emerges in commodity aesthetics as a crucial site in capital's struggle to uphold the commodity's appearance of use value—as a continuous process of "sensual organization." By shaping human sensory and psychic desires, especially sexuality, advertisers have been able to carry commodity aesthetics and aesthetic innovation deep into the self.

This pattern has extended itself into the realm of critical theory. As commodity aesthetics has extended into thought and speech, it has also been extended into bodily gesture and comportment. As David Shumway observes of postcolonial studies star Gayatri Spivak: "There is not only the distinctive voice but also the striking face, the sari, and the characteristic tics or patterns of delivery. Whatever Spivak has to say is different merely by virtue of her having spoken the words."[59] What makes the star "sexy" is her or his proximity to power: to the money machine of Hollywood, or an affiliation with one or another ideological apparatus of the state. The celebrity at the podium of a major literary studies conference functions as the embodiment of desire and "sexual promise," speaking directly to the viewing subject's own narcissistic ego.[60] For consumer demand to be endlessly generated and regenerated, the commodity must be able to find some footing "within" the subject himself.

But the star's narcissism cuts both ways, as the theorist becomes both *seducer* and *seduced*. An unembarrassed Gayatri Spivak told one reporter: "At a gay costume party in Cairo, someone came dressed as Gayatri; this is an admiring thing."[61] With its love of *jouissance* and its iconoclastic veneer, poststructuralism, or what Teresa Ebert calls "ludic" feminism, has proved especially well suited to the new eroticization of knowledge.

"TREND INNOVATION" IN THEORY

We saw in Kaldor's analysis of the baroque weapons system that the prime contractors faced with a highly competitive environment relied on "trend innovation" to maintain slight comparative advantages. In an era of post-Fordist rationalization, the key to market survival is both flexibility in production and commodity differentiation. Clyde W. Barrow argues that today's knowledge producers in the university—"flexible specialists," as he terms them—"must continuously upgrade their skills and knowledge to meet the challenge of ever new technologies and expanding information in order to avoid their own obsolescence."[62] Baroque theorists thus rely on aesthetic differentiation to distinguish their own "commodities" in the academic marketplace.

Meanwhile, the turn toward trend innovation in critical theory has led to an accelerated turnover rate of theoretical knowledge-commodities—that is, to *an increase in the circulation rate of ideas*. In *Capital*, Marx made the distinction between production time—the interval required for actual manufacture of a commodity—and circulation time—the interval needed to transform a produced commodity back into money (through exchange), when the surplus value or profit inhering in that commodity can be realized. As Marx notes, production time and circulation time are "mutually exclusive": the longer a product is in circulation, waiting for a buyer, the more this hampers production, because it means that capital is in limbo and cannot be plowed back into production.[63] This logic increasingly applies to the production and circulation of critical knowledges, for the longer a scholarly product takes to circulate, the more this limits the scholar's ability to generate value. And without the accumulation of what Pierre Bourdieu termed "academic capital"—the exchange value of intellectual labor—the scholar cannot advance in the game. But by the same token, an increase in the circulation rate of knowledges will *shorten* the interval during which the knowledge object is "in production."

As early as the 1960s, before the rationalization of the university but well into the breakdown of the barrier between the academy and the mass media, we begin to witness a shortening of the half-life of commodity concepts in theory; hence the comment of Roland Barthes about *Tel Quel* that "intellectual history moved very fast, an unfinished manuscript quickly became anachronistic and I even hesitated to publish it."[64] As Fredric Jameson notes of the latest stage in commodity fetishism, "the frantic economic urgency of producing fresh waves of ever more novel-seeming goods . . . at ever greater rates of turnover, now assigns an increasingly essential structural function and position to aesthetic innovation and experimentation."[65]

Since the 1970s, as competition in the humanities (and, to a lesser extent, the social sciences) intensified, American "critical" theorists indeed adapted to the changed conditions with *commodity aesthetics* to prop up their academic capital. However, the frantic pace of innovation (what Haug calls "incessant aesthetic revolution") has begun to yield diminishing returns.[66] First, the "exchange value" of theory has declined in inverse proportion to rising investment costs—viz., the growing capital and labor time expended to reproduce, and maintain, the professoriate, especially in the humanities. Meanwhile, the personal and institutional costs and bureaucratic overhead required to keep scholars "competitive" have never been higher, as scholars are forced to keep up with the explosion of academic presses and titles, shuttling around the country and the world to deliver an endless series of conference papers, continually "upgrading" the same basic discursive designs, in a struggle to keep their cultural capital from eroding—for example, publishing considerably more today than they did a quarter-century ago to maintain the same relative position.[67] At the same time, the very success of baroque theory as a minor publishing venture has begun to saturate its own already crowded niche markets.

Second, a strategy of commodity aesthetics depends upon a more or less expansive or open-ended market. Simon Marginson, in a study of the commodification of knowledge in Australia, observes that post-Fordist knowledge production has led to "a proliferation of a sort, as any and every market avenue is quickly exploited." But "the 'plurality' of positional goods and knowledge goods is confined to a narrow band within which exchange values can be realized." The use value of academic knowledge does not disappear; but "the nature and diversity of use values [now get] constrained by the requirements of the market" as "the overriding importance of exchange values places limits on diversity and innovation."[68] The narrowing of intellectual diversity in theory has led to the rise of baroque *commodity concepts*. Commodity concepts ostensibly bring product intelligibility to an otherwise hopelessly differentiated and segmented market. But more and more we seem to see aesthetic differentiation leading not to innovation, but rather to greater homogenization and standardization.

Consider, in this regard, the cluster of titles on "the body" in the fall 1998 book list at Routledge. Such examples can be multiplied by searching under other commodity concepts, such as hybridity, borders or border crossings, diaspora, transgression, queering, or performance.[69] The same phenomenon can be seen in conference themes. In the late 1990s, for example, organizers of an American Studies conference in the Midwest on "(Per)Forming Diasporas" circulated a notice on the Internet inviting paper submissions. Suggested themes included: "Virtual" and "Real" diasporas; National (be)longings; Cultural dispersions and (dis)appearances; Border realignments and imaginings; In(corporate) in bodies; Knowing bodies/knowing borders; Queer diasporas; "Foreign" bodies/"foreign" agents; Nativ(e)ity scenes; Reconfiguring Race; E(race)sures, and so on. Borders, diasporas, queerness, race, bodies, culture—all congeal into one indistinguishable gray mass. The baroque period of European aesthetics again comes to mind, since the repetition of established sets and patterns was a signal feature of that movement.[70]

In response to downward pressures both on the exchange value of academic capital and on the use value of theory per se, academics throughout the humanities and social sciences—including film studies, rhetoric, American studies, anthropology, political theory, ethnic studies, and women's studies—have adopted poststructuralist conventions to make "sexier" discourses and disciplines which otherwise were more and more being relegated to third-class status by university administrators. Kaldor, in her study of the weapons design process, observed that once a market has been created and stabilized, "manufacturers often revert to product improvement, to the attempt to attract customers through the extra gimmick or a new fashion, so that enormous cost may be expended in a relatively minor 'improvement.'"[71] In the 1980s,

---

BOOK TITLES ON "THE BODY" IN ROUTLEDGE BOOK LIST FOR 1998

The "Lived" Body	Body/Politics
Changing Bodies, Changing Meanings	Bodies that Matter
Embodying Charisma	Corporealities
Embodying the Social	Telling Flesh: The Substance
Embodied Progress	of the Corporeal
The Body in Everyday Life	BodyScape
Body Cultures	BodySpace
Remaking the Body	The Body and the City
Places Through the Body	Leaky Bodies and Boundaries
The Rejected Body	

mimicry of the commodity in theory could be seen in the proliferation of marketing designs, in-jokes, puns (e.g., "Putting the Anus Back in 'Coriolanus'"), and linguistic gimmicks (e.g., using parentheses and syntax in self-consciously clever ways—"Traumatic Wit(h)ness- Thing and Matrixial Co/In-habit(u)ating").[72] Such linguistic deformations at first developed out of the poststructuralist belief that Nietzschean irony and Derridean *différance* could be used to destabilize hegemonic meanings (by contininually emphasizing the semiotic indeterminacy of signs). But the "method" soon lost whatever oppositional element it might once have had, becoming more unthinking reflex—and a new species of marketing gimmickry and self-promotion—than rebel cry.

With the proliferation of news and media venues, advertisers have struggled to find new ways to inscribe commodity semiotics onto every available social surface. Edward Tufte notes of Microsoft's PowerPoint that the program replaces "serious analysis with chartjunk, over-produced lay-outs, cheerleader logotypes and branding, and corny clip art."[73] Viewed in this light, ornamental layering of syntax and grammar in baroque the-oretical texts can be seen as a form of isomorphic mimicry of mainstream commodity aesthetics. Rather than resisting the fragmentation and weak-ening of spatial reasoning, however, poststructuralists have actively sought to accelerate the society-wide trend. Sue-Ellen Case, for example, in *The Domain-Matrix: Performing Lesbian at the End of Print Culture*, overlays her text with shadowy graphics in order to disrupt linear argument and coherence, and thereby obliterate any trace of totality.[74] Case also pur-posefully fragments her narrative, a move intended, she writes, "to encourage the reader to visit each of them in any order that appeals, sug-gesting a matrix, *rather than a line of thought.*" Case advises her reader to "channel surf" through the text—the better to choose at random "the bits of narratives and images that appeal to her particular, changing impulses of the moment"; for "what used to be called fragmentation (still presum-ing there is a whole to fragment) . . . gives way to the sense of a net of notions, intersecting in different ways, depending on the style of naviga-tion. . . . 'Fragmentation' represents the dispersal of files across noncon-tiguous sectors of a disk."[75] But compare Case's description of her project to Tufte's critique of the cognitive style of PowerPoint:

> foreshortening of evidence and thought, low spatial resolution . . . breaking up nar-rative and data into slides and minimal fragments, rapid temporal sequencing of

thin information rather than focused spatial analysis, conspicuous decoration. . .
a preoccupation with format and not content, an attitude of commercialism that
turns everything into a sales pitch.[76]

PowerPoint presentations, Tufte observes, are "indifferent to content,
slice and dice the evidence into arbitrary compartments, [and produce]
an anti-narrative with choppy continuity."[77]

In the same vein, Rey Chow praises postmodernism for insisting "on
the need to detail history, in the sense of cutting it up."[78] The denial
that there is an intelligible social "whole," along with espousal of semiotic and social "fragmentation" as a virtue, is the norm throughout
poststructuralist discourse. Indeed, as Martin Jay observes, if any one
thing can be said to bind poststructuralist thinkers to one another it is
their "unremitting hostility toward totality."[79] Foucault captured this
hostility most succinctly when he declared: "'The whole of society' is
precisely that which should not be considered except as something to
be destroyed. And then, we can only hope that it will never exist
again."[80] The fragmentary "baroque" form is thus of a piece with poststructuralist first premises, since the net effect of the baroque theorist's "playful" linguistic deformations and destabilization of rational
thought is to further obscure the totality.

As Lukács puts it, fragmentation leads "to the destruction of every
image of the whole" and thus is a central feature of reification.[81] The specialization and division of labor under capitalism first of all destroys the
organic unity of the worker's labor, which gets cut up into isolated
shards of time and space. As the labor process became routinized, the
worker's own body and its motions became reduced by scientific study
into manipulable segments. This led, in turn, to the fragmentation of the
consciousness of the subject: alienation from the subject's own labor led
also to alienation from her own species being. Fragmentation finally
came to suffuse the consciousness and ideology of capitalist civilization
and culture as a whole. Even philosophical knowledge became fragmented, as the philosopher's own labor became specialized. Hence Gramsci's
observation, "Even the intellectual is a 'professional' who has his specialized 'machines,' his 'apprenticeship,' and his own Taylor system."[82]

If, as Tufte argues, the facile templates of Microsoft's ubiquitous
PowerPoint program serve to "weaken verbal and spatial reasoning," so
too does baroque theory.[83] Density of surface design plus intellectual

standardization has been a recipe for loss of communicative clarity and cognitive coherence. Baroque or postmodernist theory intentionally obscures the relative unity of power. This represents a clear disavowal or refusal of the sociological tradition. To think sociologically, C. Wright Mills argued, one must above all be able to ask: "What is the structure of this particular society as a whole? What are its essential components, and how are they related to one another?" Poststructuralists, insofar as they axiomatically reject all talk of parts and whole, refusing to countenance the possibility that seemingly diverse phenomena may relate to one another as parts of a system whose mechanisms, strategic vulnerabilities, and points of *dis*continuity can be mapped—eviscerate the "sociological imagination." And since having a view of "the whole" is also a necessary condition for thinking *strategically*, postmodernism represents a disavowal of political strategy, too. For, absent a view of the whole, however provisional that view may be, one cannot hope to develop effective modes of action.

AGAINST THE AUTONOMY OF THEORY

Some would object to the assumption that critical theory ought to be "useful." A variety of scholars have in fact questioned the necessity and wisdom of linking critical thought and action. As early as the 1930s, with Communist totalitarianism in view, Theodor Adorno argued that the critical philosopher's responsibility could only be to engage in the critique of ideas ("negative dialectics"), not to become embroiled in politics. Both Adorno and his friend Max Horkheimer felt that to demand any "usefulness" of philosophical thought was to destroy its autonomy, hence its truth value. Jürgen Habermas would later clarify this central tenet of the Frankfurt School, arguing that "the formation of theory" should be considered separately "from the compulsions of strategic action. . . . The autonomy of theory . . . is required for the sake of the independence of political action. No theory and no enlightenment can relieve us of the risks of taking a partisan position."[84]

For other intellectuals, who were perhaps more scholarly minded than political, the events of the 1960s provided another reason to be wary of the demands of practice on theory—the moralistic culture of the New Left itself. "No one who passed through the politically charged 1960s and early 1970s," writes Martin Jay, "when even the most theoretically self-conscious intellectuals still agonized over how *engagé* they were, will forget the incessant questions from the floor after every lecture demanding to know how such esoteric and abstract ideas, expressed in the jargon of an intellectual elite, could be translated into immediate emancipatory practice."[85] Finally, poststructuralist critics rejected a theory-practice dialectic on grounds not that practice corrupts theory, but rather that theory corrupts practice.

For postmodernist critics like Foucault and Lyotard, the death of the so-called universal or humanist intellectual who in the past might have presumed to arrogate for himself a public "right" to speak for society or "the people" (Emile Zola and Jean-Paul Sartre are considered the paradigm cases) is therefore something to celebrate. As Foucault declared during the protests of the 1960s, "The intellectual discovered that the masses no longer need him to gain knowledge: they know perfectly well, without illusion; they know better than he and they are certainly capable of expressing themselves. But there exists a system of power which blocks, prohibits, and invalidates this discourse and this knowledge. . . . Intellectuals are themselves agents of this system of power."[86]

In this perspective, the best theory is also the "safest," that is, the one likely to do the least amount of harm. Indeed, there is no gainsaying the fact that Marxist-Leninists often adopted an instrumental conception of truth. A theory was said to be "true" if the left was able to seize power; and this had the effect of rationalizing some of the most undemocratic and unethical political practices in history.[87] Bob Connell's comments on Louis Althusser, whose clunky theoretical apparatus purged the concept of experience and reduced the totality to a static *aggregate* of determinate structures, are helpful in reminding us of the politically fatal consequences of any theory, modernist or postmodernist, which is uncomfortable thinking seriously about practice. Althusser, he writes, "undercut any motive for participating in the available mass organisations, *and* any hope that the working class will generate its own socialist consciousness. . . . The impact of Althusserian epistemology is to discourage intellectuals from doing research that might actually be useful to unions and parties; and the impact of Althusserian language is certainly to discourage the workers from talking to *them*. What it does positively encourage them to do is to sit around and theorize, militantly."[88]

But this is not the end of the story. Within the Marxist tradition itself, there has from the start been a vital counter-tradition that has sought to realize a humanistic, democratic harmony of theory and practice. Socialists like Rosa Luxemburg and Antonio Gramsci showed that it was possible to unite theory and practice without suffering a loss of moral or intellectual integrity. Also, the notion of a critical practice informed by theoretical reflection has never been unique to Marxism, but was also the basis of anarchism, liberal and radical feminism, and antiracist and civil rights struggles of the nineteenth and early twentieth centuries.[89] The theorist who turns away from or neglects the practical dimensions of human life, whether in politics or culture, may be in danger of losing sight of the normative and ethical values that drove her or him to conduct the research in the first place.

THEORY AS PRACTICE

If, as I have suggested, poststructuralist-inspired thought is idealist, destroys our ability to think strategically, erodes the truth value of theory, and mimics the commodity, how do we account for its continued appeal—for the high values it continues to command on the academic exchange?

The answer to this question must be sought in Guy Debord's observation that because under conditions of advanced capitalism the inflation of exchange value coincides with the "tendency of use value to fall," the *appearance* of this falling use value must nonetheless be propped up. "In the inverted reality of the spectacle, use value . . . must now be explicitly proclaimed precisely because its factual reality is eroded."[90] The reason baroque theory persists is because it has been able to prop up the appearance of use value with a patina of radicalism.

In part, it has done so by presenting a teleological narrative about its symbiotic relation with the "New Social Movements." But it also sung of its own "prodigious achievements." Left unmoored after the decline of the New Left, many intellectuals flocked to postmodernism because it seemed to provide a way of being involved without being politically engaged. Theory was no longer seen as being in a dialectic with practice;it began to seem like the only conscious *practice* available at all. For if, as the poststructuralist canon goes, the enemy of human freedom is not capitalism, patriarchy, or other determinate structures of power, nor specific classes or groups of people, but rather, discursive structures or meta-narratives—the humanist myth of the subject, say, or the notion of universal truth, or "phallologocentrism" as such—then the practice of poststructuralist and deconstructionist knowledge production might bring down the whole tired edifice of modernity. If, as Lyotard suggested, "[t]he decline, perhaps the ruin, of the universal idea can free thought and life from totalizing obsessions," then logically, is it not those who set out to destroy the universal idea, through their intellectual project excavating subjugated knowledges and subjectivities, who become the agents of the new freedom?[91]

All this is not to say that poststructuralist-inspired authors have yielded no fresh or original insights whatsoever over the years. Postmodernism *has* at times been helpful in drawing attention to some of the "local" dimensions of power. Deconstructionism, for example, drew our attention to the ambiguity of the sign, showing us the meanings hidden in the interstices of language. Michel Foucault's account of the disciplinization of the body, and of the historically contingent nature of sexuality, have provided powerful insights into the nature of modern institutions and the socially constructed nature of identity and gender. The trouble is that along with these and other insights, postmodernism has also smuggled into critical thought a whole army of confused and outright bad ideas about nature, politics, identity, ontology, truth, and—above all—about praxis. On this score, postmodernism's obfuscations, misdirections, and spatial and logical distortions seriously jeopardize the future of emancipatory thought and action.

In April 2003, at a public conference at the University of Chicago, famous humanities star after famous humanities star reportedly found little to say in defense of contemporary "theory." Among the luminaries present were Bhabha, Sander Gilman, Stanley Fish, and Henry Louis Gates, Jr. One member of the audience challenged the assembled luminaries to explain what the utility of theory was today, given that those present seemed to "concede . . . how much more important the actions of Noam Chomsky are in the world than all the writings of critical theorists combined?" Stanley Fish demurred; but Gilman trotted out the now *de rigueur* warning that intellectuals weren't to be trusted as a rule, that "not only have intellectuals been wrong almost all of the time, but they have been wrong in corrosive and destructive ways." Another panelist remarked: "This particular group of intellectuals . . . has a terror of being politically irrelevant."[92] Literary and postmodernist theory has been trading at grossly inflated prices on the academic exchange for years, by propping up the appearance of use value. Might this "terror" not stem from the realization that the gig is finally up?

Terry Eagleton reminds us, "When a radical movement is making headway, its epistemology is likely to be closely conditioned by its practice. It requires no esoteric theory at such times to recognize that the material world is at least real enough to be acted upon and altered."[93] A return to a dialectic between theory and practice, in which the practical and the speculative are not set at odds to one another, would help us correct for the speculative distortions that have so confused the critical imagination. A more direct concern with collective practice might help immunize this body of knowledge against the insidious logics of the commodity.

4 The French Ideology

> Philosophy and the study of the actual world have the same relation
> to one another as masturbation and sexual love.
> — MARX AND ENGELS, *The German Ideology*

Postmodernism, hydra-headed progeny of the twentieth-century European structuralist and poststructuralist turn, must now be regarded among the more resilient and influential intellectual movements of the last half-century. From modest beginnings in the French revolt against Marxism and existentialism, postmodernism vaulted into a movement with truly global reach in the 1980s and 1990s. In the process it has attracted its share of able critics. An impressive array of thinkers over the years have taken pains to enumerate the epistemological fallacies, contradictions, and politically troubling consequences of the postmodernist project. Yet so far such critiques have failed to stanch the flow of poststructuralism and its multiple offshoots, which now include postcolonialism, postmodernist feminism, queer theory, and leading niche brands of cultural studies. In the United States and Britain, postmodernism today commands the key strategic bluffs of "critical theory" in the humanities. Works such as Hardt and Negri's *Empire* have not only been praised effusively but have interest at the grass roots. When Michael Hardt, a literary scholar at Duke University, showed up for the World Social Forum in Porto Alegre, Brazil, in 2002, activists came seeking his autograph.

We hear from these critics in the humanities that the world has in recent years undergone an unparalleled revolution. The decomposition of Marx's philosophy of socialism has developed into a universal ferment in which all the "powers of the past" are swept away. In the general chaos of postmodernity, even mighty states face inevitable doom, as "the multitude" gather strength to transform the world. The postmodern "revolution" in theory and society makes the changes of the twentieth century look like child's play. Principles have ousted one another, heroes of the mind have overthrown each other with unheard-of rapidity, and in the last several decades more of the past has been swept away than at other times in several centuries.

In the last thirty years, postmodernist theorists have claimed to solve riddles of political and social practice that vexed past generations of thinkers. The problem of popular strategy—of how to constitute a social movement adequate to the political aspirations of the oppressed—has been overthrown, by repudiating the need for strategy at all. The difficulty of reconciling thought and action, theory and practice, has been swept aside—with the warning that thought become worldly is thought corrupted by power. The relationship of the intellectuals to the powerless is ousted—by denying that leadership is necessary. The organizational question—of how to appear before others, how to manifest the world-transforming hopes of the oppressed—is disposed of as child's play, by embracing formlessness and flux.

But how often have we heard that all the powers of the past have been swept away? In the early decades of the twentieth century, the Futurists declared, "We stand on the last promontory of the centuries!"[1] "We are more inflamed than ever, tireless and rich in ideas," wrote Marinetti. "We have been prodigal in ideas and will continue to be so. . . . Humanity is marching toward anarchic individualism."[2] Technology would be the new religion, and speed our psalm. Nearly a century later, another generation of critics would unconsciously echo Marinetti. "We are living," wrote Ernesto Laclau and Chantal Mouffe in 1987, through "one of the most exhilarating moments of the twentieth century: a moment in which new generations, without the prejudices of the past, without theories presenting themselves as 'absolute truths' of History, are constructing new emancipatory discourses, more human, diversified, and democratic. The eschatological and epistemological ambitions are more modest, but the liberating aspirations are wider and deeper."[3] Years later, this same optimism of the intellect (its Hegelian roots dangling in the air) would again be carried into the future on the wings of its own irrepressible hope. In 2000, Hardt and Negri wrote that the processes of globalization "offer new possibilities to the forces of liberation," "greater possibilities for creation and liberation."[4] Set adrift by the powers of capital, the "active subject" of "the multitude" could already be seen gnawing at the system from the inside out through dispersion and exodus.[5]

Thus have the postmodernists conducted their revolution against the problems of the past. And all this is supposed to have taken place in the realm of pure thought.

In its relentless optimism and indifference to the quotidian world, postmodernism in fact bears a close enough likeness to German Idealism that my account of postmodernism could imitate the parody of German Idealism in Marx and Engels's *The German Ideology* without straining the facts. What all forms of idealism have in common is an epistemology that holds ideas or thoughts to be ontologically prior to matter, and therefore to be constitutive of reality. Another way to put it is that idealists posit an ontological identity between their own conceptual categories and the reality they purport to describe. As Engels wrote in his critique of the very bad "materialism" of Eugene Dühring, idealism is the "attempt to prove the reality of any product of thought by the identity of thinking and being."[6] What all forms of idealism, past, present, or future, have in common is the suppression of *experience* as the basis of human knowledge and practice. Whether as Young Hegelianism or as postmodernism, so-called critical philosophical thought, once it loses its grounding in sensual, embodied life and actual social reality, inevitably subordinates social reality to conceptual abstraction.

ALTHUSSER, FOUCAULT, AND THE LIQUIDATION OF EXPERIENCE

The Young Hegelians—Feuerbach, Bruno and Edgar Bauer, August Ciezskowski, Max Stirner, Karl Köppen, Arnold Ruge, Moses Hess, and, for a time, Marx—were a group of restless and liberal-minded intellectuals that formed around the Post-Doctoral Club at the University of Berlin.[7] They focused on the question of the relevance of religion and atheism to social reform in Europe. In the early 1840s, Ruge, Bauer, and Feuerbach argued that Christianity was a projection of the *actual* spiritual and historical capacities of humankind onto the *divine*, hence the self-alienation of humankind's own essence. Believing that political and social liberation would be achieved only when "Man" won release from "his" own self-abasement before God, they spoke and wrote of the need for a new, atheistic, humanist religion.

Marx finally broke with them in the mid-1840s. *The German Ideology* was composed just two short years before the great but doomed revolutions of 1848, as the first clouds of mass upheaval were gathering along the horizon of western Europe. Capitalist industrialization and urbanization had fatally weakened the old feudal order, undermining every traditional basis of political authority. At the same time, the liberal promises of the new order unleashed an almost instinctual longing for political freedom and social equality. Marx was more aware than the Hegelians of the material forces that were driving the historical crisis to a violent climax. He accused them of reducing the practical, concrete problems of human life to a series of abstractions. Where the Young Hegelians defended theoretical reflection as a form of practice—as indeed the most important form of practice—Marx argued that consciousness itself was "a social product."[8] He and Engels broke with Feuerbach by calling for a properly materialist framework, one able to make sense of the meaning of history and to account for the genesis of a new, revolutionary collective consciousness.

What Marx took to be the starting point of his philosophy was the grounding of theory in the textures of actual, sensual life. Describing their method in the *German Ideology*, Marx and Engels write:

> We do not set out from what men say, imagine, conceive, nor from men as narrated, thought of, imagined, conceived, in order to arrive at men in the flesh. We set out from real, active men, and on the basis of their real life-process we demonstrate the development of the ideological reflexes and echoes of this life-process. . . . In the first method of approach the starting point is consciousness taken as the living individual; in the second method, which conforms to real life, it is the real living individuals themselves, and consciousness is considered solely as *their* consciousness.[9]

Sensual, embodied life, Marx and Engels maintained, is the inescapable origin point of all knowledge. For Marx, Ernst Bloch observed: "Perception, not the concept that is merely taken from it, is and remains the beginning where all materialist cognition identifies itself."[10] That is, any claim to knowledge that cannot be verified by the senses is both philosophically uninteresting, epistemologically invalid, and politically useless. From this perspective, Marx sought to overcome idealism and economism by showing how each presented an ideologically distorted view of reality. Above all, Marx attempted to reveal how the division within Western philosophy between subject and object only mirrored the *actual* division in capitalist society between subjects and objects. He and Engels argued that idealism and empiricism represent different ideological manifestations of the *social* realities from which they emerged. Empiricism occludes reality by reducing all human experience to one— *use*. But the principle of utility, which reduces "all the manifold relationships of people in the *one* relation of usefulness," whether expressed in Bentham's utilitarianism, or the political theory of Locke and Hobbes, is nothing other than the abstracted, ideational form of the founding principle of bourgeois economy itself, in which "all relations are subordinated in practice to the one abstract monetary-commercial relation."[11] Capitalism turns human beings—capitalist and worker alike—into things, and empiricism follows suit.

In the *German Ideology*, then, Marx and Engels held that "the existence of living human individuals" is the "first premise of all human history."[12] Later, however, as the Western Marxist tradition drifted toward more and more esoteric concerns, the abstract, juridical notion of "the subject" came to replace the plainer language of persons and people. The French structuralist movement, influenced by Saussure's relational theory of linguistic meaning, had announced that the "subject" itself was not sovereign, not autonomous, but was an artifact of culture.

The two texts that accomplished this forced obsolescence of the human being were *For Marx* by Louis Althusser and *The Order of Things* by Michel Foucault. In *For Marx*, his revisionist account of Marx's philosophy (1965), Althusser argued that the significance of Marx's thought lay in its sharp break with philosophy, which had previously sought to uncover the "essence" of human being. What he meant by this is that Marx himself had turned against the "problematic of human nature (or the essence of man)."[13] It was therefore the "mature," anti-essentialist Marx who now showed the way toward a truly radical historicism. "It is impossible," Althusser averred, "to know anything about men except on the absolute precondition that the philosophical (theoretical) myth of man is reduced to ashes."[14] The writings of the mature Marx necessitated the rejection of any language of subjectivity, of consciousness, of essence, of nature. Instead, a "scientific" language of practice would have to be utilized.[15] Only through scientific, i.e., Marxist and Leninist, study of the superstructures of capitalist society—identification of the "characteristic

articulations" of ideological, economic, political, and scientific practices—could one determine the true movement of history.[16]

Althusser's "scientific" Marxism thus reduced the status of the
human being to that of an epiphenomenon of structure. Representations of ideology, Althusser wrote, "act functionally on men via a
process that escapes them." That is, "It is above all as structures that
[these representations] impose on the vast majority of men." Subjects
are completely determined, or rather, *over*determined by structured
practices; they can have no direct access to the meaning of their own
experiences. Our relation to the world, Althusser maintained, "is not a
simple relation but a relation between relations, a second-degree relation."[17] With this language of a "relation between relations," we find a
twofold distancing of the subject from his or her own life, and a 180-
degree turn away from the humanistic Marxist tradition.

As E. P. Thompson wrote, Althusser treated "men and women . . . not
[as] agents in their own history, but [as] träger—carriers of structures,
vectors of process."[18] In his own work, Thompson tried to be faithful to
the dialectical textures of actual working-class life, particularly (in his
monumental book of the same name) the "making" of the English
working class: its slow rise to a measure of self-consciousness and identity. But Althusser, by contrast, was unable to "understand either the
real, existential genesis of ideology, or the ways in which human *praxis*
contests this ideological imposition and presses against its bonds."[19]
Althusser's schematic functionalist framework left no room for theoretical reflection on the texture of human life, on first-order meanings.
But how would we elaborate or refine a theory of praxis without
recourse to the reservoirs of thought, feeling, and meaning that experience continually provides? For it is experience—"the experience of Fascism, Stalinism, racism, and of the contradictory phenomenon of
working-class 'affluence' within sectors of capitalist economies" that is
always "breaking in and demanding that we reconstruct our categories."[20] Thompson wrote:

> Experience is a necessary middle term between social being and social conscious-
> ness: it is experience (often class experience) which gives a coloration to culture,
> to values, and to thought: it is by means of experience that the mode of produc-
> tion exerts a determining pressure upon other activities; and it is by practice that
> production is sustained.[21]

In short, Althusser seemed to view history as a machine, and *Capital* as a technical manual for understanding its moving parts. "History," Althusser had written, "is an immense natural-human system in movement, and the motor of history is class struggle. History is a process, and a process without a subject."[22]

R. W. Connell has argued that a severe functionalism afflicted Althusser's thought, one that reproduced, in the realm of thought, the social relations implicit in the Stalinist political milieu from which it in fact sprung. In Althusser's thought lies "an abstract militancy . . . a general justification for a revolutionary vanguard party led by an educated but fairly intolerant elite who are the bearers of Marxist science; and a general devaluation of strategies connected with spontaneity, mobilization from below, incremental change, or use of the existing state."[23] As in Stalinism, "the theory works in the same direction; the priority of the structures, the bipolar functionalism, the abstract militancy that they produce." The "scientific" conception of revolution meanwhile "seems to occur behind the backs of the workers." Connell concludes:

> That terrible intervention of living, sweating, bleeding, human beings in their own history that is the basis of all radicalism, is methodologically ruled out of "marxist science" by Althusserian Marxism. Here, I think, is its fundamental affinity with Stalinist politics, which is precisely characterised by the combination of a notional militancy with a practical suppression of grass-roots socialism.[24]

Althusser's thought had an incalculably large impact on critical theory, first in Marxism, then in poststructuralist theory, identity politics and even poststructuralist feminism. Postmodernist theorists accepted Althusser's functionalist assumptions, particularly his "eviction" of agency and the subject, uncritically.[25] Although *For Marx* had an enormous influence on theory, it was the work of Foucault, his liquidation of the human individual, that would have a truly revolutionary effect on the methodology of the humanities.

Foucault, inspired in part by Heidegger's antihumanism and Bataille's philosophy of ecstatic excess and Dionysian flows, but even more by Nietzsche's project of exposing the interested nature of all knowledge, sought to obliterate once and for all the basis of humanism in the subject. What Foucault's otherwise diverse researches had in common, whether the distinction between sane and insane, transformations

in the Western mode of perception, or the disciplinization and normalization of the human body, was a fundamental antagonism toward the
"truth regimes" of modernity. For him, the human subject was an
epiphenomenon and myth cast up by the sciences, a by-product of the
very truth–regimes that had produced the prison, the madhouse, and
the tyranny of the physician's gaze over the prostrate body. From Foucault's vantage point, the discourse of the "subject" was the strategic
linchpin of the whole corrupt apparatus of disciplinary control. The
proper task of critical thought, therefore, was not to recover or rescue
the subject, but to unmask it as a *product* of discourse.

But for Foucault to effect a decisive break with the Western tradition's "return" to human origins and ontology, an act of parricide was
required: the overthrow of the two philosophers whose work had dominated the intellectual milieu of postwar France, Jean-Paul Sartre and
Maurice Merleau-Ponty. Foucault derided Sartre for his sense of self-
importance as a "universal" intellectual—i.e., a figure whose legitimacy
to speak was uniquely authorized by his status as a philosophical
thinker. Foucault saw such a posture as pretentious, elitist, and, even
more to the point, anachronistic. In an interview in 1966, Foucault
spoke for the new structuralist movement in France when he said: "We
have experienced Sartre's generation . . . as a generation that was certainly brave and generous, one that had a passion for life, politics, and
existence. But as for us, we have discovered something else, another
passion: the passion for concepts and for what I will call 'system.'"[26]

Because any attempt to recover the subject via a language of experience or ontology would remain trapped within the nightmare of reason,
Foucault reasoned, it was also necessary to turn against phenomenology, above all the lifework of Maurice Merleau-Ponty, Foucault's onetime
teacher. Foucault published *The Order of Things* in 1966, just five years
after Merleau-Ponty's death. *The Order of Things* represented the negation
of Merleau-Ponty's project of using phenomenology to describe consciousness in its encounters with the lifeworld.[27]

What kind of knowledge, then, did Foucault propose? Studying the
shift between the seventeenth and nineteenth centuries from classical
taxonomies of form to systematized, biologistic modalities of represen-
tion, Foucault claimed to have unearthed what he called the episteme
or epistemological "field"—the structure beneath the structure, so to
speak, of Western epistemology.[28] As he put it, his goal in *The Order of*

Things had been to examine the ways in which "our [own] culture has made manifest the existence of order, and how, to the modalities of that order, the exchanges owed their laws, the living beings their constants, the words their sequence and their representative value; what modalities of order have been recognized, posited, linked with space and time, in order to create the positive basis of knowledge" within the human and natural sciences.[29]

In a sense, in calling into question the underlying structure that made Western "knowing" itself possible, Foucault was merely radicalizing Husserl's phenomenological reduction. Phenomenologists "bracket" or hold at a critical distance our experiences of being-in-the-world, in order to reflect on the ways in which phenomena come to assume shape and meaning for us. Through this doubling back of consciousness, a "return" to phenomena before we thematize them, philosophy might thereby escape Western dualism. But Foucault's *epoché* was far more radical. He called into question not only the conditions for the constitution of knowledge, but also the necessity of any relation between epistemology and ontology at all. Though he left to one side the question of whether there was any logos to the lifeworld, he implied that "order" was merely a social convention.

Foucault's radical break with phenomenology was premised on a refusal of the content of our actual experiences of the world. [30] Husserl had held that experience is ontologically prior to language.[31] Foucault refused to grant experience any such special privileges. He wrote in his foreword to the English edition of *The Order of Things*:

> I [set out] to know whether the subjects responsible for scientific discourse are not determined in their situation, their function, their perceptive capacity, and their practical possibilities by conditions that dominate and even overwhelm them. In short, I tried to explore scientific discourse not from the point of view of the individuals who are speaking, nor from the point of view of the formal structures of what they are saying, but from the point of view of the rules that come into play in the very existence of such discourse.[32]

Foucault affirmed that "archaeology"—his own deconstructive reading of Western knowledge as a discourse—"does not try to restore what has been thought, wished, aimed at, experienced, desired by men in the very moment at which they expressed it in discourse. . . . It is nothing more than a rewriting: that is, in the preserved form of exteriority, a regulated transformation of what has already been written."[33] Accordingly, if our ability to "order" or render phenomena intelligible, as logos, depends upon a prior structure, one that is itself historically contingent, then the human sciences would be forced to concede that their quest for an "apodictic" knowledge of the meaning of human nature is folly. The "subject" as such, as an invention of the modern human sciences, would simply disappear. Hence the famous closing image of *Les Mots et les choses*, of a human face, "drawn in the sand at the edge of the sea," being "erased" by time.

As brilliant as Foucault's critique of Western discourse undoubtedly is, it leaves us with nothing to say about the "merely human" realm of manifest signs and meaning. Foucault's relentlessly objectivist emphasis on the "exteriority" of human phenomena—on the purely formal qualities and appearances of human sociality—bears no resemblance to life as we in fact experience it. Consequently, reading Foucault's work is at times like reading a transcript left behind by an extraterrestrial anthropologist who studied human civilization from millions of miles away. Our extraterrestrial will have recorded in great detail only the visible gestures, built structures, and glacial flows of population over the centuries, but without comprehending any of the languages of the earth's people.[34] Our anthropologist would grasp only the most superficial elements of human culture. Seeing human life and history through the long end of a telescope, he finds, not surprisingly, that the distant figures there correspond to his own functionalist, schematic view of society. But in reducing the manifold of experiences and meanings which in fact constitute human being, he leaves us with only a sediment, a reification.

Once Foucault placed consciousness and experience behind scare quotes, the effect was to adopt what Susan Bordo, in her critique of poststructuralist feminism, calls the "view from everywhere": the vantage point of a spectatorial consciousness detached from the world.[35] To the peril of his own admirable political commitments, Foucault ignored Merleau-Ponty's observation that perceptual experience "is not arrayed before me as if I were God, it is lived by me from a certain point of view; I am not the spectator, I am involved, and it is my involvement in a point of view which makes possible both the finiteness of my perception and its opening out upon the complete world as a horizon of every perception."[36] What Merleau-Ponty meant was that we cannot suspend judgment about the nature of the world—about truth and social fact—even if we want to, because we are always involved.

Foucault's refusal of the *Lebenswelt*—the quotidian world of meaning—calls to mind Plato's idealist skepticism toward perceptual knowledge. Foucault reduces the first-order meanings of human civilization—including its *sophia*, its wisdom—to the status of shadows on a wall. For ordinary people, those who naively remain enmeshed in the shadows of meaning, only the "visible" realm is available. Meanwhile, they themselves, the people, are mere shadows, shadows cast by other shadows—by *pouvoir* or by discourse. By some conjuring trick, the archaeologist turns the world of vibrant beings into a giant bed of dessicated fossils. The stringency of this approach, however, seemingly compels us to reject as uncertain or as corrupted all extant ways of interpreting our world—psychology, sociology, political theory, theology, literature.

If there are no subjects, but only discourses (Foucault) or texts (Derrida), we seem trapped in a hall of mirrors that leads only into other halls, other mirrors—an infinite regress.[37] There is then no way out of this bind of our own making—except through poststructuralism! For if the world is nothing but texts and discourses, then the only agent, the only autonomous "being" not duped into mistaking the shadows of "experience" for experience, is the archaeologist herself. She alone hovers above the *mise-en-scène* of the phenomenal realm. As Dreyfus and Rabinow observe, "the archaeologist, by a double twist," by "dispensing with truth and meaning in a double phenomenological bracketing," thereby "successfully catapults himself" beyond the positive sciences.[38] But then, the archaeologist appears to be "a split spectator, both sharing and denying the serious meaning that motivates the production of the plethora of discourse he studies."[39] In other words, only to the archaeologist does the true meaning of the world of "meaning" (of ideas, feelings, history, and everyday life and so on) reveal itself—as a "foam," a shifting pattern of "shimmers."[40]

Foucault's view of "individuals [as] the vehicles of power" later became the received wisdom of any number of social critics.[41] Laclau and Mouffe, for example, declared: "The 'human being,' without qualification, is the overdetermined effect of [a] process of multiple construction";[42] while Gayatri Spivak wrote:

A subject-effect can be briefly plotted as follows: that which seems to operate as a
subject may be part of an immense discontinuous network ("text" in the general
sense) of strands that may be termed politics, ideology, economics, history, sexuality, language, and so on. . . . Different knottings and configurations of these strands,
determined by heterogeneous determinations which are themselves dependent
upon myriad circumstances, produce the effect of an operating subject.[43]

As I suggested in chapter 2, this magical transformation from the human
being into a human *effect* is itself a symptom of reification. To Marx, even
the capitalist remained human, a person, despite treating workers as
things, and despite himself being objectified by the very structure he
profits from.[44] Today's critics, by contrast, seek to tear down the last conceptual barriers between persons and things–as when Hardt and Negri
refer to people and social movements as machines or "machinic," as
objects "produced" by desire, biopower, technology, and so on–a reductionistic, mechanistic view of human beings that resembles LaMettrie's
materialist monism in *L'homme machina* (which dismissed "mind" as an
illusion). Even as today's sciences "solve" the philosophical problem of
consciousness by reducing it to a shadow cast by a programmed code (the
genome), critics like Hardt and Negri seem anxious to evict it from one of
its last havens–the humanities.

But the human individual, even as an "effect," cannot fully be eliminated until its potential for experience has been eliminated. This is certainly why Jacques Derrida dispensed with experience on grounds that
the concept is "most unwieldy" and "belongs to the history of metaphysics": so saying, in *Of Grammatology*, Derrida averred that he would
from now on only handle the word using tongs–putting it "under erasure" as "experience."[45] Joan Scott, citing Foucault and Derrida, soli-
dified the new metaphysics by declaring: "It is not individuals who have
experience but subjects who are constituted through experience."[46]
And countless others have taken up Scott's cry since.[47]

If the claim of Scott and others was merely that experience cannot be
taken for "God's truth," as a transparent or self-evident basis of knowledge, one beyond question or doubt, then there would be nothing in the
least bit controversial about it. We know–from experience–that perception is fallible and that experience itself is shaped by discourse, by ideology and myth, by sensory distortion, and so on. What Scott is saying,
however, is that any and all knowledge based on a claim of experience

can only have second order ontological status. That is, it can never be "the origin of our explanation." Why? Because it is itself merely an epiphenomenon of something prior—"discourse" or language or power.

This is an acute form of determinism. To say that experience is only a "discourse" is to remove any basis for substantive human knowledge of any kind, including knowledge that might be helpful to the oppressed. Ironically, feminists and scholars of color have labored hard over the past half-century to bring the experiences of subaltern and oppressed individuals and groups to light. But such efforts, though intended to "negate the negation" by filling in the vast aporias of Eurocentric, masculinist history—by bringing to light previously occluded experiences—are wholly incompatible with the poststructuralist suppression of experience. What we need, Scott concludes, is a historiography in which experience—that is, as "experience"—"becomes not the origin of our explanation, not the authoritative (because seen or felt) evidence that grounds what is known, but rather that which we seek to explain, that about which knowledge is produced."[48] The problem with contemporary historiography, thus, is that it hasn't sufficiently purged itself of the language of experience. Historians today appeal to "experience" as a way to "[establish] a realm of reality outside of discourse."[49] But the "project of making experience visible precludes analysis of the workings of this system and of its historicity; instead it reproduces its terms."[50] In other words, learning about, and from, the experiences of real, flesh-and-blood people, treating those experiences as though they might actually matter, would only get in the way of the "real" work which is "analysis of the workings of this system." In this way, the human being, already humiliated, reduced to a thing-like thing by capitalism, is finally stripped of even the aura of freedom.

Hidden within this objectivist reduction of the lifeworld is the theorist's own will to power, a will to power the breadth of which is staggering. In reducing experience—i.e., human being-in-the-world, human apprehension of life—to a concept, a category of analysis, the theorist appropriates and flattens the experiences of all people who have ever lived, who now live, who will ever live. The homeopath so dilutes experience that there is nothing left, no surplus, for the subject herself. Indeed, the subject is only said to "exist" insofar as it exhibits symptoms of "experience"—i.e., only so long as it provides fodder for the archaeologist's endless researches. "Experience" only becomes intelligible, *real*, when a genealogist like Foucault or Scott or Spivak is on hand to observe it.

"TWO, THREE ... MANY GEISTS":
REIFICATION AND THE AUTOMATON EMPIRE

The French ideology's obliteration of experience stands in the way of any theory of praxis and social change. For if people are mere appurtenances or shadows of *pouvoir*, it is logical to assume that they cannot therefore be agents of history, and must always do power's (or discourse's) bidding. This, however, would leave postmodernism in an untenable position, for that project only maintains insofar as it is able to keep up the appearance of "use value" for a radical project of social change. If human beings are not the subjects of history, therefore, then someone or something else must be.

Here we encounter the figure of Hegel, who is hastily brought in on wires to solve the epistemological plot confusions of the poststructuralist drama. In Hegel's thought, reason only becomes real through the conscious choices and actions of human beings in history. *Geist*, or spirit, fuses past and present in its teleological drive toward the future. Everything that happens, all the historical choices made by individual leaders, peoples, and states, serves the larger purpose of Idea, the universal. "For the rational," Hegel writes, "which is synonymous with the idea appears (by entering through its actuality into an outward existence) in a limitless wealth of forms, appearances, and configurations, and thus encloses its kernel with a variegated rind."[51] "Universal spirit ... experiments in a multitude of dimensions and directions, developing itself, exercising itself, enjoying itself in inexhaustible abundance. For each of its creations, satisfying for the moment, presents new material, a new challenge for further elaboration. . . . What powers it possesses in itself we understand by the multiplicity of its products and formations. In this lust of activity it only deals with itself."[52]

Hegel's conception of *Weltgeist* was fundamentally expressivist. Spirit surges up from the inner, rational logic of being, of which it is itself its real expression. In this schema, the philosopher's own thought emerges as the final expression of World Spirit, as its self-consciousness: the Owl of Minerva, i.e., of self-knowing, takes flight only at "dusk," when the philosopher writing at the end of history is himself able to decode the meaning of Being as expressed in history.

The poststructuralist conception of human activity is similar, though the "message" revealed at the end of the day is simply that there *is* no message. Hegel's expressivist and idealist account of practical human activity reappears, for example, in Foucault's own account of his researches. With "genealogy," Foucault intended to unite scholarly research such as his own, which sought to bring "subjugated" or marginalized forms of knowledge to light, with "local memories," i.e., with the practices of particular subjects, in such a way that they might together achieve a "tactical" disruption of the meta-discourses of the dominant truth-regime.53

As in Hegel, the philosopher is given the privilege of completing the expressivist "circuit": it is only when thought comes to know itself (Hegel) or to free the knowledges lodged beneath the skin of modernity (Foucault) that the progress or work of history can occur. When Foucault champions the "insurrection of subjugated knowledges"—never an insurrection of actual human beings, but of knowledges, concepts—he leans heavily on an expressivist ontology. "Local" criticism, he writes, "is an autonomous, non-centralized kind of theoretical production"; it affects "*the immediate emergence* of historical contents."54

Hegel's view of human beings as the vehicles of the *Weltgeist* also receives its echo in Foucault's exhilarated comments on the events of his day:

> The contemporary world is teeming with ideas that spring up, stir around, disappear or reappear, and shake up people and things. This is not something that happens only in intellectual circles or in the universities of Western Europe; it also happens on a world scale, and it happens particularly among minorities that, because of history, have not up to now been in the habit of speaking or making themselves heard. . . .

> There are more ideas on earth than intellectuals imagine. And these ideas are more active, stronger, more resistant, more passionate than "politicians" think. We have to be there at the birth of ideas, the bursting outward of their force, in struggles carried on around ideas, for or against them. Ideas do not rule the world. But it is because the world has ideas (and because it constantly produces them) that it is not passively ruled by those who are its leaders or those who would like to teach it, once and for all, what it must think. This is the direction we want these "journalistic reports" to take. An analysis of thought linked to an analysis of what is happening. Intellectuals will work together with journalists at the point where ideas and events intersect.55

But who or what is the agent or subject in such passages? It is neither the proletariat nor the people, but "the world." Through some unseen process, this world spontaneously "produces" ideas. "This restless succession of individuals and peoples, who exist for a time and then disappear, presents to us a universal thought, a category: that of change in general"[56]—this is not Foucault, but Hegel. For Foucault, history does not contain an immanent meaning or logic. On the contrary, Habermas notes, history for Foucault consists of "meaningless kaleidoscopic changes of shape in discourse totalities that have nothing in common apart from the single characteristic of being protuberances of power in general."[57] In both Hegel and Foucault ideas and events rapidly rise and fall in shimmering effervescence.

Foucault, despite his cheerful Nietzscheanism, seemed to take it for granted that such changes were positive or even "good." Late in his life, he wanted to place himself in the middle of the "event," as if to record the magnificent tumescence of Spirit as it bloomed, or as if to place himself at the bedside of history as it continually died. "I do not know how to write the history of the future," he wrote, "I am a maladroit forecaster of the past. I would, however, like to grasp things as they are happening, because these days, nothing is finished, and the dice are still rolling."[58] Foucault's credulous wonder when confronted with *de novum* led him to lavish early and undiscriminating praise on the radical Islamists of the Iranian Revolution in the late 1970s, when Foucault identified not with left and feminist elements in that revolution, but with the Ayatollah Khomeini.[59]

Today's theorists, following Foucault, and eyeing the efflorescence of at least ostensibly "new" popular movements in the West, similarly replace Hegel's Absolute Spirit with a new metaphysic of Multiplicitous World Spirit. In the automaton *Empire*, the authors tell us that the "virtual powers of the multitude . . . *tend constantly* toward becoming possible and real";[60] that "[n]ew figures of struggle and new subjectivities are produced in the conjuncture of events, in the universal nomadism, in the general mixture and miscegenation of individuals and populations, and in the technological metamorphoses of the imperial biopolitical machine."[61] In other words, "History," with a capital *H*, may no longer be on the march, as generations of Marxists had naively supposed, but "histories" with a small *h* are triumphally on the rise everywhere. *Geist* now travels under a panoply of assumed names—"empire," "rhizome," "biopower," "discourse," "desire," and so on: as concepts that gesture toward the real but bear no direct relationship to empirical fact.

While in Hegel *Geist* manifests through the conscious freedom of human beings, acting through history, in postmodernism it is the critical theorist herself who becomes the agent of history, crisscrossing the paths of discourse, joyously lifting "subjugated knowledges" from the coffins of modernity. With its crypto-teleological narrative, postmodernism presents itself as the vanguard of change. Foucault, Lyotard, and others argue that the intellectual should no longer play the role of a "legislator" of values—a leader or educator of the people. On the contrary, what is needed is a division of labor between academics and the masses. But of the two roles, it is only the theorist who is able to exert something like a "conscious" agency. It is only, Habermas writes, "under the incorruptible gaze of geneaology, [that] discourses emerge and pop like glittering bubbles from a swamp of anonymous processes of subjugation."[62]

Poststructuralists have portrayed themselves as the counterpart and ally of the "New Social Movements" that mushroomed after the New Left. Their conceptual armory is said both to reflect and *to enable* the new forms of practice. For if the problem of power lies in "subjectification" by a form of *pouvoir* that is constituted in and through knowledge regimes, then the "solution" logically must lie in helping "subjugated knowledges" bubble up from the obscure depths of modernity. The role of the theorist is therefore not to identify more or less promising lines of practice, but to create *Lebensraum* for the spontaneous generation of new identities, new forms of "difference." Thus cultural studies theorist Kirstie McClure, who warns us "that what is at stake in . . . contests [over the proper role of theory] is a matter neither of explanatory adequacy *nor of political efficacy* . . . but a matter of breathing room for the articulation of new knowledges, new agencies, and new practices."[63]

Similarly, Homi Bhabha tells us that the subaltern's very failure to represent itself through a political project or stable identity represents a new explosion of exciting practices, "a (re)ordering of symbols becomes possible." With the sundering of sign from referent, "the sign ceases the synchronous flow of the symbol, [and] it . . . seizes the power to elaborate . . . new hybrid agencies and articulations."[64] In Bhabha's idealist version of postcolonialism the subject that "seizes the power to elaborate" is not the person or group, but *the sign*. But this habit of ascribing agency to immaterial *concepts* was also a signature characteristic of the

Young Hegelians, who, as Marx and Engels wrote, "fight only against . . . illusions of consciousness" and use "phrases" to combat "other phrases." Reality, as the spontaneous efflorescence and eruption of "difference," is in this manner rendered identical to philosophical thought.

Conflation of reality and concept has led some cultural studies critics to make fanciful claims about the powers of deconstruction. Margaret Drewal, for example, finds that camp aesthetics, as "a gay signifying practice," inherently "confounds gender codes, overrules compulsory heterosexuality, and undermines the very foundations on which democratic capitalism was built."[65] And who or what will undermine "the very foundations" of capitalism? Liberace and the dancers at the Radio City Music Hall. Because the "camp" practices of performers like Liberace and the Rockettes are "counterhegemonic" by their "very nature."[66]

Alas, having discarded dialectical and materialist thought, the author cannot hold in conceptual tension the only *apparently* contradictory propositions that camp both undermines and shores up, heterosexual norms and capitalist social relations. Here as elsewhere, the French ideologist serves as a kind of high priest of theory, one whose ritual function is to serve as medium for the mystical transubstantiation of thought into reality. The process is accomplished in three steps. First, the theorist-priest abstracts general concepts from the facts of real life. Second, she or he projects these concepts and categories back onto the world. Finally, the fact is said to be based on the concepts themselves. Marx and Engels demonstrated the procedure in *The German Ideology*:

> First of all an abstraction is made from a fact; then it is declared that the fact is based on the abstraction. . . .
>
> For example: *Fact*: The cat eats the mouse.
>
> *Reflection*: Cat = nature, mouse = nature, consumption of mouse by cat = consumption of nature by nature = self-consumption of nature.
>
> *Philosophical presentation of the fact*: Devouring of the mouse by the cat is based upon the self-consumption of nature.[67]

Michael Hardt and Antonio Negri follow the procedure in *Empire*. First they seize upon certain social facts, e.g., that human beings are displaced by capital. Second, they abstract the phenomenon from its dialectical historical context. Finally, they enshrine the *concepts* used to describe the facts as the self-originating source of the phenomenon.

Fact: Human beings are driven across borders by global capital.

Reflection: Human beings = bodies = biopower; movement of bodies = production of bodies = immanent, machinic production of new, hybrid subjectivities.

Philosophical presentation of the fact: Immigration and refugee flows are based upon the immanent, machinic production by biopower of new, hybrid bodies.

The real relations of capitalist production are thus obscured by the authors' reified jargon of desire, "machinic" bodies, "diaspora" and "hybridity." Thus are cause and effect reversed; thus is the suffering of flesh-and-blood human beings, stripped of land, home, and family, covered over and suppressed; thus are the origins of a global social process mystified.

THE CATECHISM OF PRAXIS

If postmodernism's theory of practice is essentially idealist, how then have its advocates managed to present it as such a radical and even "dangerous" theory that it continues to be heralded as a "revolution of world significance"? Without a doubt, the fountain from which postmodernism has drawn its perpetual youth receives its wellspring from the mystique of the Sixties, the last time the Western left was able to mount a utopian project of any vitality and scope. As Foucault (who often tied his own researches to what happened in the 1960s) told one interviewer:

I think what happened in the sixties and early seventies is something to be preserved. One of the things that I think should be preserved, however, is the fact that there has been political innovation, political creation, and political experimentation outside the great political parties, and outside the normal or ordinary program. It's a fact that people's everyday lives have changed from the early sixties to now, and certainly within my own life. And surely this is not due to political parties but is the result of many movements. These social movements have really changed our whole lives, our mentality, our attitudes, and the attitudes and mentality of other people—people who do not belong to these movements. And that is something very important and positive. I repeat, it is not the normal and old traditional political organizations that have led to this examination.[68]

There is an important grain of truth to this observation, though, characteristically, Foucault exaggerates its significance. May 1968, let us recall, was in large part a revolt against the PFC's moral and organizational "sclerosis"—the vanguard party, bureaucratized party structures, and so on. By the 1960s, there was indeed a crisis of Marxism. Marxism was seen to have failed as a mode of perception, as a political strategy, and as a theory of form (collective consciousness and organizational practice). Communist, unionist, and social democratic politics in France and elsewhere had reached a dead end. Thus, the upheavals of 1968 and the break with the "Catholicism" of Marx did in fact represent an important point of rupture in the history of the critical tradition; and the effect of the rupture was to yield new ways of perceiving and acting in the world. The gay and lesbian movement—to take but one example, though also the one most favorable to Foucault's argument—could not have developed within a Marxist framework.

However, Foucault and others went well beyond recognizing the limits of the Marxist paradigm to abandon dialectical and materialist thinking in toto. And this could only be accomplished by tethering the story of the emergence of poststructuralist thought to a narrative of historical necessity. According to that narrative, the devolution of state power to the most minute "capillaries" of civil society—including the human body itself, as the site of disciplinization and normalization—indicates a corresponding shift in subaltern practice. The collapse of the Marxist socialist paradigm represented the beginning of a shift from meta-theoretical, "totalizing" forms of practice to micropolitical, astrategic ones. The New Social Movements have thus been relieved of an onerous burden.[69] Shorn of its universalist and scientific pretensions, its heavy dreams of totality and grand strategy, history has been made clear for truly democratic possibilities—pluralistic, creative actions. Politics will no longer be construed in terms of a struggle for overt political power, nor as a struggle among classes or interests. Instead of dreaming of unitary frameworks and norms, subalterns will root tactical practice in chaos and indeterminacy: dispersed, local disruptions of discursive "networks," achieved through the proliferation of identities and what Foucault called "subjugated knowledges."

As Norman Rush wrote in a widely debated essay in The Nation in the early 1990s, from now on "practical and ethical critique of actually existing capitalism will arrive [only] piecemeal. It will necessarily be ad hoc,

crisis-oriented, pragmatic, pluralistic in its sources. It will lack an overar-
ching ideal. . . . It will be ungainly and will involve some competing,
unlovely propositions." Political practice in the future would therefore
be indistinguishable from practice today—it will be short-term focused,
ideologically unintegrated, formless, and so on. And all this will remain
the case forever. "Forget socialism, now," Rush concluded. "It's going to
be very postmodern in the terrain where socialists used to browse."[70]

With the end of colonialism, the collapse of the socialist project, the
metastatic encroachment of the commodity onto every intimate space
of daily life, and the shift from Fordism to more flexible forms of capital
accumulation, it seemed to many critical intellectuals that a new, post-
Marxist critical theory was needed to make sense of a topsy-turvy world.
If poststructuralism did not offer a theory of history, at least it seemed
to correspond, formally, to the transformations of culture and economy
that we have come to associate with the "postmodern condition." At a
time when working-class movements were in sharp retreat everywhere,
poststructuralism's message of the end of utopian, grand-scale movements and schemes seemed to fit the new political landscape.

Yet the poststructuralists went beyond acknowledging the value in
the new social movements; they began to prescribe a static, ahistorical
set of practices. As Shirley Pike observes, Althusser provided only "a
mechanistic set of propositions which claim to explain scientific development and the production of knowledge"; and the result was an "idealist position."[71] Poststructuralists later stripped Althusser's system of
its Leninist "scientificity" but preserved this idealism. Socialist theory,
which in its best moments comprehended practice dialectically and
historically, as a dynamic region of improvisation, was replaced with a
"catechism" of praxis—a recitation of rigid norms for proscribing collective action and critical research alike. Foucault provided a succinct
list of this catechism in the introduction to Deleuze and Guattari's *Anti-
Oedipus*, when he urged that "action, thought, and desires" be developed "by proliferation, juxtaposition, and disjunction"; that we must
"prefer what is positive and multiple, difference over uniformity, flows
over unities, mobile arrangements over systems" and embrace "not
[the] sedentary but [the] nomadic"; that we should smash the myth of
the individual subject "by means of multiplication and displacement,
diverse combinations"—and so on.[72] A more comprehensive description of this catechism as it appears not only in Foucault but in the

diverse work of dozens of other critics since his death can be summa-
rized as follows:

1. "Difference," or non-identity is (and should be) the ontologically defining princi-
    ple of human social being. The principle of difference is (and should be) the oper-
    ative principle of culture and collective action.[73]

2. Critical action in time and space is, and should be, dispersed or decentralized.
    Practice and identity is best conceived in terms of constant motion and flux,
    indeterminacy and impermanence. Corollaries: (a) Subalterns ought not to seek
    to establish permanent institutional changes, reforms, or rights, but rather to
    subvert all orders, norms, institutions. (b) Space should not to be conceived as
    public or common.[74]

3. The desire to comprehend the *totality* of society must be strenuously resisted.[75]
    Corollaries: (a) Investigating society at the level of the whole—including being
    open to the possibility that an actual empirical relation may inhere between the
    whole and its parts—is unproductive for critical research and action, and either
    does lead or may lead to totalitarianism.[76] (b) The attempt to imagine or propose
    an alternative, future society (utopianism) leads to the loss of heterogeneity.[77]

4. The principle of anti-holism should be extended to the formation of subjects
    and political projects: there must be no search for political unity or unity in
    identity.[78] Corollary: Ideas of unity, commonality, or community inevitably
    produce conflict among different groups, and indeed reproduce existing social
    hierarchies.[79]

5. Praxis is best effected through semiotic destabilization of existing social mean-
    ings, rather than through battles fought and won on the ground of overt mean-
    ing. Praxis should be based not on rendering meaning or history intelligible to
    people, but making meaning impossible.[80]

6. Communication between human beings is "always already" estranged, incom-
    plete, and distorted. Communication should take place without recourse to a
    common set of understandings. Political agents should therefore not strive for
    mutual understanding— speaking a common language.[81]

7. Sociological, historical, and geographical judgments, especially concerning who
    has power and who does not, questions of cause and effect, and so on, are to be
    scrupulously avoided. So, too, questions of group psychology, political strategy,
    and human motivation.[82]

There is a remarkable degree of concurrence among postmodernist theorists on these key points, giving the lie to frequent postmodernist claims
that their discourse is too diverse, too subtle and complex, to be vulnerable to systematic critique. What is important to note is that this catechism, which to this day remains strongly normative for praxis, serving
to prescribe certain forms of practice (dispersion, localism, spontaneism,
difference) while proscribing others (strategy, unity, analysis of totality),
codifies the "common sense" that developed with the Sixties structure of
feeling. When Michel Foucault urged those wishing to change society to
"turn away from all projects that claim to be global or radical," because
"we know from experience that the claim to escape from the system of
contemporary reality so as to produce the overall programs of another
society, of another way of thinking, another culture, another vision of
the world, has only led to the return of the most dangerous traditions"—
that is, Stalinism—he was not so much carefully working through a new
theory of historical action so much as he was engaged in automatic writing—channeling the "spirit" of his generation.[83]

   In a passage that helps us to clarify the difference between Marx's
dynamic, open-ended, phenomenological dialectic of practice, and the
closed and reified systems of critical theory today, Enzo Paci wrote in
The Function of the Sciences and the Meaning of Man:

> When philosophies are dogmatic and categorical, when they are either idealistic
> or realistic systems, they stand still. . . . But phenomenology is not a construction
> insofar as it continually departs and redeparts from actual experience where it
> reconsiders previous experiences and their results in the present for the future.
> Idealism and realism become worn out in the temporal course of praxis insofar as
> they are abstract and constructed philosophies.[84]

Everywhere today we see evidence of a disintegrating world order
whose social contradictions are already threatening every last vale of
safety and repose. We find ourselves choking on the traumas and social
dislocations of modernization and patriarchal capitalism, while bearing silent witness to the destruction of the natural order. Rather than
seeing new, wondrous, diverse subjectivities, we see instead the standardization of human consciousness and the rise of neo-fascist, racist,
and religious fundamentalist ideologies throughout the world. And
rather than challenging us to summon a collective will to respond with

sustained purpose, will, and imagination to these and other deepening crises in human society, a "leading" sector of the intelligentsia of the West asks us to put aside our instinctual horror at the vision of our dying world and to celebrate indeterminacy and "nomadism."

But the postmodernist outlook, while ostensibly innocent of the corrupted world of quotidian meaning and political choice, confirms not the death of politics and strategy, as critics like McClure and Scott believe, but merely and once more the uselessness of idealism, which has always provided false comfort against power.

5 The Prince and the Archaeologist

The new idealism in critical social thought has had the effect of compromising our ability to think *strategically* about social change. An antistrategic bias suffuses contemporary social movement culture and critical theory alike. Many in the anti-globalization movement seem to believe that leadership, or having a sense of organizational direction, are unnecessary.[1] At the same time, the notion that "critical" intellectuals and theorists ought to try to relate means to ends has largely disappeared from the agenda of Western critical theory. As Allison Jagger observes, political philosophers no longer bother to give thought to the problem of developing "a strategy for moving from the oppressive present to the liberated future."[2] Indeed, if a consensus exists today among critical theorists it is to sunder theory from practice, the better to inoculate the theorist against the threat of practical thought.

To clarify the stakes involved in the question of strategy in socialist and radical political thought, in this chapter I wish to contrast the different approaches to praxis taken by Michel Foucault, on the one hand, and Antonio Gramsci, on the other. In setting Gramsci's "Prince" against Foucault's "Archaeologist," I hope to convince the reader that Gramsci offers the far more convincing account of the nature and purposes of political life, of the relationship between knowledge and experience, and, hence, of the best way for subordinate groups to go about achieving social transformation.

EXEMPLARY LIVES

In many ways, the lives of Antonio Gramsci and Michel Foucault could hardly have been more different. Gramsci, the son of Peppina Marcias, a woman from a respected family in the Sardinian village of Ghilarza, and Franceso Gramsci, a government clerk from the Italian mainland, suffered from poverty and poor physical health most of his life. Gramsci committed his life to the revolutionary struggles of the working class, finally perishing in one of Mussolini's fascist dungeons—penniless and almost forgotten, aged only forty-six—a martyr to the working class whose premature death was only one of many engineered by the fascists who had come to power in Italy and Germany. Paul-Michel Foucault, by contrast, grew up in a wealthy home, in Poitiers, France—the son of Paul Foucault, a surgeon and professor of anatomy, and Anne Malapart, herself the wealthy daughter of a surgeon, who brought to the marriage her own château and land.3 A dandy who drove an expensive sports car, Foucault became a professor at the Ecole Supérieur Normale, rose with astonishing rapidity to the loftiest heights of the French academy, and died an international celebrity.

Yet in life and in death, Gramsci and Foucault both led lives of example to others. From his youth on, Gramsci was involved in socialist politics. In his late twenties he played a crucial role in organizing the workers' councils in the factories of Turin, as an activist and as chief editor of the socialist journal L'Ordine Nuovo. Later, after the factory councils were defeated, Gramsci was asked to help found the Italian Communist Party, which he for a time headed. Imprisoned by Mussolini in 1926 for his political activities, Gramsci spent the next decade in prison, refusing to compromise his principles. After years of intense physical suffering, he died there, in the spring of 1937.

Foucault too was a politically engaged intellectual, involved in the social movements of his day. In 1971 Foucault founded the Groupe d'Information sur les Prisons (GIP)—a movement to provide information about the inhumane carceral system in France. In the remainder of his life, Foucault publicly sided with a number of other radical political causes, from immigrant rights to the inhumane conditions in French insane asylums. Today, Foucault is often remembered as the most prominent "out" gay intellectual of the century, a courageous figure who was willing to speak out on behalf of the oppressed and to be open with his own sexuality in the face of social ridicule.4 His death, at the age of fifty-eight, a casualty of the AIDS epidemic, was, like Gramsci's, premature, one death among many resulting from malevolent state policies and the social prejudice against gays and lesbians.

Both men also suffered, and their suffering appears to have played a formative role in their politics. Foucault, as a gay man growing up in an intensely homophobic society, knew isolation and marginalization. At the elite Ecole Normale Supérieure, a place one of his biographers describes as "a pathogenic milieu, a center where the most absurd, most eccentric behavior came out, as much on a personal as on an intellectual or political level," Foucault suffered from an extreme sense of shame and rebellious rage, in large part over his closeted sexuality.[5] An unsociable and aggressive individual at that time, Foucault attempted suicide there in 1948, at the age of twenty-two.[6]

Gramsci, meanwhile, never shook off the perspective of his native Sardinia, an impoverished island historically exploited by more powerful interests in the northern mainland. (He spoke with great pride and intimate knowledge of Sardinian culture throughout his life.) He knew what it felt like to be an outsider, and learned at an early age to see the world from the point of view of those forgotten by history. Moreover, born with a severe deformity (he was hunchbacked), Gramsci could not have but felt personally isolated in his childhood. "I was forced to make too many sacrifices," Gramsci once wrote in a letter to his wife, Julia. "Because my health was so poor, I persuaded myself that I was merely something to be tolerated, an intruder in my own family. Such things are not easily forgotten, and leave much deeper traces than we might think."[7] At the University of Turin, where he had won a meager scholarship to study, Gramsci had barely enough money to pay his rent and no money for a proper coat to protect him against the cold winters. At Turin he experienced physical and psychic deprivation—chronic malnutrition, nervous exhaustion, illness, and isolation. As an adult, Gramsci compensated for his severe geographical and physical limitations by developing an extraordinarily powerful intellect, and an iron will. Yet his life remained difficult; at the age of thirty-one, after a whirlwind decade during which he completed his studies, worked as a journalist, and helped lead the failed factory council movement in Turin, he suffered a severe mental and physical breakdown, leading to a six-month stay in a Moscow sanitorium where he met his future wife, Julia Schucht, another patient.

Foucault and Gramsci were personally acquainted with isolation, marginality, and "difference." But they also experienced the phenomenology of power differently. Gramsci was more acutely aware of the effects of material deprivation—fatigue, cold, hunger—and of the overt

political violence of the state—the myriad humiliations of imprisonment—on the human body and mind. Foucault knew first-hand the
power of normativity and sexual oppression. But as someone who grew
up in the lap of luxury, and who went on to obtain a prestigious position in French intellectual life, material inequality and political repression were remote experiences. The "Prince," then, was witness to the
naked violence of the state, to the arbitrary exercise of justice, and to
the grinding brutality of capitalist exploitation. The "Archaeologist,"
by contrast, was more attuned to the subtle, hidden network of repres-
sions of disciplinary mechanisms and social norms. Gramsci became a
sociologist and linguist concerned with palpable structures of power
and overt struggles over meaning, and a revolutionary; Foucault chose
training first as a psychiatrist, then as a historian, to explore social control over the individual and the production of *signs* of the "self."

Both thinkers, it is true, were drawn intellectually to the problem of
the role of intellectuals in society, and to the relationship between
knowledge and power. Both, too, were interested in the relationship
between language and historical experience. And both had a great deal
to say on the subject of critical or oppositional practice. Yet here the
similarities between them end, and the signal differences begin. Gramsci's intellectual project was above all conditioned by his political context, which was one of severe social upheaval, the rise of fascism, and
sectarian squabbles on the left. The recurring theme in Gramsci's writings is therefore the question of how the opposition might successfully
build an effective socialist movement in the face of difficult circumstances in order to lead society toward socioeconomic justice. Foucault,
by contrast, came to his political conclusions from the immediate historical context of French postwar society. Writing at a time of extraordinary economic growth in Europe, amid the giddy, tumultuous global
upheaval of the New Left, Foucault wrote of the dangers not of fascism,
but of liberalism. Having seen the hypocrisy and emptiness of both representative democracy and of the communists, Foucault refused both.

The result of the different historical and personal contexts of the
two men's work, then, led them to nearly opposite conclusions about
the nature of political life, power, and the means of political struggle.
Indeed, Foucault's thought can be said to represent the reversal, if not
the negation, of the political vision Gramsci committed his life to
developing. While Gramsci and Foucault both hoped that their work

might be of use to the oppressed, they finally arrived at antipodal perspectives on a great many important issues relating to praxis, including subjectivity, consciousness, history, temporality, and truth.

In an essay on Gramsci and Foucault, Joan Cocks observes that the latter's political thought was hobbled by his "inability to support any movement that through its massiveness and disciplined unity would be
popular and yet powerful enough to undermine an entrenched legal-
political regime; and [second, by] the inability to stand on the side of any

COUNTER-HEGEMONY VS. ANTI-HEGEMONY:
Conceptual Differences in the Thought of Antonio Gramsci and Michel Foucault

Concept	GRAMSCI	FOUCAULT
STRATEGY	Product of human will	Product of non-conscious discursive structures or systems
OPPOSITIONAL FORM	Hegemony/alliance (unity)	Difference, dispersion (disunity)
INTELLECTUALS	Organic leaders, connected to masses	Specialized, technical ("dialectic of distincts")
HISTORICAL SUBJECT	The vast majority of human beings (i.e., the working class, with "allied" classes)	Subjugated knowledges (marginalized, abjected individuals and groups)
LEADERSHIP	Necessary (Jacobinist)	Unnecessary (Anti-Jacobinist)
ORDER/NORMATIVITY	Necessary, to be created	Inescapable, but to be resisted
MODALITY OF STRUGGLE	War of position (coordinated struggle at all levels)	Micropolitical resistance (dispersed struggles, primarily through individual cultural practices)
GEOGRAPHICAL IMAGINATION	Dialectic between local and global (synthetic)	Dispersed, local (analytic/fragmented)
HISTORICAL MEANING	Intelligible as class conflict	Intelligible as "will to power"

CONCEPT	GRAMSCI	FOUCAULT
MODE OF HISTORICAL INQUIRY	Hegelian, Marxist (*telos* of freedom) Historical, dialectical, sociological	Nietzschean, Heideggerian inquiry (myth of eternal return) Genealogical, relativist
POWER	Immanent to relations of capitalist production (hierarchical)	Coextensive with society as such (diffuse)
SOCIAL CHANGE	Shift to new "common sense," corresponding more, or less, to actual human freedom	Shift to a new but arbitrary *episteme*
TEMPORAL "TOWARDNESS"	Future-directed (possibilities are generated in the past and present)	Past-directed (determination of the present by the past)
POLITICAL TELOS	World revolution/ a new civilization	Aesthetic action, new pleasures ("stylizing" existence)
CONSCIOUSNESS	The ground of Being	Epiphenomenal
MEANING	The ground of politics	Epiphenomenal
EXPERIENCE	The basis of knowledge (phenomenological)	Epiphenomenal (an effect of power-knowledge— post-phenomenological)
TRUTH	Socially conditioned, but verifiable in practice	Socially constructed, a form and an effect of power
TOTALITY	Knowable, if only perspectivally	Unknowable and/or repressive

positive new cultural-political order at all."[8] These two elements, political unity and cultural hegemony—in Gramsci's language, the "hegemonic bloc" and "moral and intellectual leadership"—lie at the heart of what are in fact the two theorists' irreconcilable conceptions of political life.[9] If Gramsci today is largely remembered as the theorist of hegemony— the forging of political unity across cultural differences—Foucault might well be described as the theorist par excellence of *anti-hegemony*, what

Aronowitz describes as a politics "recognizing the permanence *of differ-ence*," and in which "movements for liberation . . . will remain autonomous both in the course of the struggle and in the process of cre-ating a new society."[10] While Gramsci, a Hegelian Marxist, passionately defended a politics of mass strategy, meaning, and intellectual leader-ship, Foucault, a Nietzschean, defended an antipolitics based on singular-ization, local and dispersed tactics, spontaneity, and the disruption of discourse. And where Gramsci conceived of the critical intellectual as a strategist, a leader, and an educator, Foucault argued against a politics based on education, assigning to intellectuals the more modest role of serving as technical "specialists" who would facilitate the spontaneous coming-to-expression of what he called "subjugated knowledges."

THE VIRTÙ OF THE MODERN PRINCE

As I noted in the last chapter, despite his own admirable activism, Fou-cault in his writings often seemed to conceive the proper role of theory as a form of historical *spectatorship*. It is fair to say that Gramsci had little sympathy for such passive and intellectualist approaches to human events. As he once complained: "The Socialist Party looks on like a specta-tor at the course of events, it never even passes judgment on them, it never proposes policies the mass can understand and accept."[11] But no revolutionary movement, he wrote, ever matures or "perfects itself" until it has realized "that in order to produce certain results it creates the nec-essary preconditions, and indeed devotes all its forces to the creation of these preconditions."[12] The task of the modern prince, thus, was not sim-ply "to reconstruct and reinforce" an already existing political identity, but to create a unified will "from scratch."[13] Quentin Hoare rightly describes Gramsci's Jacobinism as the "unifying thread which links all of Gramsci's prison writing on history and on politics."[14] That is, Gramsci was convinced that to achieve hegemony, the subaltern class would have to be given form by a "conscious" or directing element. We might sum up this difference in approach and emphasis in the politics of Foucault and Gramsci by saying that Foucault had no theory of what Machiavelli called *virtù*, while Gramsci made *virtù* the central feature of his work.

Machiavelli, like other Renaissance intellectuals, highly valued demonstrations of individual skill and excellence—*virtù*, or masculine will and ability. In Machiavelli's hands, *virtù* became a frank assertion of the possibility of human free will against the moralism and fatalism of Christianity. During the Renaissance, human freedom was yet seen as finite, limited to particular spheres of excellence and kept in check by the play of contingent forces by *fortuna,* or fortune—forces beyond human control. Machiavelli, however, held that the skilled political leader could push against the constraints dictated by those forces. Many, he wrote, are of "the opinion that the things of this world are, in a manner, controlled by Fortune and by God, that men with their wisdom cannot control them." In Machiavelli's famous metaphor, fortune resembled "one of those ruinous rivers that, when they become enraged, flood the plains, tear down the trees and buildings, taking up earth from one spot and placing it upon another; everyone flees from them, everyone yields to their onslaught, unable to oppose them in any way." Yet, he wrote, those who properly exercise *virtù* need not be controlled by *fortuna.* The skillful prince or leader thus plans in advance, preparing the people to defend their city-state against foreign enemies:

> [For] although [rivers] are of such a nature, it does not follow that when the weather is calm we cannot take precautions with embankments and dikes, so that when they rise up again either the waters will be channeled off or their impetus will not be either so disastrous or so damaging. The same things happen where Fortune is concerned: she shows her force where there is no organized strength to resist her; and she directs her impact there where she knows that dikes and embankments are not constructed to hold her. And if you will consider Italy, the seat of these changes and the nation which has set them in motion, you will see a country without embankments and without a single bastion.[15]

In this manner, Machiavelli essentially folds *fortuna* into *virtù.* "*Fortuna* now no longer appears as an external power," Fontana observes, "but rather as an aspect of *virtù.*"[16] Hence the significance of the conclusion of *The Prince,* when Machiavelli calls for a unified Italy.[17] The narrator encourages the people to unite in order to create the basis of a stable republic, one capable of repelling foreign invaders and achieving greatness. But such a unity, a *colletiva voluntà* to make Italy great once more, perhaps even to surpass the glory of imperial Rome, could only be realized through the creative leadership of a clever and forceful prince able to win the admiration and loyalty of the people, a prince exercising *virtù.* Only a skillful prince could transform the *res privata,* an order dominated by ruthless private interests, into a *res publica,* a "public thing."[18]

As a theorist working within the Italian tradition, Gramsci could not help but absorb Machiavelli's emphasis on active, conscious *will* in political life. Gramsci recognized that Machiavelli was the first theorist to fully appreciate the significance of *il popolo*, the people, as a new force in history. Indeed, Machiavelli himself was himself but a "precocious" Jacobin (as he termed him), a practical theorist with a keen sense of the conscious element needed to give shape to that form.[19] Hence, in Gramsci's politics, the "modern" prince exercises a *socialist virtù*."

Like Machiavelli's Prince, the modern prince cannot make history any which way it likes. Critical historical practice represents a movement from "what is" (*essere*) to what "ought to be" (*dover essere*), taking the given organic and conjunctural relations and working them to political advantage.[20] Just as *fortuna* or nature conditions the prince's choices, objective or structural forces shape the context in which the modern prince's conscious actions and appearances unfold. Gramsci essentially historicizes Machiavelli's dialectic between *fortuna* and *virtù* with his distinction between "organic" and "conjunctural" historical movements. In an elaboration of Marx's theory of base and superstructure, Gramsci describes "organic" crises as epochal transitions rooted in fundamental structural changes in the underlying mode of economy, and "conjunctural" ones as occurring, more immediately, in the spheres of politics and culture.

"Organic crisis" thus becomes analogous to *fortuna* in Machiavelli's thought. What is key is that the contradictions of capitalism always play themselves out in *conjunctural* terms, in the sphere of *virtù*. That is, organic changes in the mode of economic reproduction constitute a certain *horizon* of historical action, providing an objective context with unique opportunities and challenges. *But the outcome of this transition is never predetermined.* Economics may indeed define the fate of civilization in "the last instance," but political power is always the accomplishment of a determined protagonist. Synthesizing Machiavelli's political theory with Marx's historical materialism, then, Gramsci maintained a feeling both for human freedom and for the structural limits of that freedom.

Politics is not a "science," but a struggle based on intuition and the rational calculation of probabilities. To deny the rational, directing element of politics is therefore as much folly as to deny the play of unconscious and irrational factors in the political realm. In any political struggle, but especially in the poorly matched struggle of the weak against the powerful, it is necessary to bring one's scarce resources to bear on the most vulnerable points of one's antagonist's defenses if one hopes to achieve certain objectives, and this requires leadership. "One speaks of generals without an army," Gramsci observed, "but in reality it is easier to form an army than to form generals. So much is this true that an already existing army is destroyed if it loses its generals, while the existence of a united group of generals who agree among themselves and have common aims soon creates an army even where none exists."[21]

STRATEGY AND THE MODERN PRINCE

Thus, Gramsci's emphasis on human *will* in political action, almost wholly absent (as we will see in a moment) from Foucault's politics and epistemology, accounts for Gramsci's extraordinarily focused interest in questions of *strategy*. The word *strategy*, the science or art of commanding forces in battle in fact comes from the Greek, *strategia*, for "office of a general" (*strategos*), which in turn derives from stratos, a "spread" (or encamped) army, and *agein*, to drive or lead. From earliest usage, then, a "strategist" was a leader capable of perceiving the whole field of action in order to guide available forces in a struggle to achieve a desired outcome— a new balance of power. These elements—bold leadership (*virtù*) and a view of the totality of forces with a view toward imposing a new order— were central to Gramsci's conception of a counter-hegemonic politics.

Gramsci was himself a master strategist, one who never wavered in his belief that leadership was essential to effective social struggle, and who was almost obsessed with understanding the phenomenon of political action. The *Notebooks* are in fact strewn with numerous critical commentaries by Gramsci on political campaigns that still stand out as practical exemplars of how subaltern movements ought to go about analyzing the political balance of forces. Of India's struggle for independence against the British, for example, Gramsci wrote:

Gandhi's passive resistance is a war of position, which becomes a war of movement at certain moments and an underground war at others: the boycott is a war of position, strikes are a war of movement, the clandestine gathering of arms and of assault combat groups is underground war. A kind of *arditismo* is present, but it is employed very cautiously. If the English became convinced that a great insurgent movement was being planned, destined to annihilate their current strategic superiority (which, in a certain sense, consists of their ability to maneuver along internal lines and to concentrate their forces at the "sporadically" most dangerous place) by smothering it through mass action, that is, by obliging them to spread their forces thinly over a theatre of war which had become simultaneously widespread, then it would be to their advantage to provoke a premature sortie of the Indian fighting forces in order to identify them and decapitate the general movement.[22]

In this brief passage we can identify several key elements of Gramsci's strategic thought. First, we see Gramsci's attunement to the complexity and force of contending wills and assessment of the strengths and weaknesses of the antagonists involved. Like Clausewitz, who argued that the strategist must avoid so-called timeless formulas, Gramsci rooted political knowledge experientially. That is, he saw strategy not as an inquiry into the essence of war "as such," but rather (to quote Clausewitz) an "attempt to investigate the *essence of the phenomena* of war and to indicate the links between these phenomena and the nature of their component parts."[23] A strategist is not a metaphysician, therefore, but a *phenomenologist* of conflict, insofar as she or he must "suspend" the naturalistic attitude, or "common sense," in order to perceive what is really there. It is for this reason Clausewitz begins *On War* by "bracketing" received or orthodox notions about what warfare "is." What is important, he suggests, is that we grasp the structure of our experiences in the activity of war.[24]

In the comments on Gandhi we also see evidence of Gramsci's keen empiricist's eye for the whole field of action. The complexity of *class* struggle places especially great hermeneutical responsibilities on the shoulders of the counter-hegemonist, for whom the "field of action" must constitute the whole of society and culture, past and present—i.e., the *totality*.[25] Since the meaning of any given political act only accrues in relation to the wider context or background of prior meanings, such a strategist must be exquisitely sensitive to context. In Gramsci's terms, the responsibility of the leader is to discern patterns in the total field of significations, social and economic structures, cultural objects, and so on, which together constitute the background or horizon of action. The counter-hegemonist must be able to map, as accurately as possible, the complex terrain of parties, movements, institutions, economic forces— in short, the dynamic balance and relations of will and force—in order to exploit places in the hierarchical network of power, nodes, where hegemony is unstable or breaks down. As Kerry Whiteside observes of Merleau-Ponty's phenomenology of politics, "Understanding power itself depends on grasping the meaning of social conditions "; hence, "the effectiveness of political leadership depends on the leader's ability to perceive these structures accurately."[26] She or he must be able to discern, in the rapidly shifting sands of meaning, hidden patterns that might indicate promising or perilous lines of action.

We might finally note that Gramsci's very interest in the anti-imperialist movement in British India exemplifies his stance toward knowledge, which was not that of the putatively impartial or objective social "scientist" but of a revolutionary, an intellectual, and a political leader. The strategist is a partisan geographer who maps the social with normative (ethical and political objectives) in mind and in heart. She applies her will to an existing set of conditions, in order to perceive, and work in harmony with, the tendencies that correspond to her own plans and desires. Only in the attempt to "see" the possible, the potential that is immanent to the real, in the present, can the possible be coaxed into being. Seeing is possible only when the strategist's own subjective emotion and feeling are involved—"strong passions are necessary to sharpen the intellect and help make intuition more penetrating."[27]

"Only the man who wills something strongly can identify the elements which are necessary to the realisation of his will."[28] Paradoxically, accurate or "objective" prediction of political outcomes or events is only possible *subjectively*, through the exertion of a particular *will*. At first, prediction seems to be a relatively simple matter, namely, "seeing the present and past clearly as movement." But Gramsci comments: "Seeing them clearly: in other words, accurately identifying the fundamental and permanent elements of the process."[29] And only a particular subject will be able to sort out the essential from the inessential:

> When a particular program has to be realized, it is only the existence of somebody to "predict" it which will ensure that it deals with what is essential—with those elements which, being "organizable" and susceptible of being directed or deflected, are in reality alone predictable. This is in contrast with the habitual way of looking at the problem. For it is generally thought that every act of prediction presupposes the determination of laws of regularity similar to those of the natural sciences. But since these laws do not exist in the absolute or mechanical sense that is imagined, no account is taken of the will of others, nor is its application "predicted." Consequently everything is built on an arbitrary hypothesis and not on reality.[30]

In other words, "reality is a product of the application of human will to the society of things."[31] This phenomenological insight into the means by which agents can act in order to transform their lifeworld lies at the heart of every epistemology of strategy. The strategists of ancient China, for example, held that "one 'knows' a world not only passively in the sense of recognizing it, but also in the active shaping and 'realizing' of it. It is the capacity to anticipate the patterned flow of circumstance, to encourage those dispositions most conducive to a productive harmony."[32] This participatory conception of knowledge was central to Sun Tzu's use of the Taoist concept of *shih*, or strategic advantage:

> All determinate situations can be turned to advantage. The able commander is able to create differentials and thus opportunities by manipulating his position and the position of his enemies. By developing a full understanding of those factors that define one's relationship with the enemy, and by actively controlling and shaping the situation so that the weaknesses of the enemy are exposed to one's acquired strength, one is able to ride the force of circumstances to victory.[33]

FOUCAULT'S "GREAT REFUSAL" OF STRATEGY

Even Foucault's most sympathetic critics concede that he offered neither a theory of social change nor a strategy for challenging power.[34] As Foucault told one interviewer:

> If someone should ask me what it is I think I am doing, I would answer: if the strategist is a man who says, "what importance does a particular death, a particular cry, a particular uprising have in relation to the great necessity of the whole, and of what importance to me is such-and-such a general principle in the specific situation in which we find ourselves?" then it is indifferent to me whether the strategist is a politician, a historian, a revolutionary, someone who supports the Shah or ayatollah. My theoretical morality is the opposite. It is "antistrategic": be respectful when singularity rises up, and intransigent when power infringes on the universal.[35]

As we have seen, while Gramsci viewed experience as the ultimate basis of politics and truth, Foucault, as a leading figure in the structuralist and, later, poststructuralist revolt against phenomenology, saw experience largely as epiphenomenal—as an object whose appearance as something real and "foundational" (a ground for knowing) was precisely that which demands explanation (see my discussion in chapter 4). But having refused the language of experience and consciousness, Foucault could speak only of emancipating knowledges, never human beings. Working in their separate spheres, intellectuals and people would "attempt to emancipate historical knowledges from [their] subjection, to render them . . . capable of opposition and of struggle against the coercion of a theoretical, unitary, formal and scientific discourse."[36] Such subjugated knowledges, or "local memories" as Foucault termed them, once freed, would go on to "struggle against the coercion" of unitary discursive systems. Because the "struggle" was not against particular classes or social groups, only vague "discourses" or even *pouvoir*, the genealogist is freed from having to worry about the intentions or plans of potential antagonists—those who seek to repress particular discourses, say.

Foucault's skepticism toward experience and phenomenology led him to refuse five key principles which, together, constitute a good deal of the foundation of the strategic tradition: 1) the idea that leadership is necessary in political and military struggle; 2) that it is essential to study motives and interests and other objects of consciousness; 3) that having a view of the "totality" or relations within the functional whole of society is required for effective political action; 4) that one cannot know "doctrinally," i.e., in advance of a given situation, what kinds of tactics or particular actions are appropriate; and 5) that the goal of agonism is *normative*, i.e., that it results in the transformation of a *situation* whereby one political or social order gives way to another.

Because Foucault held that meaning, like the subject, is a chimera—an effect produced by impersonal structures of power—he concluded that there could be no epistemological basis for intellectuals to exercise cultural or political hegemony. Indeed, intellectuals themselves, whether mainstream social scientists or corrupt union leaders or Communist Party hacks, stood (or stand) in the way of the eruption of the "knowledges" of those marginalized by power. What "blocks, prohibits, and invalidates this discourse and this knowledge," Foucault wrote in the early 1970s, was "a system of power" whose "agents" were the intellectuals themselves. As for the people, "the intellectual discovered that the masses no longer need him to gain knowledge: they know perfectly well, without illusion; they know better than he and they are certainly capable of expressing themselves."[37]

It was this ostensibly populist sentiment that led Foucault to reject all forms of leadership and strategy. Foucault understood his own scholarly project as a lifelong effort *"to shut the mouths* of prophets and legislators: all those who speak *for* others and *above* others."[38] Foucault thus argued that intellectuals were required to renounce their past roles as "bearers of universal values," whether as public intellectuals like Jean-Paul Sartre, or as strategists and leaders, like Lenin or Gramsci. Instead, he argued, the intellectual ought to conceive of herself as a "specialist." As specialists of knowledge—the expert working in the university, in the prison, in the school, the laboratory, and so on: in short, as "the person occupying a specific position—but whose specificity is linked . . . to the general functioning of the apparatus of truth"[39]—intellectuals occupy key nodal locations of the power-knowledge network. They therefore "can operate and struggle at the general level of that régime of truth which is so essential to the structure and functioning of our society."[40] That is, by conducting genealogies of the present, they might worm out hegemonic truth-regimes from the inside, thus creating more space for subjugated knowledges to proliferate.

Second, if meaning is a chimera, and if what really matters in the history of modernity are the obscure machinations of a power/knowledge nexus, then it is safe to assume that the assumptions governing all subaltern struggles heretofore have been misguided and wrong. Especially wrong would be the assumption in strategic discourse that political struggle was a struggle for "hearts and minds," i.e., a struggle for control of *meaning.* "The problem," Foucault insisted on more than one occasion, "is not changing people's consciousness—or what's in their heads—but the political, economic, institutional régime of the production of truth."[41] Foucault was unequivocal on this score. "Let us not," he wrote, "ask why certain people want to dominate, what they seek, what is their overall strategy. Let us ask, instead, how things work at the level of ongoing subjugation, at the level of those continuous and uninterrupted processes which subject our bodies, govern our gestures, dictate our behaviors, etc."[42]

Third, because Foucault located the problem of power in the operations of discourse, especially the discourses of the human sciences, discourses of the social "whole," which arose out of modernity and Enlightenment, were part of the problem. Foucault rejected humanism on the grounds that the myth of a human essence had obscured social difference and led to the repression of non-normative forms of subjectivity. On similar grounds, he faulted Marxists for positing a "totality" whose causal structures and relations could be reliably known. The discourse of totality was used to suppress forms of subjectivity and modes of action and knowledge that failed to fit the Marxist metaphysics of the working-class subject. On these grounds, Foucault advocated the end to every thought about the relationship between parts and whole, particular actions and long-term goals. Or as he put it: "'The whole of society' is precisely that which should not be considered except as something to be destroyed. And then, we can only hope that it will never exist again."[43]

Fourth, Foucault asked us to adopt a particular and idiosyncratic set of tactics—nomadism, dispersion, difference, etc.—seemingly irrespective of every actual historical situation that might confront us. As I noted in chapter 4, Foucault embraced Deleuze and Guattari's *Anti-Oedipus*, calling it a "manual or guide to everyday life." Summing up this guide, Foucault wrote:

- Develop action, thought, and desires by proliferation, juxtaposition, and disjunction, and not by subdivision and pyramidal hierarchization.

- Withdraw allegiance from the old categories of the Negative (law, limit, castration, lack, lacuna). . . . Prefer instead what is positive and multiple, difference over uniformity, flows over unities, mobile arrangements over systems. Believe that what is productive is not sedentary but nomadic.

- Do not think that one has to be sad in order to be militant. . . . It is the connection of desire to reality . . . that possesses revolutionary force.

- Do not use thought to ground a political practice in Truth; nor political action to discredit, as mere speculation, a line of thought. Use political practice as an intensifier of thought, and analysis as a multiplier of the forms and domains for the intervention of political action.

- Do not demand of politics that it restore "rights" of the individual. . . . The individual is the product of power. What is needed is to "de-individualize" by means of multiplication and displacement, diverse combinations. The group must not be the organic bond uniting hierarchized individuals, but a constant generator of de-individualization.[44]

Such a categorical menu proscribing certain *means* of action cannot be reconciled with strategic reflection. Strategy by its nature requires flexibility on the part of the strategist, i.e., a dynamic, improvisatory,

empirical approach. Hence Clausewitz's careful disavowal of any inten-
tion on his part to establish a "complete system and comprehensive
doctrine" grounded in unchanging laws: any commander who does
battle by following bookish prescriptions will soon find himself dead.[45]
But of course what makes the very existence of such a list surprising is
that it chafes against Foucault's declared aversion to *normativity* of any
kind, especially the imposition of new norms by self-described "leaders" and intellectuals.

Let us consider some further difficulties that Foucault's rejection of
these elements poses for the subaltern.

Foucault's assault on a politics based on *meaning* would seem to prevent us from thinking through the significance and likely impact of
our actions, especially how those actions may be *perceived* and reacted
to by others. He remained categorical about the irrelevance of taking
interests and wills into account. As Alex Honneth observes, Foucault
seemed to view "the classes that dominate at any given time . . . as the
mere bearers of systemic processes, that is, as a quantity that can in
principle be ignored."[46] Unfortunately, Foucault never explained just
how it would be in the interest of a subaltern group struggling to
change society to ask what others' "overall strategy" is.[47] The trouble is
that in war and other forms of agonism, "the will is directed at an animate object that reacts."[48] Our antagonist, like us, also has a will, also
has conscious intentions. The leadership of a revolutionary or resistance movement therefore has *no choice* but to grapple with an extremely fluid and dynamic field of action, i.e., one in which one's antagonist
also improvises, also acts. Sun Tzu wrote that the "ability to gain victo-
ry by changing and adapting according to the opponent is called
genius."[49] But Foucault leaves us no room for the exercise of our
genius—nor, for that matter, for the possibility that we might *make mistakes* that we can learn from.

But by the same token, Foucault cannot help us know who our friends
are: in a world riven by injustice, violence, and unspeakable suffering,
knowing who one's friends are—the problem that sets in motion Plato's
long dialogue about justice in *The Republic*—is not a trivial issue. But Foucault had few words in his otherwise copious writings for such fundamental features of the human condition as friendship, intimacy,
solidarity, empathy, or love. Indeed, Foucault lacked any proper theory of
intersubjectivity as such—except, that is, for an affinity for Nietzsche's

philosophy of mutual objectification and domination. But without a way to distinguish between truth and lies, friend and enemy, good and evil, it is hard to know how the oppressed are to come to terms with the life-world—a living world teeming with people, situations, parties, ideologies, and choices of life-and-death significance.

"The masses," Foucault told Duccio Trombadori, a Gramscian Marxist whose critical questions to Foucault about his lack of a proper theory of politics put Foucault on the defensive, "have come of age, politically and morally. They are the ones who've got to choose individually and collectively. . . . [They] have to make a choice."[50] On the one hand, sympathetic critics point to passages like this in Foucault's work as evidence of an admirably radical, democratic, and pluralistic politics. In his theory, after all, there are no leaders and no led, no authoritarian types bossing people around. Since the subjugation of marginalized subjects (prisoners, the mad, immigrants, homosexuals, and so on) owes not to oppression by a particular class or social interests, but to regimes of power-knowledge, it follows that intellectuals ought to stand down from making either universal claims or strategic ones. As Foucault wrote: "The intellectual no longer has to play the role of an advisor. The project, tactics and goals to be adopted are a matter for those who do the fighting. What the intellectual can do is to provide instruments of analysis, and at present this is the historian's essential role. . . . But as for saying, 'Here is what you must do!' certainly not."[51]

To Gramsci, though, to unburden the people of knowledge of certain carefully concealed social facts was not to do them any great favor. He therefore resisted the false flattery that the people "already know what is to be done." If it were in fact true that the people knew what needed to be done, then structures of oppression would, presumably, be overcome quickly or easily. That they have not been so easily overcome is something that needs to be looked at. Few people have more than a tentative grasp on the sociology of power or the history of political struggle, let alone a sense of how to go about changing the world. On the contrary, it is probably more typical for the masses to identify with their oppressors, since the dominant ideas in a society are also the ideas of its ruling class. "The class which has the means of production at its disposal, has control at the same time over the means of mental production," as Marx and Engels noted.[52] Hence Gramsci's crucial distinction between *chi sa*, those who "know," and *chi non sa*, those who do not. The responsibility of the modern prince was not to pretend that such a distinction did not in fact exist, but instead to dissolve it by raising the people "up." The key thing was that Marxism must be "the opposite of the Catholic," by which he meant only that the philosophy of praxis must not

> leave the "simple" in their primitive philosophy of common sense, but rather. . . lead them to a higher conception of life. If it affirms the need for contact between intellectuals and simple it is not in order to restrict scientific activity and pre- serve unity at the low level of the masses, but precisely in order to construct an intellectual-moral bloc which can make politically possible the intellectual progress of the mass and not only of small intellectual groups.[53]

To oppose leadership on principle, therefore, as Foucault did, seems lit- tle more than moralistic and, potentially, quite harmful posturing. The question is not whether one should act as though there were leaders and led—that distinction is a given—but whether one's goal is "to create the conditions in which this division is no longer necessary," i.e., through revolution.[54] Social movements are neither 100 percent spon- taneous nor 100 percent directed. Every movement, every organization, develops its own leadership, whether formally, through procedural vote, or informally, via personal charisma or influence.[55] There are always "conscious" elements, which is to say leading elements in any movement, a core of activist-intellectuals who must actively decide which lines of action to pursue, how the movement is going to repre- sent itself, when and where to initiate actions, to relate means to ends, and so on—even in erstwhile anarchistic or "purely" democratic move- ments.[56] To pretend otherwise is simply to sweep the question of *legiti- mate* and *illegitimate* forms of leadership under the rug. What is paramount is that the modern prince leads in such a way that the dis- tinction between prince and people, leaders and led, finally disappears.

TEACHING LITERACIES OF POWER

This brings us at last to the pivotal source of the differences between Gramsci and Foucault on the question of politics—the possibility and desirability of imposing *a new normative order*. As Joan Cocks observes, Gramsci and Foucault "represent . . . polar positions . . . on the question of whether an [oppositional] movement should have as its end the imposition of a new positive hegemonic culture—including a new system of classification, a new range of sensibilities, new possibilities of action, new norms of conduct, new institutions, canons, and traditions, and even a new legal-political state."[57]

For Gramsci, successful counter-hegemonic struggle hinges on the patient cultivation of a new basis of social consent, through leadership by a class or social group over the other, diverse elements of society. In one of Machiavelli's more famous metaphors, he suggested that the Prince must exhibit, by turns, the character of the fox and the lion. That is, the leader must rule by cunning as well as by force, bringing both into harmony in the figure of the Centaur, i.e., "a half-man and half beast." Gramsci incorporated this notion into his theory of hegemony. Hegemony, he argued, involved moments of both democratic consent or education (fox) and coercion or force (the lion). We might say that the modern prince wages political struggle as a "fox" when he engages in political debate, rational discourse, and consciousness-raising, but acts as a "lion" insofar as his goal is finally to impose a new set of norms and values upon a given people or society.

Hegemony cannot in fact be achieved through purely democratic or consensual means, simply because politics unfolds not only on the level of consciousness (the mythical Kantian plane of autonomous or practical reason) but pre-categorically as well, at the level of unconscious structures of meaning.[58] Hegemony is a strategy, that is, for creating a new "common sense." As Fontana puts it, the hegemonic movement succeeds only when it has sucessfully transformed the "subordinate, particularistic mass of disaggregated individuals into a leading and hegemonic subject whose thought and values have become the prevailing conception of the world."[59] Hegemony is ultimately not merely a struggle among "ideas," but a struggle over what we might call the means of perception. Fontana writes:

> Since, for Gramsci, reality is perceived, and knowledge is acquired, through moral, cultural, and ideological "prisms" or "filters" by means of which society acquires form and meaning, hegemony necessarily implies the creation of a particular structure of knowledge and a particular system of values. The social group or class [which] is capable of forming its own particular knowledge and value systems, and of transforming them into general and universally applicable conceptions of the world, is the group that exercises intellectual and moral leadership.[60]

A hegemonic movement or project is thus successful to the degree that it has succeeded in altering the underlying *Gestalten* or perceptual structures that shape our daily experiences of reality—when its own values and norms have become the underlying "common sense" of the society at large, thus permanently altering the "cognitive and affective structures" of human reality itself. In Femia's words, hegemony is achieved via "the institutions of civil society" which together "operate to shape, directly or indirectly, the cognitive and affective structures whereby [people] perceive and evaluate problematic social reality." The modern prince is therefore the figure who "organizes and forms the disparate impressions of reality into a unified and stable totality."[61] *Il politico*, the political strategist or leader, must unify otherwise "disparate" phenomenal impressions of reality. We might even describe the modern prince as a *Gestalter* or *conformator*—the subject who shapes or organizes the perceptual structures (*Gestalten*) of reality, so long as it is understood that this "organization" of perception is itself accomplished only on the basis of what Gramsci calls "effective reality"—the "what-is-thereness" of the world.[62] In short, hegemony is always the imposition of a new normality.[63]

The movement of the modern prince is thus only complete when the prince becomes indistinguishable from the movement of society as such. "The development and expansion of the *particular* group are conceived of, and presented, as being the motor force of a *universal* expansion, of a development of all the 'national' energies. In other words, the dominant group is coordinated concretely with the general interests of the subordinate groups."[64] In its very coming to form as a party, the *colletiva voluntà* of the working class spreads its practical, worldly philosophy until it has "become universal and total," encompassing the whole of civilization.[65] Or, as Fontana puts it, when it has successfully transformed the "subordinate, particularistic mass of disaggregated individuals into a leading and hegemonic subject whose thought and values have become the prevailing conception of the world."[66]

Like Machiavelli's "new" prince, then, the modern prince would have a dual character. To use Gramsci's phrase, in coming to form the modern prince would be the equivalent to "the nexus [of] Protestant Reformation plus French Revolution: it is a philosophy which is also politics, and a politics which is also philosophy."[67] In other words, the prince would lead boldly, even forcefully, as the "conscious" element of the hegemonic

bloc. But it would also lead "morally," by virtue of its character as an educator of the people. "In a very real sense," Fontana writes, "the democratic philosopher is the hegemon of the people, the teacher and guide who
leads the people to a new way of life and a new practice."[68] In one of the
most important passages in the *Notebooks*, Gramsci writes:

> An important part of the Modern Prince will have to be devoted to the question of
> intellectual and moral reform, that is, to the question of religion or world-view. . .
> . The Modern Prince must be and cannot but be the proclaimer and organizer of
> an intellectual and moral reform, which also means creative terrain for a subse-
> quent development of the national-popular collective will toward the realisation
> of a superior, total form of modern civilization.[69]

As this passage suggests, counter-hegemonic struggle must be understood to be a form of pedagogy, a *strategy* of mass education. "Every relationship of 'hegemony,'" Gramsci wrote, "is necessarily an educational
relationship," in the sense that every social group seeks to "educate"
others into its way of viewing the world.[70] Unlike reactionary or liberal
movements, which lead through mystifying the nature of power, the
modern prince would seek to raise the people "up" through mass education or consciousness-raising, by cultivating in the people basic literacies about power. When Gramsci and other radical leaders were
imprisoned on Ustica, a tiny island in the south of Italy, in 1926, the
first thing they did was to set up a school for the illiterate prisoners.
Their curriculum (which they also made available to uneducated local
officials and impoverished local islanders) consisted not of Marx's or
Engels's work, but basic literacy, mathematics, history, and French and
German. "You can't imagine," Gramsci wrote to his friend Piero Sraffa
in one of his first letters from prison, "the physical and moral state of
degradation to which the ordinary prisoners have been reduced." Only
teaching, he wrote, kept him and the other political prisoners from
"becoming demoralized."[71]

The word *hegemony*, so pivotal to Gramsci's thought, derives from the
Greek *hegemon*. The word originally had two related meanings: the first
was "leader," in the traditional sense of one who rules; the second, however, was one who leads as a "guide," i.e., one who seeks or "shows" the
way. An early prefix compound of the Greek *hegeisthai* (to guide or to lead)
was *exegeisthai*, meaning guiding or leading someone out of complexity,

from which we get the modern word *exegesis* (critical explanation or interpretation of a text). We might say that for Gramsci, hegemonic leadership consists both of leadership in the sense of rule, and leadership in the sense of *guiding* the people out of confusion, i.e., helping them to make sense out of the otherwise unintelligible chaos of social reality.

The prince accomplishes this chiefly through a struggle to make what was "background" become "figure," i.e., by denaturalizing social phenomena that are otherwise presented as already given, natural facts.[72] It is in this sense that socialism would come to resemble a second Reformation: it would seek to translate the liturgy of capitalist power into a vernacular so that ordinary people would be able to comprehend and employ it in order to remake human civilization. The modern prince would seek to lead the people out of confusion by teaching them basic literacies for "seeing," hence for overcoming, power.[73]

Like the Reformation, too, the coming of the prince would therefore effect the coming to consciousness of the people themselves: prince and people would complete and constitute one another.[74] In this dialectic of the "democratic philosopher," in Fontana's words, the theorist establishes a "triadic" relationship among the people, the prince, and a novel form of political knowledge, showing the people the cynical ways of the prince, but also showing how the Prince himself might achieve greatness by helping the people achieve autonomy in the form of a new, national subject. As Fontana writes, the plan of the modern prince is to become "a system of never-ending and open-ended concentric circles," in such a way that the consciousness of the led, the people, and the consciousness of the leaders mutually augment one another and expand to other sectors of the population, as "the people's action on its intellectuals produces a more historically rooted and more critical knowledge of the world, and where intellectuals' action on the people results in the raising and widening of the cultural level of the people." The "democratic philosopher" directly addresses and eventually merges with the people, constituting in effect a new type of knowledge and social being.[75] The form of "address" is one of "I–thou": a mutual exchange from you to me, me to you.[76]

AGAINST PEDAGOGY

While Gramsci's thought was directed toward the establishment of a new, positive culture— even a "new civilization"—Foucault was deeply skeptical that normative distinctions could be drawn between one kind of social order and another. For this reason, *contra* Gramsci, not only did Foucault make no distinction between those who "know" and those who do not, nor between "teachers" and "taught"; he also wrote *against* educative practices as such, on grounds that the very notion of pedagogy implied a "truth regime" needing to be subverted. In this he was in good company. Deleuze and Guattari held the same position, as did Jean François Lyotard, who defended "apedagogy," as he called it, on grounds that "all pedagogy participates in . . . repression, including that which is implied in the internal and external relations of the 'political' organizations."[77]

The poststructuralists' avowed hostility to pedagogy and leadership was one key factor in the eventual emergence of speculative and "baroque" manifestations in theory. Rather than translate theory into the "vernacular," by making ideas accessible to ordinary people, cultural studies critics chose to translate the vernacular of mass culture into high Latin. If the Gramscian intellectual is an *exegete* who tries to help the people out of their confusion by teaching them the ways of princes, we might say that postmodernists are "*eisegetes*"—intellectuals who mislead the people by sowing confusion and mystifying actual social relations. To take one example out of thousands available: Laura Kipnis has used expensive and elaborate theoretical tools to argue that *Hustler* magazine, perhaps the most openly misogynistic, racist, and anti-Semitic mass circulation pornography magazine in the United States, is "counter-hegemonic" (as she put it) because it lampoons bourgeois norms and values. But arguing that *Hustler* is "counter-hegemonic" because it embodies a working-class attack on middle-class values ("taste") is like arguing that Hitler was a communist because he championed "the little man" and appealed to the German working class for national unity.[78] As the late Edward Said, who was a shrewd critic of Foucault, observed: "Cults like post-modernism, discourse analysis, New Historicism, deconstructionism, neo-pragmatism transport them into the country of the blue; an astonishing sense of weightlessness with regard to the gravity of history and individual responsibility fritters away attention to public matters, and to public discourse. The result is a kind of floundering about that is most dispiriting to witness, even as society as a whole drifts without direction or coherence."[79]

Foucault's "apedagogical" outlook was, so to say, *Crocean*. As Fontana shows in *Hegemony and Power*, his brilliant study of Machiavelli and Gramsci, Benedetto Croce held that the Protestant Reformation, with its degraded spectacle of the entry of the masses into history—its leveling of cultural and socioeconomic distinctions—compared poorly with the Italian Renaissance, which Croce viewed as the apex of European civilizational advance. The stunning aesthetic and political achievements of the Renaissance, Croce believed, had been the product of the "high culture" of the bourgeois intelligentsia, who had effectively held themselves aloof from the culture of the common people. The lesson Croce drew from the Renaissance, therefore, was that only such a distinterested, "pure" philosophy, one removed both from historical necessity and from the hoi polloi, could approach universal truth. Like Nietzsche, who was appalled at the idea of mass education, Croce hence defended what he called a "dialectic of distincts," i.e., separate spheres of practice for intellectuals on one side and masses on the other.

Gramsci (who devoted a great deal of the *Notebooks* to showing the serious flaws in Croce's philosophy of politics and history) took a different view. It was the Reformation, not the Renaissance—whose aesthetic achievements remained limited to a narrow cultural and social sphere: a "rebirth" benefitting only an intellectual elite—that stood as the truly pivotal event in the history of civilization. In smashing the Catholic church's monopoly on power and ideology and mediating between the people and "higher" ideas, intellectuals like Luther and Calvin had created the opening for Enlightenment, the French Revolution, and nineteenth-century socialist and democratic movements.[81] The Reformation was thus *the* historical example of how a "high" culture and ideology might be disseminated to the masses. While Luther was no democrat, in asserting that every man was his own priest he imbued ordinary people with the sense that they themselves were authorized to speak with God. As autonomous agents, they could participate in the community of faith without mediation by the Catholic church.[82] Hence, Gramsci's comparison of the modern prince to a "new priest," i.e., a leader who, in *teaching* the people the ways of power, would spread the "religion" of socialism (in much the same manner as Machiavelli had termed his "Prince" the "new Prince").[83]

Croce, however, saw *The Prince* as a demonstration of the necessity of separating politics from ethics and the realm of truth.[84] Political life, Croce held, would always remain (in Fontana's words) "an activity and an art whose particular sphere is the manipulation and control of the appetitive and economic interests of self-regarding individuals."[85] In shielding philosophical, contemplative knowledge from the "instrumental" realm of political life, Croce had accepted the bifurcation of knowledge between *chi sa* and *chi non sa*. Croce essentially "Hegelianized" Augustine's *City of God*, arguing not that theoretical and practical realms were opposites, or that practice and contemplation could not condition one another, but that together they constituted a "duality-unity." At the same time, Croce excluded labor (economic activity) as a form of practice, and privileged the individual over the collective as the primary vehicle of world spirit.[86] In reinvigorating the traditional "Christian and Augustinian distinction between the state, conceived as the result and remedy of the earthly bellum omnium, and the spiritual-ethical realm, seen as the sphere where 'true' justice reigns," Croce effectively reduced the working classes to one "appetitive" interest group among others, a subject whose apparent fate was to remain in a condition of perpetual ignorance and submission to their supposed betters.[87]

Let us return, at this point, to Foucault. I argued in the previous chapter that Foucault's theory of social change was carried by a strong undertow of Hegelian idealism. History, he held, continually tosses up myriad, superficial appearances and "singularities," events that arise spontaneously, whose meaning cannot be reduced to any single narrative or set of narratives, and whose movement can be neither forecast nor directed. Overawed, it seems, by the mass movements of his time, from the insurrections in Paris to the upheaval of the Iranian Revolution, Foucault articulated a "spontaneist" position of political action, eschewing leadership and strategy.[88] Croce, too, turned to Hegel to justify the autonomy of a universal and disinterested knowledge, while Foucault looked to Nietzsche to deny the very possibility of universal truth (but also to justify the autonomy of his own "archaeology"). The theoretical result in both cases was the same—a fatalistic and essentially "tragic" conception of politics, a conception that negated every "conscious" element and stripped political life of its ethical significance.

Recently, poststructuralist critic Wendy Brown has, perhaps inadvertently, drawn our attention to the hidden intellectual affinity between Croce's conception of politics and Foucault's. In *Politics Out of History*, Brown argues that the meta-narratives of modernity having been exhausted, it is useless and reactionary for the left any longer to cling to worn-out and nostalgic visions of revolution and emancipation. Wielding Nietzsche's genealogical method like a club, but against socialism, feminism, and identity politics, i.e., not, as one might have expected from a self-described leftist, against capitalism, patriarchy, racism, or other jeje-une social formations, Brown chides contemporary political theorists for their credulous and largely celebratory treatment of social movements whose *ressentiment,* or vengeful, "wounded attachments" to past historical traumas prevent them from moving forward—that is, from obtaining the kind of cognitive distance necessary for true critical reflection.

Significantly, Brown turns to Croce's Hegelian philosophy of history to bolster her case for a *disengaged* political theory. "Croce's argument for a literal and figural separation between political life and intellectual inquiry," she writes, "suggests possibilities both for the rejuvenation of a rich moral political vision and for abatement of the moralizing by which contemporary intellectual and political formations currently infect each other."[89] Quoting at length from Croce's "Politics and Morals" (1941), which she describes as a "remarkable little essay," Brown writes:

> Why have I insisted on pointing out, with the greatest care, the distinction between theory and practice, between the philosophy of politics and politics? To urge the philosophers to be modest and not to confuse political life, already sufficiently confused, with inopportune and feebly argued philosophy? Yes of course. . . . But I confess that I was moved, above all, by the opposite desire, name-ly, to save historical judgement from contamination with practical politics, a con-tamination which deprives historical judgement of tolerance and fairness.[90]

In yet another work, Brown similarly echoes Croce's view of practical politics as a "contamination" of speculative thought:

> Political theory . . . runs a great risk of losing its distinctive value in intellectual life and even its offerings to political life, if it becomes trapped by responding to events. . . . It runs the risk of limiting its capacity as a domain of inquiry capable of disrupting the tyranny or givenness of the present, and expanding the range of possible futures. It runs the risk as well of substituting political positions for political thinking, thereby sacrificing its capacity to call into question the terms of the present. This does not mean that expansive political theory requires a retreat from political life. But it does require distinguishing the theorization of political life from acting within it: this means not only refusing the identification of action with theory, but refusing the notion that one is superior to the other, or even more important to politics than the other.[91]

Brown is not merely saying that political theorists should resist responding in knee-jerk fashion to contemporary events—a sensible view. Rather, she is saying that they should also leave off weighing in as theorists on *any* of the political issues of the day. Indeed, empirical concerns, she strongly implies, are better left to properly trained experts. Referring to the complexities of the post-Communist political order in Europe, Brown writes: "Why not leave actual analyses of the events and aftermath of 1989 to those fluent in the relevant languages and erudite in the relevant historical, economic, political and cultural formations?"[92] By this logic, ordinary people probably shouldn't delve too deeply into such questions, either. For if a tenured professor of politics feels unworthy to express an opinion about such events, how much more unqualified is the uneducated public?

Having breathed new life into Croce's apolitical idealism, Brown goes on to link Croce with Foucault. She praises Foucault for "[distinguishing] the value of critical thinking from position taking, policy formulation, or blueprints for action."[93] But this was not quite correct. Foucault often engaged in commentary on unfolding historical events (and often in just the wrong-headed ways Brown would caution us against). Still, Brown is not mistaken in intuiting a connection between the French historian and the Italian philosopher and critic. Her categorical rejection of any dialectic between theory and practice derives more immediately not from Croce at all but from Foucault. What Brown takes away from her reading of Foucault is the latter's rejection of *strategy* as a proper sphere of philosophical contemplation. For, like Croce, whose thought represents a return to the terms of the Augustinian distinction between the *civitas dei* and the *civitas terrena*—that is, between the distinct spheres of God's kingdom, the spiritual, moral, and contemplative, on one side, and worldly authority and power, on the other—Foucault, too, accepts a distinction between spheres of knowledge.

REVERSAL OF FORTUNE

"It is the task of theory . . . to study the nature of ends and means," Carl Von Clausewitz wrote in *On War*.[94] From the mid-nineteenth to mid-twentieth centuries, radical social and political movements took seriously this dictum of the founder of modern strategy. Left discourse was dominated by strategic questions as radicals struggled with the question of *how* revolutions occurred, why they failed, and how the chances

for achieving them might be bettered. Marx and Engels studied international relations, war, and political economy from the point of view
of developing democratic revolutionary movements in Europe: Engels
was particularly expert in military affairs and strategic doctrine, and
demonstrated extraordinary command over minute and technical matters of warfare; Marx published extensively on international military
and political affairs.[95] In the early twentieth century, Lenin studied the
writings of Clausewitz. Both he and Trotsky proved brilliant strategists
and tacticians during the Soviet Revolution and the civil war consoli-
dating Bolshevik rule.[96] Throughout the remainder of the next century, revolutionary intellectuals heeded Clausewitz's advice, bringing
strategic reflection to bear on concrete political movements throughout Africa, Asia, and Latin America. By the late twentieth century, third
world anticolonial struggles—all informed by strategic doctrine—had
shattered the European imperial and colonial system.

The situation was different in the "advanced" or overdeveloped capitalist societies. There, after World War II, the ideological and cultural
superstructures of oppression became increasingly complex, and strategic theory languished. The important but singular exception was the
U.S. civil rights movement, where a strategic (Gandhian) orientation
was more or less dictated by the situation in the South, where blacks
confronted visible institutions of segregation and state-sanctioned terror. But elsewhere, in the United States as well as in Western Europe,
Japan, and a few other places, the postwar liberal, patriarchal, capitalist order had evolved such impressive mechanisms of social control—
what Herbert Marcuse in *One-Dimensional Man* (1964) portrayed chillingly
as a subtle, westernized version of totalitarianism—that traditional
strategic theories seemed hopelessly inadequate if not obsolete. The
postwar economic boom lulled organized labor in the United States
into a state of quiescence, while in Western Europe, labor militancy was
channeled into increasingly powerful but also bureaucratized and technocratic labor and social democratic parties, ones that by the 1980s had
become virtually indistinguishable from their more conservative counterparts. The rise of mass consumerism, a strong middle class, and the
"society of the spectacle," among other things, also made it more
difficult for radicals in the West to make a case for "total" alternatives to
an economic and social system that most ordinary people identified
with, at least on a conscious level.

Later, it is true, second wave feminists and gay rights activists demonstrated tactical brilliance in challenging sexual oppression and gender inequality.

Alas, the events of subsequent decades dashed any realistic hope that this "new" approach, based on dispersion and "difference," would alone prove sufficient to dismantle existing structures of power. By the 1990s, the "amazing efficacy of discontinuous, particular and local criticism," as Foucault called it, no longer seemed as amazing as it had twenty years before.[98] It was the political and religious right, not the left, which was to succeed in mobilizing a transformative hegemonic political project with truly global reach.

That the right and not the left has made such headway is in part due to the left's own rejection of a *hegemonic*, which is to say, strategic, conception of praxis.[99] Missing is an effective leadership willing and able to organize the scattered and isolated movements of the powerless into a coherent whole. "The absence of political leadership on the left is striking," an American activist observed in the early 1990s. "We have few national figures, few leaders who transcend narrow sectoral issues. The left must ask why this is so. . . . In a society as large and complex as ours, with its enormous backlog of problems, we will need intellectual, moral, and political figures to inspire cohesive political action."[100] So long as many on the left continue to refuse leadership and to neglect a *strategic* orientation, i.e., a sense of a meaningful alternative to the present order, and of the concrete objectives necessary to get there, social movements will continue to lurch from crisis to crisis.

The erosion of the use value of theory has meanwhile led some critics to turn Machiavelli and Gramsci on their heads, e.g., inverting the relationship between *virtù* and *fortuna* to suggest that agency is impossible and the social whole is no longer subject to meaningful description. Foucauldtian cultural studies critic Kirstie McClure, for example, demands that intellectuals give up their obsolete interest in trying to reveal something about "the truth of the world." We must thus resist looking for a "comprehensive causal theory," a theory of "'truth,'" a theory that might serve as "a guarantor of practical imperatives, a find of justifications for instrumental action, and an authoritative foundation."[101]

Thus do postmodernists continue to suppress or abolish the "directive" or active element from our politics. In so doing they exert a subtle but unmistakable pressure on *chi sa*—those with at least some knowledge of the actual origins of social crises—not to educate *chi non sa*—those who do not. The effect of this only apparent populism is to confine the critical intelligentsia to a narrow, cosmopolitan, sectarian sphere, while at the same time maintaining the people themselves in perpetual ignorance both of the mechanisms of power and of the tried (if, certainly, contested) historical methods for challenging that power. But should we heed the postmodernists' advice, we would resemble that prince who, during calm weather, neglects to take the opportunity to reinforce the dam, build levies, and prepare the people by bringing them to higher ground. We would thus give our will completely over to the play of chance and fortune, and so leave the future of the earth in the hands precisely of those most lacking in scruples, and in humanity.

6 The Postmodern Prince

Gramsci's theory of the modern prince reminds us that action without appearance is action *in obscura*, a gesture signifying nothing. What we call political life is presupposed by our ability to appear before one another as potential equals in the space of appearances. Only on the phenomenal ground of seeing and being seen can our actions assume meaning, becoming intelligible to others. Hence Machiavelli's remark in *The Prince* that people "in general judge more by their eyes than their hands; for everyone can see but few can feel."[1] Political life, as Hannah Arendt observed, "depends utterly upon . . . the existence of a public realm in which things can appear out of the darkness of sheltered existence."[2] What we call reality "is guaranteed by the presence of others, by its appearing at all . . . and whatever lacks this appearance comes and passes away like a dream, intimately and exclusively our own but without reality."[3] Action without appearance is not *political* action.

In order for subalterns to "exist" politically, therefore, they must first have to assume some determinate shape. Hence Gramsci's description of the modern prince as "an organism, a complex element in society in which a collective will . . . begins to take *concrete form*."[4] Only by organizing themselves as a "permanently organized and long-prepared force," one able to be deployed "when it is judged that a situation is favorable," could they hope to withstand the buffeting winds of conflict and fate alike, and thus come to vie for political power.[5] Part political party, part social movement, part worldly philosophy, part evangelical religion, the modern prince would form the kernel or germ of an utterly new form of human civilization.

The "postmodern prince," similarly, would be a "collective intellectual" that would gather up the dispersed energies of existing liberation movements throughout the world and provide them with the *form* of a single world historical movement. Through its articulation of a moral ontology of freedom, and its exercise of strategic *virtù*, the prince would seek to win the loyalties of other movements and groups in society, exerting a hegemonic influence over culture and state. In its coming-to-form as a unified subject, the postmodern prince would illuminate the many- sided nature of power and domination—capitalism, patriarchy, racism, and other distorting institutions—and also prefigure the just society to come.

Such a conception, as I have shown in this work, cuts against the grain of existing theoretical orthodoxy. A variety of critics have pointed to the rise of the so-called New Social Movements in the wake of the New Left period as evidence that the problem of oppositional unity—the discourse of unity, along with the practical question of *how* to go about establishing a coherent movement—is now obsolete. Iris Marion Young, for example, argues that "desire for political unity will suppress difference, and tend to exclude some voices and perspectives from the public."[6] Postmodernist rhetorician Judith Butler, similarly, dismisses the ideal of unity in the women's movement as a dangerous distraction from the more pressing concern of deconstructing essentialism within the movement:

> Is "unity" necessary for effective political action? Is the premature insistence on the goal of unity precisely [not] the cause of an ever more bitter fragmentation among the ranks? Certain forms of acknowledged fragmentation might facilitate coalitional action precisely because the "unity" of the category of women is neither presupposed nor desired. Does "unity" [not] set up an exclusionary norm of solidarity at the level of identity that rules out the possibility of a set of actions which disrupt the very borders of identity concepts, or which seek to accomplish precisely that disruption as an explicit political aim?[7]

Butler poses these questions rhetorically, apparently assuming that the perils of unity are sufficiently well established not to require further argument (nor *empirical* investigation). Certainly, some discourses of unity *are* "exclusionary." But it is also true that most successful social movements in history drew freely on images and metaphors of unity, solidarity, and even "sameness" of identity. Making "difference" the *summum bonum* and guiding principle of practice, as poststructuralists like Butler do, only condemns subaltern subjects—in the present instance, women—to invisibility in the realm of appearances.

Notwithstanding the rise of poststructuralism as a new orthodoxy in the humanities, however, a variety of other critics over the years have dissented from the fetish of difference and disunity to call openly for a new, common project of the left, a new *form* for bringing disparate elements together. As early as 1973, New Left author Bruce Brown took note of the strategic weakness of "highly dispersed and atomized" forces of the opposition and wrote that "it is crucial that they transcend the limitations of their particularity and work out, in practice and in theory, a new, unifying perspective capable of linking partial struggles and specific oppressions to their common objective roots and of joining them within a totalizing revolutionary project."[8] In the same period, but writing from France, Henri Lefebvre similarly called for a movement whose "basic principle and objective" would be the "bringing-together of dissociated aspects, the unification of disparate tendencies and factors."[9] Lefebvre wrote:

> Inasmuch as it tries to take the planetary experiment in which humanity is engaged for what it is—that is to say, a series of separate and distinct assays of the world's space—this hypothesis sets itself up in clear opposition to the homogenizing efforts of the state, of political power, of the world market, and of the commodity world. . . . It implies the mobilization of differences in a single movement (including differences of natural origin, each of which ecology tends to emphasize in isolation): differences of regime, country, location, ethnic group, natural resources, and so on. . . . The reconstruction of a spatial "code"—that is, of a language common to practice and theory, as also to inhabitants, architects and scientists—may be considered from the practical point of view....The first thing such a code would do is *recapture the unity of dissociated elements*, breaking down such barriers as that between private and public, and identifying both confluences and opposition in space that are at present indiscernible.[10]

Other critics, too, writing in later years, called for a new conception of unity, a new syncretic unity that would bring together "dissociated elements," but without calling for a return to the Marxist language of the working class as the only subject of history.[11]

Most notably, in 1986, a group of veteran left intellectuals and activists clustered around South End Press and *Z Magazine* in Boston, Massachusetts—Michael Albert, Leslie Cagan, Noam Chomsky, Robin Hamel, Mel King, Lydia Sargent, and Holly Sklar—issued a manifesto

entitled *Liberating Theory*. The authors called for a new "holism" in theory and practice —what they called a "new humanism"—and urged nomi-
nally distinct social movements to learn to "function in the context of
one another."[12] Because seemingly different forms of power and domination are in fact intertwined and constitute a single functional whole,
the authors suggested that a material and historical basis already exist-
ed for the unification of diverse movement elements. Social movements,
they argued, must *"recognize that they themselves are essentially different facets
of one still larger movement all of whose parts must relate positively to one another if the whole and any of the parts will succeed—not only in defeating a shared
enemy, but in gaining interdependent aims and creating a new liberatory society."*
Different movements must converge in "a trajectory of demands, means
of struggle, and organizational forms" such as workers councils. The
authors—most of whom had been activists during the New Left era—
implicitly broke with the antinomian urge that had characterized
much of the 1960s protests by calling for an expansive, *outward-* orient-
ed, and *majoritarian* strategy in which the movement "progressively
increases the numbers of people who wish to transform society."[13]

This vision—of a unified movement in which many diverse movements come together to form the nucleus of a new civilizational order—
corresponds in broad terms to the vision of what I call the *postmodern
prince.* Before saying more about this conception, however, it is first necessary that we have in view the history of how modern political theorists, above all Antonio Gramsci, have gone about theorizing *form* as a
way of talking about democracy, power, and the meaning of history.

FORM IN MODERN POLITICAL THOUGHT

Form is the manner in which a given political community sustains
itself through time. Form is to a polity or movement as the body is to
the soul: it is through form that a particular subject comes into being.
Aristotle held that the *morphé* or "form" of the polis is equivalent to its
constitution, i.e., whether as a monarchy, democracy, oligarchy, and so
on. Form plus a specific *hulé* or "matter"—the inhabitants themselves—
constituted a *polis* as such.[14]

This ancient theory of form remains suggestive at a general level;
however, it is not terribly useful in helping us grasp the key features of
form in the modern era. The various forms of the modern polity, unlike
the ancient, cannot be pegged to unchanging categories. Modernity, as

ceaseless historical change, constantly destabilizes political community, making its "nature" something of a moving target. However, one pattern that can be discerned in modern politics is the tension between two kinds of form: on the one hand, liberal constitutionalism; on the other, the radical politics of "the mass." Understanding the origin of this tension will put us in a position not only to evaluate Gramsci's contribution to a theory of *radical* form, but will prepare us for our discussion of a new form adequate to the political and social challenges of our postmodern times.

Prior to the modern era, political "form" was largely an extension of the personalities and ambitions of the various monarchs and despots who ruled Europe and Asia. Political thought barely advanced from the time of Augustine's *City of God*. With the waning of divine right at the end of the late medieval period, however, ensuring the legitimacy of political authority and the continuity of power became a quite pressing concern in intellectual circles. After the beheading of Charles I in the English revolution, Thomas Hobbes developed the earliest recognizably modern and "liberal" conception of form. *Leviathan* became the paradigmatic case for all subsequent modern theories of the state. The state was no longer tied to God's will, but was recast as little more than a rational accommodation for the individual to accept out of fear of her neighbors. However, in Hobbes's conception, only a negative freedom was possible. Political subjects, though "equal" before the absolutist power of the sovereign state, were "free" only to pursue their own individual interests, without reference to common values or projects. The result, then, was a fragmented polity that utterly belied the apparent picture of unity famously depicted in the frontispiece of *Leviathan*. In that classic image, a giant, benign monarch towered over a landscape wielding the sword of absolute authority, while on closer inspection, one saw that the monarch's own body and limbs were composed of the king's subjects themselves. The *form* of political authority (the king) emerged only on the basis of the individual bodies of the people.

This image of an identity between the people and their government, however, represented a mystification of the true nature of absolutism. Subsequent liberal theorists of course rejected Hobbes's absolutism and began to lay the basis for the modern democratic state as we know it today. Equality in representation, what we think of today as *the* essential feature of the liberal polity, became enshrined constitutionally. For a time, theoretical debates raged over the question of how representative

Frontispiece to Hobbes's *Leviathan*, (1651)

institutions might be made permanent enough to ensure the stability of the polity, but also flexible enough to adapt to changing needs. (This was at the heart of the disagreement between Hamilton and Jefferson over federalism, during the founding of the American republic.) By the late eighteenth and early nineteenth centuries, however, a consensus had been reached on the central narrative of liberalism. But that narrative, which told of the triumph of representative democracy and the inevitable spread of Western "civilizational" norms through secularization and the consolidation of the liberal nation-state, told only half the story.

Paradoxically, the constitutional rights that became the set pieces of liberal bourgeois theory also had the effect, not unintended, of safely containing the otherwise dangerous aspirations of the masses. From the eighteenth century on, liberal and republican theorists like John Locke and Jean-Jacques Rousseau grounded political authority in a social, racial, and sexual contract—a white fraternity—that excluded women and non-whites.[15] In Immanuel Wallerstein's words, "Liberalism was invented to counter democracy."[16] Up until the onset of World War I, in fact, the debate between liberals and conservatives revolved around the question of which small group of propertied white men was to control the state.

The liberal narrative of form thus effectively suppressed the existence of a potent *counter*-tradition within modernity. That tradition, the
radical tradition in political thought, is typically portrayed as originating in the French Revolution. Unlike the revolution in the Atlantic
colonies, where the political struggle remained largely within the cau-
tious limits set by elites within the rising merchant class, the revolution
in France quickly overflowed all the bounds of this class project. As Jules
Michelet wrote in his paean to France, in words chosen to convey the
sense of a new *dramatis persona* on the world stage, "I come to establish
against all mankind the personality of the people."[17] The storming of
the Bastille was a lightning bolt of history that illuminated all at once
"the multitude of the poor and downtrodden, whom every century
before had hidden in darkness and shame." It was this figure, Arendt
writes, that now "[appeared] for the first time in broad daylight."[18]

Rousseau is credited with having provided the philosophical basis
for the French Revolution, particularly with his mystical fusion of the
polity, the so-called general will, in the *Social Contract*. Yet the intellectual roots of the revolution extend further back in history, to the early
sixteenth century and the republicanism of Machiavelli. No less an
authority on the matter than Robespierre wrote that "the plan of the
French Revolution was written large in the books . . . of Machiavelli."[19]
For it was in fact Machiavelli's originality and genius that he alone saw
that only a prince capable of focusing the mass, this dangerous but
exhilarating force, could found a new order. Hence Gramsci's admiring
reference to Machiavelli as a "precocious Jacobin."

At the time Machiavelli wrote *The Prince*, two interrelated historical
developments were transforming the social and political terrain of
early modern Europe. The first was the decline of traditional sources of
political authority; the second was emergence of "the people" or mass
as a power in its own right. Machiavelli's political theory represented
the first cogent attempt to come to terms with both phenomena.[20]
Machiavelli's republican politics (above all, in the *Discourses*) might be
described as a "controlled fusion" of politics: he sought to preserve
what he saw as the dynamic, invigorating antagonism of class blocs,
while keeping this antagonism from reaching an explosive level. A
civic, pagan religion, and a project of national greatness won through
collective, masculinist *virtù*, together would serve to regulate and stabi-
lize the polity. In contrast to Hobbes, then, who at about the same time

theorized a distant sovereign and a fragmented, privatized civil society, Machiavelli imagined a unified people striving together to achieve collective glory. This, however, raised the question of how, precisely, the people are to be bound into a coherent form, capable of holding in check the chaos of a brutal order dominated by ruthless, powerful, private interests.[21] Machiavelli concluded that this could happen only if a leader emerged who could impose his will on the chaos.

As Gramsci observed, Machiavelli sought "to represent the process whereby a given collective will, directed toward a given political objective, is formed." Unlike his predecessors, Machiavelli had indulged neither in "long-winded arguments" nor "pedantic classifications of principles and criteria for a method of action," but instead had ingeniously "represented this process in terms of the qualities, characteristics, duties, and requirements of a concrete individual. Such a procedure stimulates the artistic imagination of those who have to be convinced, and gives political passions a more *concrete form.*"[22] At the end of *The Prince*, Machiavelli abruptly launches into a proto-nationalist exhortation in which he invokes the prince-figure to unite the people of Italy, "In Italy there is no lack of material to be given a *form*: here there is great ability in her members, were it not for the lack of it in her leaders."[23] Gramsci argued that this sudden ending was in fact integral to the meaning of Machiavelli's whole. "In the conclusion, Machiavelli merges with the people, becomes the people; not, however, some 'generic' people, but the people whom he, Machiavelli, has convinced by the preceding argument—the people whose consciousness and whose expression he becomes and feels himself to be, with whom he has become identified." People, prince, and theorist, in short, become one. "The entire 'logical' argument now appears as nothing other than *auto-reflection* on the part of the people—an inner reasoning worked out in the popular consciousness, whose conclusion is a cry of passionate urgency."[24] The "prince" thus becomes the *medium* or *form* for the people themselves—a way for the people to become manifest in the space of political appearances. The character of the prince "represents physically and 'anthropomorphically' the symbol of the 'collective will,'" the historical figure who unites the multitude of dispersed wills in Italy.[25]

Hegel later took up Machiavelli's proto-nationalist conception of the collective will of the people and transformed it into a metaphysics of universal freedom. In Machiavelli's thought it is clear that once the "prince" completes his historic mission, he becomes superfluous or dispensable—much like Rousseau's "Lawgiver," who creates the primordial conditions for the polity by shaping a people into a moral community. In the thought of Hegel, the "German Machiavelli," something similar occurs. Hegel describes at length the "world-historical individuals," great individuals who "see the very truth of their age and their world, the next genus . . . which is already formed in the womb of time." These are the modern heroes who instinctively sense the "universal, the next stage of their world" and "make it their own aim and put all their energy into it." But, Hegel writes, once "their objective is attained. . . [they] fall like empty hulls from the kernel."[26] Great deeds, in short, fall from the grasp of individuals, even from groups, to become instances of the artistic "cunning" of History itself. The problem of form is no longer a problem of strategy, as it was for Machiavelli, but a problem of interpreting the metaphysics of history.

Hegel argued that human and physical reality was rational. Idea or *geist*, he held, was immanent in nature but remained "objective" so long as it remained merely an "in-itself." As "God's own eternal life," as Hegel put it, Spirit "still lacks at this point the *form of being which is actuality*."[27] Idea contains within itself potential "self-consciousness" and subjective activity; but as Nature, it remains "the universal."[28] Spirit is thus divided against itself. And so it remains until it externalizes itself: realization of Absolute Spirit unfolds as *expression*.[29] Hegel's genius was to join this metaphysics of expression to the play of subjective human passion and will. Through the unfolding of *human history*, that is, Spirit becomes manifest. *Geist*, through civilizational struggle and evolution, eventually assumes phenomenal form. The *state* is "embodiment of the universe in human life," as synthesis of real subjective will and universal Reason.[30] The state alone is "the form [Reason] assumes in the realm of the actual."[31]

But by "state," it is to be understood, Hegel meant not only the political and juridical apparatus, but "the moral whole" of a people—the *Gestalt* or totality that constituted a people's essence. The spirit of a people, he writes, is a people's "consciousness of itself, of its own truth, its own essence, the spiritual powers which live and rule in it," a feeling of mutual identification.[32] Drawing heavily on ancient Greek ideals of a unity between politics and ethics, Hegel conceives the state as the living embodiment, in the form of its laws and constitution, of a religious morality, a concretization of the "spirit of a people." Here it is pointless to try to distinguish, analytically, between people and state, because they constitute dialectical moments in the unfolding of a single onto-logical essence.[33] The state expresses the unity of subjective freedom—"knowledge and volition"—and objective necessity. It *gives shape* to individual wills, through a common will.[34] The state embodies a "rational and self-conscious freedom, objectively knowing itself." Yet this "definite national spirit itself is only one individual in the course of world history"—i.e., it is but one state-spirit among others in the grand design of Absolute Spirit.[35]

Nationalists and socialists alike seized upon Hegel's ontology of free-dom in the form of the state as a way to focus the inarticulate feelings of whole peoples and classes.[36] In the late eighteenth and early nineteenth centuries, the Romantics—chiefly Herder, Fichte, and Novalis—reacting against the rationalism of the Enlightenment, began to dream of har-nessing the mass of the people to the *expressivist* form of the nation-state. In their naturalistic ontology, language and "soil" were seen as the essen-tial bases for a spiritual, hence political, entity—the *volk*. Each *volk*, through its act of nation-building, would give collective expression to a prior natural essence. Liberals assimilated this Romantic perspective and cast the nation-state as the *particular* form of the *universal* spirit of human progress. For such nationalists there was as yet no contradiction between nationalist and universalist conceptions of form. But in point of fact, by the mid-nineteenth century the conflict between liberal and radical visions of civil society was coming into the open. The failed popular revo-lutions of 1848 served ominous notice to the ruling classes that future revolutions might not be so easy to contain. To liberals, meanwhile, they demonstrated the need to offset the social contradictions of capitalism with temporizing concessions to the working class. But to socialists and trade unionists—who were ruthlessly crushed—the aborted revolutions were an object lesson in the need for a more strategic orientation.[37]

One result of the soul-searching among workers and radical intellec-tuals following the catastrophe of 1848 was the founding of the First International, a federation of workers' parties and movements called the Working Men's International Association, in a meeting in London on September 28, 1864. Just as Machiavelli conjured the figure of the prince as a transitional figure who founds the republican order and then disap-pears, socialists now began to conjure a "form within the form" through which the working class might manifest its self-consciousness as a collective will. The major theorist of this new form was Karl Marx.

Marx saw the major agent of revolutionary praxis as a universal *class*. By his own account, Marx set Hegel "on his feet" by grounding the German philosopher's abstract renderings of form and state in the sensuous, material activity of human beings, viz., in a concrete account of human labor. For Hegel, the evolution of the state parallels and is constitutive of the evolution of human consciousness, because the becoming of Spirit is nothing other than "its increasing self-knowledge in the temporal sequence of its shapes, i.e., in history."[38] For Marx, history was indeed intelligible; but its intelligibility could be observed not in the movement of the state, nor of history *qua* history, but in the conflict of social classes in civil society. This conflict, Marx and Engels wrote in the *Manifesto*, was now "hidden," now "open," a dialectic between immanent and manifest that continually resolved at a higher and higher level. Through the objective social contradictions generated by capitalism itself, the working class would eventually realize its essence as the harbinger and agent of universal free species being. The inner meaning of history would thus be revealed.

Despite these surface similarities between Marx and Hegel, however, the significance of the proletariat for Marx was primarily strategic, not metaphysical. In one of the more famous passages of The Eighteenth Brumaire of Louis Bonaparte, his analysis of the failed French revolution of 1848 that brought Napoleon III to power, Marx wrote:

> Their mode of production isolates them from one another, instead of bringing them into mutual intercourse. The isolation is increased by France's bad means of communication and by the poverty of the peasants. . . . In this way, the great mass of the French nation is formed by simple addition of homologous magnitudes, much as potatoes in a sack form a sackful of potatoes. In so far as millions of families live under economic conditions of existence that divide their mode of life, their interests and their culture from those of the other classes, and put them into hostile contrast to the latter, they form a class. In so far as there is merely a local interconnection among these small peasants, and the identity of their interests begets no unity, no national union and no political organisation, they do not form a class.[39]

Because the working classes, through their labor, control the machinery of production, hence the reproduction of life itself, Marx believed they stood in a uniquely privileged position to overthrow the system of exploitation by withdrawing their collective consent to capitalism. For this universal potential to be realized, the working class would have to develop consciousness of its historical burden *as* a class, moving from a class merely "in-itself"—immanent, objective—to a class "for-itself"— coherent, self-conscious, strategic.

In France, objective circumstance had stranded the peasants on the ideological shoals of reaction. Only with the proper conditions could the peasants realize some new phenomenal *form* ("unity" or a "national union"). Meanwhile, at the time Marx penned the *Brumaire*, class strug- gle in most of Europe had begun to assume a more definite and regular shape. Previously random strikes, revolts, and local acts of resistance were being replaced by mass revolutionary upheavals, nationalist move- ments, planned utopian communities, and the formation of more or less stable political parties representing the working classes. Of these experiments in form, only one, the modern political party, seemed to offer the mix of permanence and flexibility necessary for revolutionary praxis. To avowed communists like Marx and Engels, the state would never be an adequate vehicle for carrying the values of those who made up the majority of humankind, the working classes. The rise of the nation-state had been accompanied by global colonialism and bloody internecine struggles among the imperial powers. And it had been achieved by sublating the aspirations of the vast majority into national projects whose function had been to preserve and expand the privileges of the bourgeois elite. This left only the political party as a counter to the nation-state as a vehicle of mass aspirations and universal significance.

At the end of the nineteenth century, then, there were only *two* major forms of the modern polity: the nation-state and the political party. Both forms had been set in motion by the political and techno- logical advances following the Reformation, "a historical phase linked to the standardization of broad masses of the population (communica- tions, newspapers, big cities, etc.)," as Gramsci put it.[40] Through these "imagined communities," a form emerged through which particular peoples or social classes could participate in political life.[41]

LENIN'S LEVIATHAN

The Bolshevik Revolution in Russia transformed Marxist political thought. Lenin's famous notion of the party "vanguard"—a secretive and highly disciplined organization to help the working class move from in-itself to for-itself through strategic leadership—effectively became the paradigmatic model of radical form for at least two generations. Mao, Che, and numerous other revolutionaries in the third world adapted Lenin's strategic doctrine to local conditions, typically yoking Marxist-Leninism to peasant-based movements for national liberation.

Lenin believed that the primitive political and economic conditions prevailing in Russia made a peaceful transition to a more socially equi-table order impossible. Some sort of "conscious" intervention, he con-cluded, was necessary to overcome the brutal institutions and feudal social relations in tsarist Russia. In *What Is to Be Done?* Lenin argued that the working class had a revolutionary consciousness, but a conscious-ness only in "embryonic form."[42] This merely "spontaneous" and "instinctive" consciousness awaited proper cultivation and chan-nelling by "*professional* revolutionaries"—a party "vanguard" of highly trained leaders who would train the proletariat away from "corpo-ratist" (local or trade unionist) efforts toward a truly internationalist, communist consciousness.[43] Such a vanguard would, in essence, catch up with the masses, who in their militancy and readiness for revolu-tion were far ahead of the Social Democrats.

The Leninist conception of form came to be articulated philosophi-cally by the Hungarian Marxist Georg Lukács. In *History and Class Con-sciousness,* Lukács showed how consciousness and culture had become vulnerable to the totalizing process of commodification under capital-ism. Only the proletariat, as the "subject-object" of history, could reverse this process of reification, overcoming extant antinomies (apparent con-tradictions) in civil society between subject/object, fact/value, phenome-na/noumena, freedom/necessity through its revolutionary praxis. Like Lenin, Lukács faulted both economic determinists, who saw revolution as inevitable, and economic pessimists, who asserted that the condi-tions were not yet ripe for revolution in Europe. The self-consciousness of the proletariat, he argued, would not arise spontaneously "in any fatalistic and automatic way."[44] The objective crisis of capitalism would only "tend" to create the necessary conditions for revolution.[45] The movement therefore needed leadership to enable the proletariat to come to "full consciousness" of itself and its historic mission. Hence the centrality in all varieties of Leninist thought of the "organizational" question. As "both producer and product of the dialectical process,"

Lukács wrote, the working class was already generating a "world of which it is the *conscious form*"—i.e., the Marxist-Leninist party.[46]

Just as Hegel saw reason as split within itself, Lukács perceived the universal consciousness of the proletariat as internally divided between the particular and the universal. The proletariat in its primitive or naive state could not yet overcome internal ideological and perspectival differences. Leadership was necessary in order to overcome "the reified divisions according to nation, profession, etc."[47] The party would be the point of "*concrete mediation between man and history.*"[48] Without the party "as the free and conscious deed of the most conscious element," the working-class movement would unravel "into a loose aggregate of individuals incapable of action." What had weakened radical groups affiliated with the International outside Russia, Lukács contended, was that "they were neither able nor willing to give them any concrete organizational form," by which he meant the Communist Party.[49] If the Communists were "the tangible embodiment of proletarian class-consciousness," then the party itself must be, ontologically and politically, "the independent expression of that class consciousness."[50] The party, Lukács wrote, is "the *form* of this consciousness and the form of *this* consciousness: i.e., it is both an independent and a subordinate phenomenon." The party form alone allows the working class to "see its own class consciousness given historical shape."[51] The Communist International, meanwhile, was nothing other than "Lenin's concept of the party—on a world scale," i.e., "organ and focus of the struggle of the oppressed people throughout the world for their liberation."[52]

However, because the working classes could not have epistemological access to their own experiences, it would fall to the party to comprehend their experiences for them. As to how workers could be confident that the party, as their ontological "expression," was on the right path, Lukács offered the following dubious argument: The party would not be able to survive if it did *not* in fact have the correct view of history, "for otherwise the consequences of a false theory would soon destroy it."[53] The party, however, has not been destroyed. Therefore, it *must* really have the correct view of things, must really manifest the truth of history.

This syllogism reduces truth to an instrumentalist criterion and leaves no room for questioning the party leadership. Lenin boasted that the very strength of the Bolsheviks lay in their ability "to build up and successfully maintain the strictest centralization and iron discipline" necessary to seize the czarist state.[54] Because the material exigencies of late-imperial Russia required secrecy and organizational hierarchy inside the party, Lenin gave virtually no thought to the problem of mediating the relation between the party-state and the individual. As with Hobbes's *Leviathan,* there was, then, no check on the sovereign's (Party's) power. The party was "subordinate" to the masses in theory, but never in fact. The practical effect of this was to obliterate the freedom of the individual. Although "the fully developed communist society" would in practice "be the first society" in history to enable real freedom, Lukács wrote, in the meantime the struggle "must entail the renunciation of individual freedom. It implies the conscious subordination of the self to that collective will that is destined to bring real freedom. . . . This conscious will is the Communist Party."[55]

In such passages, Lukács articulates a Marxist-Leninist version of Rousseau's "General Will." In *The Social Contract,* Rousseau presented his skeptical view of representative government, introducing his mystical notion of a self-identical general consciousness. "Sovereignty," he wrote, "cannot be represented, for the same reason that it cannot be alienated; its essence is the general will, and will cannot be represented—either it is the general will or it is something else; there is no intermediate possibility."[56] "Each one of us puts into the community his person and all his powers under the supreme direction of the general will; and as a body, we incorporate every member as an indivisible part of the whole."[57] Lukács's view was virtually identical. "The separation of rights and duties," Lukács wrote, "is only feasible where the leaders are divorced from the masses, and act as *their representatives,* i.e., where the stance adopted by the masses is one of contemplative fatalism. True democracy, the abolition of the split between rights and duties is, however, no formal freedom but the *activity* of the members of the collective will, closely integrated and collaborating in a spirit of solidarity."[58] Lukács did warn against reducing the party to "a hierarchy of officials isolated from the mass of ordinary members who are . . . given the role of passive onlookers."[59] But there was nothing in his theory to shield the vulnerable individual from the savage machinery of the state.

Leninism, which began as the most "materialist" of Marxist doctrines, thus ended up with a metaphysics of its own, hypostatizing *Geist*—that is, a universal, expressive, self-identical subject—in the form of the party. In theory, like Machiavelli's "Prince" and Hegel's "men of destiny," the party vanguard, becoming the state en route to communism, would disappear once its historical mission had been fulfilled. In practice, however, this proved harder than anyone (except the anarchists, who predicted it) imagined. The result was the most severe rigidification of political form in the history of the *polis*—Soviet totalitarianism—and the bureaucratized killing and repression of millions of people.

ENTER, STAGE LEFT: THE MODERN PRINCE

By the end of the twentieth century, Lenin's hierarchical and authoritarian conception of form had been thoroughly repudiated by most political theorists on the left. This was an inevitable and, from the standpoint of those committed to a democratic conception of social revolution, welcome development. Nonetheless, it left a gaping hole in the theory of praxis and the theory of form. "What is now in crisis," Laclau and Mouffe later wrote in *Hegemony and Socialist Strategy*, "is a whole conception of socialism which rests upon the ontological centrality of the working class, upon the role of Revolution, with a capital 'r,' as the founding moment in the transition from one type of society to another, and upon the illusory prospect of a perfectly unitary and homogeneous collective will that will render pointless the moment of politics."[60]

But this notion of a "perfectly unitary and homogeneous collective will," while not an inaccurate representation of Leninism, was not at all a fair depiction of Antonio Gramsci's considerably more nuanced—and strange—conception of form. The modern prince, Gramsci wrote, was indeed to have the "Jacobinist" character of Machiavelli's Prince and the disciplined and internationalist character of Lenin's vanguard. But it would also have the religious character of the Reformation and the qualities of Rousseau's Lawgiver, founding a new, universal *Sittlichkeit*, or moral order. Or as Gramsci himself put it, the objective of the modern prince was to create "*an integral new culture* which [would] have both the mass character of the Protestant Reformation or the French Enlightenment and the classical cultural character of Greek civilization or the Italian Renaissance—a culture which . . . synthesizes Maximilien Robespierre and Immanuel Kant, politics and philosophy, in a dialectical unity which belongs no longer to one particular French or German social class, but to Europe and the world."[61] It is to this fascinating, if confusing melding of elements that we must turn for insight into the basis of a possible new political form today.

Gramsci, like Lenin, concluded that the modern political party—as the direct homologue in the sphere of civil society to the state—was destined to replace the individual as history's "protagonist."[62] While Gramsci considered himself a Marxist-Leninist, however, and borrowed a great deal from Lenin, his theory of hegemony and its conception of the party represents a qualitative and not merely quantitative departure from Lenin. That Gramsci was in fact aware of the limits, and dangerous implications, of Lenin's party vanguard is suggested in his key distinction between "bureaucratic centralism"—an authoritarian, top-down organizational party structure—and what he termed "democratic centralism," a more "organic" and democratic form. The superiority of the latter, he wrote, lay in the fact that it offered "an elastic formula, which can be embodied in many diverse forms . . . [and which] comes alive in so far as it is interpreted and continually adapted to necessity."[63]

Clues to what Gramsci meant by "democratic centralism" can be seen in those passages in the *Notebooks* where he offers his own empirical analysis of some historical political or military conflict. One such passage is Gramsci's analysis of a pivotal naval campaign between England and Germany during World War I. In the Battle of Jutland, Gramsci relates (in a comment on an analysis of the battle by Winston Churchill), the German admiral entrusted the execution of his plan to the subordinate units in the field, explaining in advance "the general strategic plan to all the subaltern commanders and [allowing] the individual units the kind of freedom of maneuver that could be required by circumstances." The British admiralty, by contrast, relied on a rigid, centralized command structure that required ships to "'wait for orders' every time." The local German units' freedom of maneuver was key in helping them defeat the English fleet, which "in spite of its superiority . . . was unable to attain its positive strategic goals because at a certain point the admiral lost communication with the fighting units and they committed error upon error."[64]

Gramsci's interest in this particular battle undoubtedly stemmed from his reflections on the problems of the Communist International. As Stalin formalized Moscow's control over the Comintern, the "satellite" national parties more and more came to resemble the British fleet. The Comintern's failure, in other words, was not to entrust local forces to carry out tactical decisions autonomously, in ways appropriate to their specific contexts. Gramsci was perhaps suggesting that whatever form the political struggle was to take, the leadership should allow local forces to operate with considerable autonomy. At the same time, Gramsci felt that while local forces should be allowed to act autonomously, to be effective they would nonetheless have to be "shaped" within an overall strategic framework. In an advanced capitalist context, where the "superstructure" of society and culture had become highly differentiated, this framework or strategy would have to resemble trench warfare, i.e., a "war of position," in which the subaltern classes would wage their struggle for strategic territory piece by piece along the periphery, rather than in an all-out "frontal" military attack on the state—a "war of maneuver." Such a war of position would be cultural and political as well as economic, a decentralized yet coordinated struggle with "positive strategic goals."

Democratic centralism also differed from Lenin's vanguard party in another important respect: Gramsci interpolates a crucial mediating element between leaders and led, the so-called organic intellectuals. Where Lenin reduced communist praxis to a dualism between leaders and led, Gramsci introduced *three* elements in dialectic with one another. The first of these was a "mass element, composed of ordinary, average men, whose participation takes the form of discipline and loyalty, rather than any creative spirit or organisational ability." The "collective will" at this stage, however, remains only a "rudimentary . . . formation." The mass only becomes a "force in so far as there is somebody to centralize, organize, and discipline them." Like Lenin, Gramsci thus introduces a second element—the disciplined revolutionaries or leaders who together form a "principal cohesive element," an element without which there could only be "a scattering into an infinity of wills." The responsibility of this, the Jacobin element, would be to create this will "from scratch" and guide it "toward goals which are concrete and rational." This directing element "centralizes nationally and renders effective and powerful a complex of forces which left to themselves would count for little or nothing."[65]

So far, this conception is scarcely distinguishable from Lenin's. But Gramsci now introduces a third element, implied in Lenin's theory but never adequately theorized there: an *"intermediate element, which articulates the first element with the second and maintains contact between them, not only physically but also morally and intellectually."*[66] By "intermediate element"

Gramsci meant intellectuals or militants from within the mass itself. While "traditional" intellectuals are linked to a declining social formation, organic intellectuals arise out of a class that has close ties to the dominant mode of production. In Gramsci's conception, such intellectuals rise to positions of authority or leadership from within the working class, playing a key role in helping the class define itself.[67] The overall effect thus would be "continual adaptation of the organization to the real movement, a matching of thrusts from below with orders from above, a continuous insertion of elements thrown up from the depths of the rank and file into the solid framework of the leadership which ensures continuity and the regular accumulation of experience."[68]

Whether this mediating element alone is enough to temper Gramsci's ominous description of a party leadership endowed with (as he writes) "great centralizing and disciplinary powers" is an open question, one that has led some commentators to see Gramsci as an authoritarian thinker. But to see Gramsci as an authoritarian thinker is to overlook the sharp departure from all previous theorizations of form, not excluding Lenin's, implicit in his complex conception of the party.

To Gramsci's way of thinking, what was even more essential than proper organizational discipline and a professional "cadre" in realizing an effective praxis was the prior experiential basis necessary to lend the modern prince its political, psychic, and moral unity, a unity without which no "party," Leninist or otherwise, could exist at all. The modern prince would "[take] account of that which is relatively stable and permanent," without, however, becoming reified in the *static* form of a bureaucratic, purely "mechanical" institution.[69] The prince, Gramsci wrote, "presupposes 'continuity,' either with the past, or tradition, or with the future; that is, it presupposes that every act is a moment in a complex process, which has already begun and which will continue." The collective will would then be able to develop a sense of its own "'duration,'" as something "concrete and not abstract, that is to say in a certain sense it must not go beyond certain limits." Gramsci even assigned a life span to this figure: "Let us say the narrowest limits are a generation back and a generation to come."[70]

Gramsci described Machiavelli's *Prince* as the "concrete myth" of an "anthropomorphic" figure who would embody and symbolize the "collective will" of the Italian nation. The modern prince, similarly, was Gramsci's concrete "myth" or symbol of a new historical form that would catalyze the collective will of the proletariat and their allied classes. The ontogenesis of this "collective will" would unfold in over-lapping phases. In the "economic-corporate" stage, the group develops a sense of "unity and homogeneity," on the basis of individuals' iden-tification with others in an immediate professional group or associa-tion—e.g., one's shop or union. Next, workers develop consciousness of economic solidarity: the "solidarity of interests among all the members of a social class—but still only in the purely economic field." Workers seek economic rights *qua* workers, but only within the context of the existing system and still on the basis of "self" interest. Finally, a class arrives at the "highest" form of consciousness, what might be called transcendental solidarity. Here "one becomes aware that one's own cor-porate interests, in their present and future development, transcend the corporate limits of the purely economic class, and can and must become the interests of other subordinate groups too."[71] At this stage, "previously germinated ideologies become 'party,' come into con-frontation and conflict until only one of them, or at least a single com-bination of them, tends to prevail, to gain the upper hand, to propagate itself throughout society."

In other words, the different *Weltanschauungen* of the subjugated classes, heretofore inchoate and contradictory, are carefully turned on the lathe of praxis until they assume the honed clarity of a single com-mon philosophy, thus forming the ideological basis of a genuinely *polit-ical* movement. Now, functioning as a "party"—i.e., as a more or less coherent national entity—the "collective will" generates "not only a unison of economic and political aims, but also intellectual and moral unity." In sum, the party's influence has become so strong that it suc-ceeds in "posing all the questions around which the struggle rages not on a corporate but on a 'universal' plane, and thus [creates] the hege-mony of a fundamental social group over a series of subordinate groups." Meanwhile, "the life of the state is conceived of as a continu-ous process of formation and superseding of unstable equilibria . . . between the interests of the fundamental group and those of the subor-dinated group." That is, the functional and policy posture of the state comes more and more to coincide with the interests of the hegemonic class. Yet it never *completely* coincides with those interests, "stopping short of" complete identity between the state and "corporate economic interest," i.e., a particular class interest.[72]

Gramsci often compared the universal morality of the modern prince to a supreme moral law. In this, he may have been inspired by Mazzini's Hegelian nationalism (Mazzini once urged Italy's workers, "Do not accept any other formula, any other moral law. . . . Let the secondary laws for the gradual regulation of your existence be the progressive application of this supreme law").[73] The universalism of the modern prince implied "precisely that any given act is seen as useful or harmful, as virtuous or wicked, only in so far as it has as its point of reference the modern prince itself, and helps to strengthen or oppose it. In men's consciences, the prince takes the place of the divinity or the categorical imperative, and becomes the basis for a modern laicism and for a complete laicization of all aspects of life and of all customary relationships."[74]

This conception has enough of a "totalizing," if not indeed totalitarian, ring to it that it perhaps ought to worry us. Lukács, too, after all, spoke of socialism in terms of a devotional, totalistic commitment—a commitment necessitated by the fact that the nature of the revolution was to break down all distinctions between individual "rights" and collective "duties."[75] Militants, Lukács wrote, would have to commit "their whole personalities" to "a living relationship with the whole of the life of the party and of the revolution."[76] To the extent that Gramsci's absolutist formulation of a "categorical imperative" of the party resembles such Leninist catechisms of a "correct party line," then, there is reason to proceed cautiously, even skeptically, in the shadow of Gramsci's socialist Kantianism.

This said, however, it is reasonably clear from Gramsci's references to religion, and in particular his appreciation of the democratic aspects of the Reformation, that the last thing he would have defended is a conception of the "party" in which the party leadership acts by "holy" fiat—a fundamentalist clergy enforcing communist *Shariah*. Notwithstanding the many shades of ambiguity in Gramsci's prison writings, there is no question that the classes and groups *within* the hegemonic bloc who would effectively be subordinated to a single class (the working class) would *consent* to being led. They would participate, in other words, because the modern prince, in its "moral and intellectual leadership," had convinced them that a new civilizational order was not only possible, but desirable and in keeping with their own conception of a just world.

UNITY AND DIFFERENCE:
THE CHALLENGE OF TRANSLATION

As we have seen, the modern prince represents that effort (to quote Richard Bellamy) *"through which a multiplicity of dispersed wills, heterogeneous aims, are welded together with a single aim, on the basis of an equal and common conception of the world."*[77] If this vision of a homogeneous collective will (the counter-hegemonic bloc) is controversial today, it is due in part to the widespread but mistaken perception that the classes and social groups allied with, and finally incorporated into the modern prince, would find their "differences," the specificities of their identities, suppressed. In fact, there is strong evidence that Gramsci envisioned not some "absolute" incorporation of subordinated elements (mythical fusion in a general will) but merely a *practical* coherence, i.e., one able to achieve particular, concrete historical goals.

Indeed, arguably, the *colletiva voluntà* resembles Hegel's totalizing idealism less than it does Aristotle's holist dialectic between particular and universal. Aristotle held that "the whole is necessarily prior [in nature] to the parts."[78] To be a *polis*, however, this "whole" would need to have both homogeneous and heterogeneous qualities. Aristotle wrote:

> It is true that unity is to some extent necessary, alike in a household and a polis; but total unity is not. There is a point at which a polis, by advancing in unity, will cease to be a polis: there is another point, short of that, at which it may still remain a polis, but will none the less come near to losing its essence, and will thus be a worse polis. It is as if you were to turn harmony into mere unison, or to reduce a theme to a single beat.[79]

A polis, properly speaking, must be "composed of unlike elements," because "there cannot be a single excellence common to all citizens, any more than there can be a single excellence common to the leader of a dramatic chorus and his assistants."[80] Every political form can be said to rest at some distinct coordinate on the continuum of identity and difference. Just as there can be no absolute identity between parts and whole—ontological fusion—there also cannot be complete "difference" or non-identity, for then we could no longer even speak meaningfully of society or community.

Gramsci's hegemonic bloc, similarly, expresses both sameness and difference. Like Lenin, Gramsci affirmed the need for a disciplined and organized party to turn the dispersed interests of the working class into a potent "collective will," lending it shape and direction. The "essential task" facing the modern prince, he wrote, was "that of systematically and patiently ensuring that this force is formed, developed, and rendered ever more homogeneous, compact, and self-aware."[81] Unlike Lenin, though, at no time did Gramsci describe the counter-hegemonic bloc in terms of an absolute identity among its constituent subjects. Gramsci's reference to forging a "single aim," therefore, was not metaphysical but pragmatic. The praxis of the modern prince, he wrote, would be a "long labor which gives birth to a collective will with a *certain degree* of homogeneity—with *the degree necessary and sufficient* to achieve an action which is coordinated and simultaneous in the time and the geographical space in which the historical event takes place."[82]

Counter-hegemonic praxis, moreover, would require the leading class to take account "of the interests and the tendencies of the groups over which hegemony is to be exercised, and that a certain compromise equilibrium be formed."[83] The guiding organizational principle of the modern prince would therefore not be the achievement of absolute identity, but rather pursuit of "*what is identical in seeming diversity of form* and on the other hand of *what is distinct and even opposed in apparent uniformity*, in order to organise and interconnect closely that which is *similar*."[84] The task of the leadership of the modern prince would be to identify regions of commonality between and among different social groups, commonalities obscured by *seeming* differences, as well as to acknowledge actual or substantive differences among these groups (i.e., "what is distinct and even opposed in apparent uniformity"). Only after careful "evaluation of the degree of homogeneity, self-awareness, and organization attained by various social classes,"[85] does the modern prince then organize and "interconnect" the elements which are in fact similar to one another.

To see Gramsci as defending a "totalizing" conception of homogeneity that would simply paper over existing differences between groups and movements is thus to miss what remains unique and useful in his theory of politics. Gramsci saw that without a unified form, subalterns would have little ability to affect national and international events. But his dialectic of unity and difference, while by no means resolving the essential tension between the two, represented a major revolution in radical social thought.

That an "attunement" to difference was implicit in Gramsci's politics can be seen in his extensive theoretical writings on language.[86] During his investigations into Italian sociolinguistics, Gramsci had been struck by the fact that written European Middle Latin (ca. 400–1300 C.E.) had split into two distinct languages, "one of them popular or dialectical and the other the learned language of the intellectuals and cultured classes."[87] Whereas elsewhere in Europe the Reformation had quickly erased this distinction, creating a basis for popular consciousness, especially nationalism, to flourish, this had not been the case in Italy. The coexistence of numerous regional dialects, coupled with the desire of liberal, bourgeois intellectuals to maintain their "European" linguistic traditions (which separated them from the masses, and which indeed was decisive in cementing their class hegemony) severely retarded the formation of Italian national unity. Italian linguistic history thus contained a signal lesson in the importance of language in forming an effective "national popular will." As in the "first" Reformation, socialist idiom would have to be such as to allow both for a universal element and recognition of the people's self-consciousness and autonomy. In the face of vast local and regional cultural and linguistic differences, the modern prince would have to incubate the germ of a new, universal civilization. Just as Luther had translated the Latinate, liturgical texts of the church—previously accessible only to the "traditional" intellectual functionaries of that institution—into German and other comprehensible popular languages; and just as Machiavelli—the "Italian Luther"—had sought to make the knowledge of princes (i.e., power) accessible to the laity, the modern prince "translates" the obscure "Latin" of power into a language able to be grasped by ordinary people. At the same time, the people themselves would "translate" their own experiences into a worldview that, in turn, would form the intellectual and perceptual horizon of the modern prince itself.

Gramsci held that nationalism and the fetishism of differences prevented the people from perceiving the true nature of reality, hence too from seeing what needed to be done. Remaining rooted in one's own local caste or region leads to a parochialism blind to the wider world— the context of all historical action. As Gramsci wrote, "'It is possible to judge the greater or lesser complexity of one's conception of the world from one's particular language. Whoever speaks only a dialect . . . necessarily partakes in an intuition of the world that is more or less restricted and provincial.'"[88] Language, as ideology, draws the world; the narrower the language, the narrower the world. What Gramsci theorized, however, was not the "return" to mythically perfect language—the transparent correspondence between words and things of gnosticism—but rather a form of universal *translation* adequate to achieving a concrete social and ethical objective in the world, namely the patient, laborious construction of a new political and moral identity rooted in (in Martin Jay's words) "a linguistically unified community with shared meanings."[89]

Even in his early writings, we see hints of Gramsci's later vision of the modern prince as a new historical figure that establishes its hegemony linguistically not by eradicating local differences and dialects, but rather by "translating" its own vision into an intelligible vernacular—into a political syntax to articulate organically to the actual, diverse conditions and lived experiences of the people in all their diversity. The challenge was to invent a universal language without obliterating local dialects, a problem Gramsci was acutely aware of as someone familiar with proposed cosmopolitan "solutions" to language distinctions in the late nineteenth and early twentieth centuries. For example, in a 1918 essay on "One Language and Esperanto" (*La lingua unica e l'esperanto*), Gramsci criticized a proposed plan by the nineteenth-century novelist Alessandro Manzoni to unify Italy through a single language. Such a language, Manzoni argued, would have to be imposed "from above," by the newly formed Italian state. Gramsci wrote:

> The advocates of a single language are worried by the fact that while the world contains a number of people who would like to communicate directly with one another, there is an endless number of different languages which restrict the ability to communicate. This is a cosmopolitan, not an international anxiety, that of the bourgeoisie who travels for business or pleasure, of nomads more than of stable productive citizens. . . . They would like artificially to create a definitely inflexible language which will not admit changes in space and time.

Gramsci continued: "Manzoni asked himself: now that Italy is formed, how can the Italian language be created? He answered: all Italians will have to speak Tuscan and the Italian state will have to recruit its elementary teachers in Tuscany." But such indifference to geographical and cultural distinctions would not do. Gramsci was most passionate

on the *ethical* need to defend local dialects against the totalizing imperialism of bourgeois cosmopolitanism:

> If a single language, one that is also spoken in a given region and has a living source
> to which it can refer, cannot be imposed on the limited field of the nation, how
> then could an international language take root when it is completely artificial and
> mechanical, completely ahistorical, not fed by great writers, lacking the expressive
> richness which comes from the variety of dialects, from the variety of forms
> assumed in different times...? Let us have no doubt about it: Esperanto, the single
> language, is nothing but a vain idea, an illusion of cosmopolitan, humanitarian,
> democratic mentalities which have not yet been made fertile and been shaken by
> historical critical thinking.... Only by working for the coming of the International
> will Socialists be working for the possible coming of a single language.[90]

Two years later, Gramsci reluctantly admitted that many workers were
attracted to the bourgeois fantasy of Esperanto. Their interest, he
acknowledged, was indicative of "a real desire for and a historical push
toward the formation of verbal complexes that transcend national limits
and in relation to which current national languages will have the same
role as dialects now have."[91] But it was socialism, Gramsci felt, not
Esperanto, that would truly serve the function of a new "verbal complex."

The historical role of the modern prince, then, was to serve as
exegete—i.e., as a guide showing the people how to make sense out of the
non-sense of their violent world, in order to change it. In a way, Gramsci's narrative represented not merely a retelling of Machiavelli's myth
of a new prince, but an evocation of the mythic image of Babel and its
dream of a universal language. We might say, however, that the responsibility of the modern prince, as Gramsci conceived it, was not to tell
the people how to build their tower, but rather to bring them to the site
of history, there to teach them a common tongue so that, *juntos*, they
might figure out how to get construction under way, and to decide
what it is they want to build.

THE POSTMODERN PRINCE

Let us turn, finally, to the question of form today. A *postmodern prince*
would represent the single, transcendental consciousness of today's
diverse social movements, hence also the *social needs* of civil society. As I
wrote at the outset of this chapter, such a prince would look a great

deal like the unified movement described by Albert, Cagan, Chomsky et al, in *Liberating Theory*: it would come into being at that moment when existing movements had come to "recognize that they themselves are essentially different facets of one still larger movement all of whose parts must relate positively to one another if the whole and any of the parts will succeed." This theme bears some resemblance to another work as well—Laclau and Mouffe's *Hegemony and Socialist Strategy*, which had been published just the year before *Liberating Theory*, in 1985.

In *Hegemony and Socialist Strategy*, Laclau and Mouffe had similarly called for an "articulation" of diverse movement elements without reducing their distinct causes and identities to the sole historical antagonism of labor or class exploitation. But Laclau and Mouffe had failed to specify the content of this articulation—i.e., the underlying phenomenological, sociological, and psychic "ground" that might bring diverse movements together. Their account of the "articulation" of elements was purely "negative," i.e., based on the essentially theoreticist and alienated notion that each movement would relate to every other solely as an "other." In *Liberating Theory*, the authors hinted at a "positive" articulation of elements based on what they held in common as human beings enmeshed in a shared historical *reality*, and driven by a shared sense of values. In their view, a "meshing of strategies into encompassing plans for the development of the whole left [must] occur at every level.... It is precisely this linking of insights and their connection within holistic perspectives that will become the highest priority of these types of interchange."[92]

In contrast, Laclau and Mouffe's "hegemonic bloc" was to be based neither on a common experience of oppression nor on a shared *transcendental* constellation of ethical values and political goals, but on the "equivalence" of what made each movement "different."[93] Laclau and Mouffe, in short, offered no *practical* reasons in *Hegemony and Socialist Strategy* why different organizations and movements might work together. However, because *Liberating Theory* was published by a nonacademic press and was written in unadorned theoretical language (which put it at odds with the baroque theory prevalent at the time) that book generated little debate in theoretical circles, while Laclau and Mouffe's more academic-minded book, a work as dense as a black hole, went on to influence critical theory in subsequent years. Yet *Liberating Theory* in fact represented the greater advance in the theory of form and unity.

The fatal flaw in Laclau and Mouffe's book was its essentially formalistic approach to the problem. As Gramsci repeatedly warned, the task of building a unified will must not to be conceived as "a rationalistic, deductive, abstract process—i.e., one typical of pure intellectuals (or pure asses)," but rather must be presented "in such a way that the organizing and the interconnecting appear to be a practical and 'inductive' necessity, experimental."[94] In other words, the unification of diverse elements of the polity—e.g., urban and rural workers, peasants and middle-class intellectuals—cannot occur on the basis of *thought* alone, but on the basis of actual commonalities in the *lived reality* of the different groups. To do otherwise, to attempt to unite the people on the basis of an artificial or dictatorial vision of how things "should" be, is to succumb to a "bureaucratic conception, where in the end there is no unity but a stagnant swamp, on the surface calm and 'mute,' and no federation but a 'sack of potatoes,' i.e. a mechanical juxtaposition of single 'units' without any connection between them."[95] What is essential is that the "collective organism [be] made up of single individuals, who form the organism in as much as they have *given themselves*, and *actively accept*, a particular hierarchy and leadership." Gramsci continues:

> If each of the individual members sees the collective organism as an entity *external* to himself, it is evident that this organism no longer in fact exists, it becomes a phantasm of the mind, a fetish. . . . What is astonishing, and typical, is that fetishism of this kind occurs [not only in organs of the State but also] . . . in "voluntary" organisms . . . like parties and trade unions. . . . The tendency is . . . toward an external, critical attitude of the individual towards the organism. . . . In any case, a fetishistic relationship. This individual expects the organism to act, even if he does not do anything himself. . . . [Moreover] . . . each individual, seeing that despite his non-intervention something still does happen, tends to think that there indeed exists, over and above individuals, a phantasmagorical being, the abstraction of the collective organism, a kind of autonomous divinity, which does not think with any concrete brain but thinks, which does not move with specific human legs but still moves, etc.[96]

Just such "phantasmagorical" beings and "autonomous divinities" have been conjured every time a poststructuralist critic has gone on the fool's errand of trying to redeem Gramsci and his theory of a hegemony for the poststructuralist project. The halls of critical theory are now crowded with these spirits, who shuffle around under such names as "the multitude," "rhizomes," or (in Laclau and Mouffe's version) "autonomization of spheres."

What is essential, then, is that the postmodern prince in no way be construed as a "coalition" in the usual sense of that term—i.e., as an assemblage of groups who retain their autonomy and identity even at the end of a long period of joint action. The collective will of the prince cannot be reduced to an aggregate or "series" of disparate parts. Rather, it represents the *organic coalescence* of the various diverse movements for human and nonhuman liberation into a single universal project to cultivate the basis of a new social order. Originally, the words *coalition* and *coalescence* meant the same thing—the process by which separate entities grew or combined together to form an organic whole. During the modern period, however, the words drifted apart. Today, the word *coalition* connotes "an alliance for combined action of distinct parties, persons, or states, without permanent incorporation into one body" (*Oxford English Dictionary*), while *coalesce* still retains its original sense of unity: in modern biology, *to coalesce* still signifies the "growing together of separate parts." It is in the latter sense, of a "growing together," that the postmodern prince must be conceived and summoned into being. And the "earth" of this coalescence, as it were, can only be lived human experience.

Contra postmodernism, one of the themes in this work has been the importance of grounding a theory of radical politics in a *phenomenological* approach. Gramsci, I have emphasized, was a phenomenological thinker. In fact, Gramsci's view of identity and meaning as being rooted in experience was quite close to that later adopted by the French phenomenologist Maurice Merleau-Ponty. Both theorists, as Renate Holub has observed, shared an appreciation for the absolute centrality of "the production of meaning and value" in human affairs.[97] Both too saw consciousness or "forms of knowing" as "embedded in . . . interrelationality, rather than merely either in the subject (subjectivism) or in the object (objectivism)."[98] As far as we know, Gramsci never actually encountered the works of Husserl or Brentano. His generally unremarked closeness to the phenomenological tradition, therefore, must have emerged naturally out of his personal political and ethical involvements as a revolutionary. As a strategic thinker and politician, that is, Gramsci could not help but think practically, hence also "sensuously." Gramsci was simply not concerned about defending the "ontological centrality" of the working class; he sought a politics not which would manipulate preexisting essences, but which would patiently and laboriously construct new political formations.

This sensitivity to the *experiential* nature of human identity pervades Gramsci's work—most famously, perhaps, in his essay, "On the Southern Question," where he wrote eloquently of the need to bring the rural peasants of southern Italy into historic alliance with the urban workers of the north. The cultivation of such a "collective will" of proletariat and peasants was to be based not on some shared "essence," but rather on the basis of shared sociopolitical and existential conditions, which produced a *latent* common political interest in seeing the ruling classes of Italy overthrown. In short, form must always be rooted in the lived experiences of actual flesh-and-blood human beings, i.e., in a *phenomenological* relationship between a form and the perceiving beings who together constitute it.

One of the main findings of phenomenology is that the lifeworld is an active accomplishment by particular subjects who have an "intentional" or meaningful relationship to it. As Merleau-Ponty showed in his critique of behaviorism, the living organism, in its ontological "comportment" toward the world, cannot be meaningfully separated from that world. Reality, that is, exists for an organism as a *Gestalt* or total pattern of meaning that or means something to the organism itself: "The organism itself measures the action of things upon it and itself delimits its milieu by a circular process which is without analogy in the [inanimate] physical world."[99] The "behavior" of an organism thus can only be grasped as a whole, not, as in the Cartesianist view, as the sum of aggregate parts, or as reflexes or "responses" to "external stimuli." There is a continual tension between the subject and its milieu, such that each simultaneously acts upon and conditions the other—the "living organism . . . is related to everything else."[100] Gramsci's view of the modern prince was essentially just this. Insofar as the modern prince, in its coming-to-form, its "appearing," would gather around itself the *existing* forces and meanings of society, and transform them, in no way could it be said to be something separate or distinct from society. Rather, in its intercourse or dialectical exchange with its *ümwelt*—its surrounding milieu—the prince would resemble the "living organism," existing as a tissue of intentions and actions intertwined with the lifeworld.[101]

If we try to conceive of a *new* political subject, a postmodern prince, in this way, i.e., as an *organism*, we find that it is not so easy to do so. In large measure, perhaps, this is because the familiar political forms, whether they be the nation-state, political parties, or unions, strike us as historically exhausted and outmoded, or simply corrupted ("one big union," anyone?). But it is also because we lack an *idea-image* of the form such a new collective subject might take today. The early modern political theorists, as we saw, used various metaphors to represent the new political form they proposed to become the basis of the modern secular polity. For Hobbes, as we have seen, that form was to resemble a sword-wielding sovereign whose body was made up of the people themselves, while for Machiavelli, it was the figure of a prince that would serve metaphorically as the vehicle for the development of the people's national consciousness. What would our *postmodern prince* look like?

I want to suggest that Octavio Ocampo's painting of Cesar Chavez may be of help in envisioning a new, radical theory of political form. Cesar Chavez, the epitomy of an "organic" intellectual in Gramscian terms, was the son of Mexican migrant laborers who organized migrant farm workers and founded the United Farm Workers Union. Looking closely at Ocampo's painting, one sees with surprise that Chavez's visage is in fact an illusion: his face, shoulders, and chest are composed entirely of hundreds of farmers and workers, women and men, brown and white, all marching together. His hair is made of plowed fields, his lips of doves, the highlights on his face, protest banners. The farm workers' movement is depicted diachronically: marchers stream into the present from the past, marching "through" or past the viewer. Skulls lining the left side of the painting are really figures of women and children burying the dead— victims of poverty and pesticide poisoning. As the painting's title suggests—*Portrait of La Causa*—Ocampo sought to capture the complex morphology of mass counterpower. Chavez the individual, like Machiavelli's *Prince*, is thus portrayed as a transitional figure, one whose form briefly serves as a vehicle through which a collective will manifests itself. We might say that the United Farm Workers Union was the *form* of the workers' struggle; Cesar Chavez was merely its "face." In Ocampo's painting, unity in form is built on the foundation of diverse elements. Rather than being a hindrance to unity, diversity turns out to be its *precondition*.

Ocampo's portrait hints at a new vision of political form that would go beyond both the modern liberal conception of representational government as well as the homogeneous party "vanguard" of Marxist-Leninism. While his portrait of the United Farm Workers Union portrays unity-in-diversity only within a *single* movement, we might extend it metonymically to stand in as a figure for the unity of *multiple* movements united in a common utopian project. In the broader instance, too, homogeneous form would emerge not in spite of the different elements, but on their basis. That is to say, following Aristotle, the relationship between whole and parts would be seen to be dialectical. On the one hand, the diverse ele-

Cesar Chavez: Portrait of la Causa, OCTAVIO OCAMPO

ments would shine light on a normative "whole" that is to become post-modern prince. At the same time, however, the postmodern prince, in its own *bildung* and unfolding, would reveal the erstwhile "different" elements to be facets of the same larger whole. The "prince" is the *positive* articulation of otherwise discrete elements in such a way that together they "paint" the visible realm—the totality of power, "what is"—as well as the incipient totality of what "ought to be"—a healed world.

The unity of the postmodern prince is a *spiritual* and *historical* unity, in the sense that its constitutive parts come to view themselves as "organically" and not merely functionally related to one another. To be politically efficacious, moreover, the prince must be able to exploit strategic opportunities by acting, at times, like a *single organism*. That is, it must be able to pursue long-term goals with some consistency of purpose, and these goals must be pursued not just locally and globally, but with a certain degree of simultaneity and tactical coordination. In practical terms, this means that something *like* a new International is required. Like the Internationals of old, this one too would conceive of itself in utopian terms, as a bid to remake human life. Unlike the old, however, it would be rooted in a critical life-philosophy rather than merely in opposition to capitalism per se. It would also be thoroughly democratic, eschewing the centralization of political authority.

It is crucial, however, to understand that the *form* of the postmodern prince is dialectical, dynamic, and in constant motion. The prince is form *and* formlessness. The prince *cannot be reduced to* its mere official or "governmental" bodies or proxies. Nor can it even be conceived in terms of *a single political party*. Once our utopian imaginary is *bounded* or contained within a single organizational structure, it becomes reified—that is, it becomes vulnerable to attack from without and corruption and bureaucratization from within. As the Chinese strategist Sun Tzu observed, "The consummation of forming an army is to arrive at form-lessness. When you have no form, undercover espionage cannot find out anything, intelligence cannot form a strategy."[102] Just as "water has no constant shape," one's forces should have "no constant formation."[103]

In this regard, one of the persistent challenges facing the critic who would explain Gramsci's idiosyncratic notion of the "modern" prince is determining to what extent the entity he had in mind would resemble an ordinary political party, and to what extent it would resemble a movement. In fact, it would be both. On the one hand, to the extent that the prince symbolizes the "psychic" aspirations of the people, it is essentially *immaterial* and even boundless. On the other hand, it is clear from Gramsci's remarks that it would also have the quality of a functioning political party in the formal sense of an organized, centralized, and disciplined structure. What can be confusing about Gramsci's conception of the party is that, following Marx, he saw the state largely as a battleground for interests and conflicts rooted in society itself, and denied that there was more than a "methodological" distinction between state and civil society.[104] For this reason, he did not limit the term "party" only to a formal organization, i.e., the registered party replete with offices, an official name, seats in the parliament, and so on. In his theory, *any* coherent or intelligible group "interest," provided that it was capable of acting in a concerted way to vie with other groups for cultural, economic, or political power, could be construed as a party. Formal parties, i.e., electoral organs, on this view, are merely crystallizations in determinate form of the interests of particular "parties"—i.e., social classes or groupings—in civil society. A hegemonic class achieves and maintains power not merely through cunning or force, but more important by winning the consent of other groups in society.

In short, the ruling class does not "rule" directly. Typically, it does not even assume the form of a single political party; if it did, if there was an identity between a party and a dominant social group, it would be vulnerable to criticism and even direct assault. Rather, the hegemonic group prefers to stand over and above *multiple* parties, wielding a "moral" and ideological influence over many different social groups:

> Hence the intellectual General Staff of the organic party often does not belong to any of these fractions, but operates as if it were a directive force standing on its own, above the parties, and sometimes is even believed to be such by the public. This function can be studied with greater precision if one starts from the point of view that a newspaper too (a group of newspapers), a review (or group of reviews), is a "party" or "fraction of a party."[105]

This formulation of Gramsci's remains useful to this day, in helping us comprehend even the most basic features of our polity—for example, corporate funding of the major U.S. political parties and patriarchal rule.[106]

The *counter-hegemonic* movement or movements similarly "rule" without "governing"—at least in the near- and medium-term. When

Gramsci described the need for cultural and political "trench warfare," the so-called war of position, rather than a frontal assault on state power ("war of maneuver"), what he had in mind was not *uncoordinated* activity, but rather a mix of Jacobinist direction and grassroots cultural dissemination à la the Reformation. Stuart Hall explains:

> [Hegemony is] the struggle to contest and dis-organize an existing political formation; the taking of the "leading position". . . . over a number of different spheres of society at once — economy, civil society, intellectual and moral life, culture; the conduct of a wide and differentiated type of struggle; the winning of a strategic measure of popular consent; and, thus, the securing of a social authority sufficiently deep to conform society into a new historic project.[107]

The postmodern prince, hence, must be visible and invisible, and must have form *and* formlessness. On the one hand, the postmodern prince must show its "face" to the world (how else to win the people's respect—consent?) and be organized with the degree of homogeneity and authority needed to engage in transnational campaigns. For example, the postmodern prince might assume shape in the form of a body akin to the UN General Assembly, a "shadow" authority rooted organically in global civil society, rather than in the nation-state. Such a body might thus elect rotating members of a decision-making Security Council each year. But a postmodern prince would also have to organize itself along *national* and *regional* axes of identity—e.g., in the United States, taking on the form of a "third party" effort.

On the other hand, however, the prince must also be fluid and subtle, as much a *moral* force as a political one. As Sun Tzu wrote: "Military formation is like water—the form of water is to avoid the high and go to the low, the form of a military force is to avoid the full and attack the empty."[108] Those who constitute the prince must conceive of their movement's mission in the broadest of ideological and cultural terms; and they must take up the entire panoply of oppositional and transformative historical "equipment" lying at their disposal.

TOTALITY AND PERCEPTION

Samir Amin writes that while "the fragmented [universal] social movement has not yet found a strong formula for crystallization, capable of meeting the challenges posed . . . it has made remarkable breakthroughs, in directions that enrich its impact: principally, women's powerful entry into social life, as well as a new awareness of environmental destruction on a scale which, for the first time in history, threatens the entire planet."[109] The question Amin's formulation begs, however, is whether it is really possible for such a "strong formula" for "crystallizing" a unified movement to be discovered, or invented.

I want to argue, in fact, that without a new theory of *totality*, and with it, a new *paradigm* of the whole, it is virtually useless to try to envision the basis of a new collective subject and its corresponding phenomenal form. In this regard, one of the more unfortunate consequences of the theoretical debates between Marxism and postmodernism in the 1980s and 1990s is that they obscured the possibility of formulating a completely new paradigm of the *totality* of social and natural relations. In fact, if we want to establish an epistemological framework for contemporary praxis, one adequate to the demands of practice, neither Marxism nor poststructuralism will do. The former, despite its formidable power and continuing relevance, is reductionist, while the latter is idealist and scholastic, the semiotician's version of the ancient metaphysics of *actio in distans*. The theory of knowledge we need must steer clear of all arbitrary doctrines and metaphysical conceits, while remaining as flexible and open-ended as possible. Our task is to construct a theory of the whole that will enable us to "see" more fully the dimensions and textures of social life, particularly structures of power and their points of internal contradiction and, hence, strategic vulnerability.

The need for a proper theory of totality can be readily apprehended by considering the facts of our existence, that is, by reflecting on our actual experience of the *phenomenal world* or *Lebenswelt*. And above all, this existence and the experiences which constitute it are only possible because we are essentially *perceiving* beings. "Sense experience," as Merleau-Ponty wrote, "is that vital communication with the world which makes it present as a familiar setting of our life."[110] Sensory perception, a capacity we have in common with all other nonhuman beings-in-the-world, therefore must constitute the epistemological ground of all and every theory of action. What made Marx a "materialist" thinker was not his ontology of labor per se, but his methodological and *ethical* commitment or attentiveness to the experiences of actual human beings as they encountered the phenomenal world. "Perception," as Bloch observed of Marx's thought, "not the concept that is merely taken from it, is and remains the beginning where all materialist cognition identifies itself."[111] Among other things, taking perception seriously means dwelling on perhaps the most important empirical finding of phenomenology, which is that *we see in wholes*. The discovery that perception is structured *holistically*—i.e., that the whole, perceptually speaking, is always prior to the parts—was first made by a group of experimental psychologists in Germany in the early twentieth century. Gestaltists like Wolfgang Köhler demonstrated that humans, like other animals, perceive in structural wholes or "forms" (*Gestalten*): that is, that every phenomenal object acquires meaning or "sens" for subject only as part of an overall structure or form (*Gestalt*).

It is a characteristic of the gestalt that no discrete figure can be perceived except in relation to a "background" or "ground" (*fond*), as Merleau-Ponty put it: "The perceptual 'something' is always in the middle of something else, it always forms part of a 'field.' An isolated datum of perception is inconceivable."[112] The holistic nature of perception has important implications for our politics. What in fact differentiates "radical" or critical social praxis from most other varieties of human action is that the practitioner assumes that a condition of perceptual occlusion prevails.[113] Radical pedagogy as such functions literally to reveal or bring to light what would otherwise remain unseen—the hidden structures of meaning and power that shape our lives—and this can only happen by revealing the *whole*.[114] Every so-called critical social movement seeks to *reveal the background itself*—that is, to make the background, as it were, *become figure*. For only once the background becomes figure does the perceiver comprehend that what she or he first took to be an "isolated datum"—e.g., a rape, a layoff of workers, a cleared rain forest—is in fact nothing of the kind, but rather a "moment" in a larger structure of meaning that can be known, analyzed, and potentially defeated.[115]

Every radical movement instructs the people in *epistemology*, insofar as it seeks to "denaturalize" existing facts. As Gramsci put it, "No movement becomes aware of its global character all at once, but only gradually through experience—in other words, when it learns from the facts that nothing which exists is natural...but rather exists because of the existence of certain conditions, whose disappearance cannot remain without consequences."[116] And the main consequence of praxis is to change the dominant filters structuring the perception of reality.

But there is a further significance to the gestaltists' finding that a *figure* can only be perceived within a particular context or field. In order for us to be able to perceive *any* phenomenal figure, whether it be a person, an inanimate object, or a social fact, we need a prior set of perceptual rules and normative expectations to help us sort through the enormous amount of inchoate sense data that continually bombards us, in order to make sense of what is "there." We cannot "see" what is in the world—whether a form of power or a path toward political revolution—until we have a sense of what it is we are looking for. One needs a principle of selection, as it were, a way of sorting out the perceptual wheat from the chaff.

For many years, from about the late nineteenth to the mid-twentieth century, Marxism provided just such a principle of selection, a powerful perceptual "frame" or system that made it possible to "see" all manner of social objects. Marxism in fact closely resembled a paradigm, in Thomas Kuhn's sense of that word—i.e., a framework for perception, a means for tying critical inquiry to experimental result, and a set of historical "exemplars" for defining effective political practice. Marx argued that human civilization could be grasped as a coherent whole, changing through time. With the aid of his dialectical categories, one could go out and investigate the world and perceive meaningful patterns woven into the warp and woof of history—provided, however, that one knew how and where to look. And what lent Marxism its paradigmatic quality was not Marx and Engels's "scientific" approach to history, but rather their capacious notion of *totality*. That is to say, only in the attempt to *grasp the whole* of social relations could the socialist revolutionary "see" *particular* structures and patterns in the lifeworld.

Nothing was "epiphenomenal" to Gramsci; everything was "phenomenological." That is, every phenomenon was a key or part of a key to unlock the hidden meanings, and probable temporal flows, of society and politics. Hence Gramsci's insatiable appetite for knowledge and information of any and all kinds. In prison, he analyzed agricultural surveys, Russian novels, economic histories of inflation and the Italian financial system, essays by De Sanctis, accounts of travel in Latin America, and so on—even ordinary postcards.[117] Out of this seemingly inchoate mass, stuff brimming with an infinity of possible interpretive possibilities, Gramsci was able to perceive patterns of society and culture that would have been invisible to anyone else. Even a mass-produced romance novel might hold a key to the meaning of a social formation—not crudely, as in some trivial reflection of an economic "base" (the Hegelian "appearance" of a pre-given, homogenous essence of "Spirit") but as a phenomenon deserving to be investigated in its right in its open relation to a whole constellation of other objects and social relations in time. The very intellectual diversity of Gramsci's *Notebooks* is suggestive of his effort to grasp enough of the complex, dynamic whole of social reality that he might better theorize *how* it might be changed.[118]

Marxism, to sum up, provided intellectuals and activists not only with a "theory" of history and a utopian dream (socialist revolution) but with a way of *perceiving the gestalt*. As Merleau-Ponty wrote in *Humanism and Terror* (during his Marxist period):

> In essence Marxism is the idea that history has a *sens*—in other words, that it is intelligible and has a direction—that it is moving toward the power of the proletariat, which as the essential factor of production is capable of resolving the contradictions of capitalism, of organizing a humane appropriation of nature, and, as the "universal class," able to transcend national and social conflicts as well as the struggle between man and man. To be a Marxist... is to believe that history has a *Gestalt*... a holistic system moving toward a state of equilibrium, the classless society which cannot be achieved without individual effort and action, but which is outlined in the present crisis as its solution.[119]

Later in his life, after falling out with Sartre over communism, Merleau-Ponty rejected the problematic teleology implicit in this Marxist theory of the gestalt. Affirming the open- endedness of human action, Merleau-Ponty denied that Marxism provided an infallible science of history, only a certain horizon of intelligibility. As he put it, socialism "presupposes a concrete view of particular circumstances and of their probable significance, a certain reading of history in terms of what is likely—and with whatever errors such a reading may imply—and it cannot, in any case, be mechanically deduced from theory."[120] He concluded that Marxism, i.e., dialectical critique of capitalism, could no longer serve as an adequate paradigm of the whole. However, he never disavowed his view that the *meaning* of any given political act was constituted through its organic participation in a *gestalt* or ensemble of historical relations.

Here we must pause to note one of the paradoxical qualities of paradigms: when they become truly dominant, the background framework provided by the paradigm serves to *conceal* as well as *reveal*. That is, truly "paradigmatic" theories work only by providing a principle of selection for perceiving social objects, allowing those who work within them to select out a tiny portion of the otherwise infinite data available, while ignoring or suppressing the rest. As Kuhn observed, the effectiveness of a given paradigm derives from its ability to "restrict the phenomenological field accessible for scientific investigation at any given time."[121] Marx's paradigm similarly restricted the perceptual field on the basis of its an ontology of economic production, which placed the working class at the center of all social meaning as the potential subject-object of history. This essentialist and reductionistic conception of totality at times led socialists to ignore or degrade identity formations not reducible to class exploitation, as well as to pay insufficient heed to the psychological and affective dimensions of solidarity.

Marxism indeed proved blind to whole regions of human experience and oppression. Feminist social critique was especially blunted by the economistic assumption in Marx that all salient aspects of history and consciousness could be reduced to class conflict and exploitation. As Barbara Taylor notes in her study of feminism in the nineteenth century, Robert Owen's utopian "call for a multifaceted offensive against all forms of social hierarchy" was "replaced with a dogmatic insistence on the primacy of class-based issues, a demand for sexual unity in the face of a common class enemy, and a vague promise of improved status for women 'after the revolution.'"[122] As "scientific" socialism began to be consolidated as the dominant paradigm, feminist issues were "either ignored, attacked as bourgeois deviationism, or relegated to the category of secondary issues."[123] In short, Marxist accounts of totality and identity set out from *one* social experience, one form of alienation and objectification—that of human labor. Even today, some Marxists persist in reducing racism and sexism to epiphenomena of class, or pin the emergence of civil rights movements to changes in capitalist strategies of accumulation.[124]

The question is whether it is possible, or even desirable, to try to arrive today at a *new* paradigm of critique and practice, one able to articulate a non-reductionistic concept of totality. In his late writings, Merleau-Ponty went beyond rejecting Marxism as a total paradigm to concluding that critical philosophy could no longer aspire to the sort of encompassing paradigm of historical change that Marxism represented. While his pessimism, in this regard, is understandable in light of the Cold War and the corruption of French intellectual thought by Communism, not having *any* view of the whole is proving to be a severe obstacle to practice today. The difficulty faced by activists and critical intellectuals who dream of changing the world is that ongoing processes of reification lead to progressive cognitive fragmentation, making it exceedingly difficult for any given historical subject to escape being portrayed as anything other than a mere "datum." Loss of a coherent sense of geographical and temporal distance (and difference) under capitalism effectively destroys the subject's ability to *perceive any image of the whole*. History is reduced to a series of unintelligible "events"—singularities or fragments whose obscure, even irrational origins frighten ordinary people.

To be sure, the well-organized social movement can still turn out tens or even hundreds of thousands of protesters in the streets, resulting in a five-second blip of coverage in the national news media. Yet to the viewer at home, such demonstrations leave only fleeting impressions. The viewer "sees" only one "protest"—one more seemingly self-interested spectacle of expression among too many others to count—protests, moreover, that apparently have nothing to do with one another: protests come and go with each passing season, without apparent rationale or program. Effectual political "appearance" thus is not to be confused with *spectacle*. "Spectacular" protests, which is to say, expressivist demonstrations that emphasize aesthetics over content and privilege tactics over strategy, interpellate people as members of a passive "audience." Rather than illuminating a *totality* of social relations that has led to pervasive conditions of injustice, they provide only discrete, "serial" moments of representation—fleeting furies signifying nothing. "Stand-alone" movements and forms of action thus sink back into the operational and "semiotic" obscurity whence they came. Because seeing, or perceiving, is "believing," political action lacking phenomenal *form* is literally "unbelievable"—it is ghostly action, a play of shadows upon other shadows. Thus, if we desire to have effects on the world, we must take careful stock of how our actions affect others at the level of "seeming," which in politics is *virtually* the same thing as "being." It follows, then, that the movement unable to illuminate its own perceptual "ground" is also incapable of emerging truly as "figure." In a liberal or pluralist polity, the single-issue social movement, if it is perceived at all, will likely be seen as an "interest group"—i.e., as a self- interested actor indifferent to the common good or the public interest. It will certainly not be seen for what it actually is, viz., *a herald of a new form of life*.

What I mean is that political fragmentation occludes the true radical significance, the *universal* significance, of *every* particular movement. And this, of course, is just the way that dominant regimes of power want it. Power thrives through perpetual occlusion of truth and the forced forgetting of the *totality*, i.e., the whole ensemble of social relations and its patterns of significance through time.[125] Enormous energies, indeed, are continually summoned and expended in order to ensure the destruction of truth (every move by the counter-hegemonist is met with a countermove by the dominant power, every feint with a counter-feint, and so on).

If, however, political fragmentation occludes the *totality*, i.e., the actual, interrelated mechanisms of repressive power, for spectators, it also occludes the totality for movement activists and strategists themselves. Without the ability to fill in the details of what Frederic Jameson calls the "cognitive map" of the empirical whole, each movement risks being blind to the necessary and sufficient conditions of social change. Environmentalists, say, will be unable to understand the reasons for the destruction of Brazil's rain forests or global warming until they understand the expansionist nature of capitalism as a world system that reduces "nature" to the status of a commodity. Similarly, unless civil rights activists learn to see the ways in which class stratification, which is *presupposed by* the capitalist mode of development, reinforces and perpetuates patterns of racial segregation, they will fail to make much headway in overcoming racism. By the same token, socialists who reduce the complex psychic and symbolic economy of racism to class exploitation will misapprehend the actual nature of racism. So long as each movement is seen as *fundamentally* distinct and separate from every other, then, it not only remains invisible, it also occludes its own historical significance—i.e., the full reach of its critique and the panoply of social changes required to alter the present facts.

In short, without a sense of the whole, we cannot know what "the left" is or indeed whether such a term still means anything. Nor can we have a clear sense of how to go about choosing our strategic priorities—i.e., why we should prefer one mode of action to another, one campaign to the next. We also can't possibly know, or know clearly enough, who our allies and enemies are. It was essential to Marxism's power as a paradigm, let us recall, that its practitioners or adherents had a practical framework for evaluating the bases of political and social unity.

Marxism provided a way of discerning "what is identical in seeming diversity of form and on the other hand of what is distinct and even opposed in apparent uniformity... in order to organize and interconnect closely that which is similar."[126] If we hope similarly to *see* the whole, and to achieve a new "whole" ourselves, we will need some new principle of perceptual selection for distinguishing between like and unlike elements. Without a theory of totality we cannot hope to arrive at the kind of effective synthesis of diverse elements and perspectives needed to establish a postmodern prince.

TOWARD A NEW THEORY OF THE WHOLE

Marxism, as a form of "materialist cognition," represented the systematic phenomenological investigation of the essence of capitalism, viz., disocclusion of the commodity form.[127] But where Marx and Engels reduced sensuous existence to one dimension of existence, human labor, the paradigm of praxis underlying the postmodern prince must be based in a general phenomenological "reduction" of *all* forms of sensual experience, including the experiences of other, nonhuman animal beings. The *actual facts* of the totality—the autonomous and semi-autonomous logics of patriarchy, racism, species imperialism, and so on—*require* this. Simply, we know that class exploitation is neither the only form of oppression nor *necessarily* (i.e., a priori, before empirical investigation) the ontologically primary one. Patriarchy antedates the formation of capitalism, and male rule will survive its destruction unless it is rooted out of the libidinal economy of masculine and feminine identity. Much depends, therefore, on our continuing ability to extend existing research efforts to map the patterns of the social structure that give rise to experiences of oppression. Merleau-Ponty wrote that the goal of a phenomenology of politics was to "show how the phenomenon of perceptual structures makes social class comprehensible."[128] Today, our task is more difficult: we must show how perceptual structures make the various structures of *power* as such comprehensible. Our task is to reveal the workings of capitalism, but also to disocclude the structures of racist consciousness and to bring to light the occluded, naturalized habitus, or structuring structures, of patriarchy—and so on. As veteran grassroots organizer Leslie Cagan writes: "One priority for the progressive movement [therefore] is to begin articulating a more thorough analysis of how issues, struggles, and people are connected. . . . We are battling an intricate, interdependent series of oppressions, structures of domination, and hierarchies of control."[129] It is to be hoped that as we begin *to see* the connections that link one movement to another, we will find new avenues of praxis illuminated, and hence surer forms of political strategy.

In a sense, the unification of elements implied in the construction of a postmodern prince would resemble the intentional matrix of ordinary perception.[130] As Merleau-Ponty showed, while each individual subject perceives the world slightly differently from everyone else, the *Lebenswelt* or lifeworld, despite its essential "ambiguity," is not for that merely an arbitrary play of signs, but provides the basis for the consensual apprehension of meaning. In his use of Merleau-Ponty's phenomenology to illuminate our relations with other beings in the natural world, David Abram describes perception as the "mutual inscription of others in my experience, and . . . of myself in their experiences." Only through this web of relations with one another can we effect "the interweaving of our individual phenomenal fields into a single, ever-shifting fabric, a single phenomenal world or 'reality.'"[131] Kerry Whiteside similarly observes of Merleau-Ponty's theory of ordinary perception that the "challenge of understanding is always that of making our partial perspectives come together to 'announce' a whole."[132]

The gestaltists showed that a subject shown a picture drawn ambiguously will perceive one image or meaning one moment, then suddenly see it as something else entirely—as a duck one moment, say, and a rabbit the next. By analogy, the coming to appearance of the postmodern prince would represent a "gestalt switch" of global proportions. In rendering the social totality suddenly visible, as "background," the prince draws existing liberationist movements themselves into the realm of appearances as a single "figure." The convergence of social *critiques* makes the totality itself visible as a social construct—i.e., as a set of social relations whose existence is conditional. In turn, the revealed whole illuminates each individual "facet"—each movement—and lends it intelligibility as part of a coherent system of oppression and domination. Meanwhile, to repeat my quote from Albert, Cagan et al. in *Liberating Theory*, recognizing themselves as "essentially different facets of one still larger movement all of whose parts must relate positively to one another if the whole and any of the parts will succeed," social movements attempt to build "a new liberatory society." In developing a prefigurative culture, the erstwhile separate movements symbolically render or "announce" a new social whole. In this way, the postmodern prince constitutes the germ or core of a new civilization.

A lovely metaphor for this process can be seen in the ancient Sufi tale about a group of Sikh men who are invited into a darkened room where an elephant has been hidden. None of the men has ever seen an elephant before. Each, therefore, feels around in the dark with his arms outstretched, interpreting what he senses in terms of his own past experiences. Thus, one, feeling the trunk, thinks it is a water pipe, while another, feeling the elephant's moving ears, determines that it is a type of fan. One touches the elephant's feet, mistaking them for columns of a great temple, while another feels one of the elephant's tusks and announces that it must be a sword made of porcelain. The great Sufi poet Rumi, in his retelling of this tale, wrote:

> Each of us touches one place
> and understands the whole in that way.
>
> The palm and the feeling in the dark are
> how the senses explore the reality of the elephant.
>
> If each of us held a candle there,
> and if we went in together,
> we could see it.[133]

Enlightenment, as disocclusion of the totality of the phenomenal world, is available to us only if we can first learn to converse with one another. Every social movement offers a partial view of the *whole* of suffering: like shards of a hologram, each contains the refracted image of the whole—but from a particular perspective. One individual sees this suffering and thinks that it is exploitation of the worker, while another sees it as male domination of women, and a third sees it as the enslavement and mass extermination of other species beings. None of them is mistaken: each perceives a particular, irreducible aspect of the totality of oppression. Yet once they come together in the same room to share perspectives—each holding her own "candle" to the totality—each comes to *see* in the practical activity of the others common work on an interdependent whole. Only in coming together do their different perceptual fields begin to cohere into one. Together they are able to map the whole, and thus to perceive patterns of power, common traditions of resistance, ideological coherences. Socialists come to *see* that the objectification of women is *like* the objectification of the worker; gays and lesbians come to see that the humiliation and degradation of the worker is *like* the diminishment of the queer; Jews and people of color come to *see* that the maltreatment of animals—their enslavement and violation and suffering—constitutes the discursive horizon and exemplary practicum for their own reduction to "subhuman" status. What is key is that only in combining their unique perspectives can the scattered forces of the opposition come to see what confronts each and all— as a practical problem and a spiritual challenge.

7 Metahumanism

Nothing in this book is meant to imply that we must or should abandon Marx's critique of capitalism. Rather, we must broaden and deepen it. The postmodern prince *is* the direct historical successor to the international socialist movement. Five hundred years of global capitalism has left one out of two human beings living in severe poverty. Hundreds of millions of people in Africa, Latin America, Southeast Asia, and within the overdeveloped countries themselves, die prematurely of malnutrition and entirely preventable diseases, the "normal" casualties of an economic system that enriches the few at the expense of the many. But even were the most egregious forms of suffering under the world capitalist regime eliminated, the division of labor presupposed by capitalist property relations would remain, hence exploitation and alienation as universal features of human life. As the young Marx noted a century and a half ago, capitalism leads to the alienation of the worker from the object and process of her labor, alienation of the individual and the human species from the rest of nature, alienation of each of us from all of us. Capitalism *by its nature* is an expansionary system that thrives off social inequality and reduces all of nature to "standing reserve" for the ceaseless production of exchange value. Because the monopoly of a small elite over the means of production distorts representative government, capitalism also thwarts the development of a genuine, which is to say, a participatory democracy. Only with a radical restructuring of the world economy leading ultimately to the abolition of large-scale private property and the democratization of the labor process, then, might poverty and the "hidden injuries" of class be overcome, and the social and ecological crises continually being spun off by the world system be brought under collective human control. For these and numerous other reasons, the postmodern prince cannot be conceived

as *other* than a socialist movement. It must ceaselessly strive for the abolition of capitalism as a world system, which is to say that it must seek to
democratize control over the means of production.

What is clear, however, is that democratizing the means of production and dissolving the division of labor *is not enough*. This may strike the
reader as an astonishing thing to say, since even the dissolution of capitalism as a world system seems like a wildly utopian and perhaps impossible undertaking. Yet it is my earnest conviction that our dreams of the
future, like our partial critiques of the present, have if anything not
been ambitious enough. Challenging the capitalist elite's monopoly of
the means of production is a "spiritually"—hence *morally* and *politically*—
hollow goal unless it is integrated with a movement to create what
Sartre called a new "image" of humanity. Such an image is unlikely to
be discovered merely in the goal of popular control over production,
however worthy that is; it can only become "concrete" in a total life-philosophy that eschews domination in all its forms.

Gramsci, we have seen, wrote that socialism, "with its vast mass
movement, has represented and does represent an historical process
similar to the Reformation."[1] The modern prince would seek to win the
"souls" of the citizens. Its leaders would be teachers, the clergy of a new
world religion. Like Martin Luther, who made knowledge of the scriptures accessible to the people by translating the scriptures into the vernacular—but also like the Prince of "the Italian Luther," Machiavelli,
who educates the people into the "ways of princes"—the modern prince
involves the people in the cultivation of a new, "worldly" philosophy
that treats of both the particular and temporal, i.e., in a sociology of the
existing order of domination and hierarchy, and the universal, ethical,
and global project of socialism. This dialectic of theory and practice
incorporates both practical and, as it were, "spiritual" dimensions.
Gramsci indeed compares Marx to Christ, and Lenin to Christ's apostle
Paul: "Christ—*Weltanschauung*, and St. Paul—organizer, action, expansion
of the *Weltanschauung*—are both necessary to the same degree and therefore of the same historical stature. Christianity could be called historically 'Christianity-Paulism,' and this would indeed be a more exact title."[2]

We cannot know how literally Gramsci intended this comparison of
socialism to an evangelical movement. Clearly, Gramsci felt strongly
that socialism ought to conceive itself as the vehicle of a world-changing
ethics, an ambition he perhaps learned from Hegel. In Hegel's phenome-

nology, the final unfolding of *Geist*, ethics and politics, being and becoming, would finally coincide in the ideal state. Essentially, human beings would now only *choose* to will, morally and subjectively, what was objectively or actually true and rational. Hegel even had an historical exemplar of a fully realized dialectic in which subjective freedom would be seamlessly joined with an ethical, "objective" culture: ancient Athens. "For the Athenians," Hegel wrote, "Athens had a double meaning, the totality of their institutions as well as the goddess which represented the spirit and the unity of the people."[3] In the *polis*, the Athenians maximized the free and conscious participation of individuals in a community with a coherent moral order. Hegel thus saw the polis, in Taylor's words, as the ideal of a community "which somehow combines the universal subjectivity of Socrates and Christ with the *Sittlichkeit*," insofar as it revealed "that dimension of our ethical obligations which are to a larger life which we have to sustain and continue."[4]

Gramsci evidently had something similar in mind, hence his tantalizing depiction of the modern prince as having "both the mass character of the Protestant Reformation or the French Enlightenment and the classical cultural character of Greek civilization or the Italian Renaissance." In expanding outward in its wider and wider dialectic, forging alliances with different groups in society in order to universalize its worldview and values, so that they eventually became—like Christianity or Islam—the perceptual substructure or "frame" for all (or at least most) of humankind—the prince would perceive itself, and be perceived by others, essentially as a *redemptive* force, one worthy of assuming "moral and intellectual" leadership of the society as a whole.

The postmodern prince, similarly, must be conceived from the start as a morally redemptive world historical movement, not simply as a "resistance" or "oppositional" movement (i.e., the negation of the negation). We might even say that just as Machiavelli's "Prince" prefigured Rousseau's notion of the "Lawgiver" who creates the moral conditions for the polity, Gramsci's "Modern Prince," as the socialist lawgiver who founds a new moral order or *Sittlichkeit* on the basis of socialized labor, prefigures the postmodern prince.

The trouble with such a formulation, of course, instantly shows itself. We have already begged the question of the *kind* of "moral order" at stake. One of the weaknesses of the left, in fact, has been its historical reluctance to declare itself openly as a *moral* and *spiritual* movement, hence to put forth a bold ontology and ethics of its own. Gramsci, like Marx, failed to specify the normative or ethical content of his "religious" vision, apart from socializing production through an ethical relation between leaders and led. But socialism cannot give us our ethics; our ethics gives us our socialism. That is, because our foundational moral beliefs and commitments define our perceptual objects for us, they play a crucial role in shaping the specific forms of action that we end up with. It is therefore important that we take care to spell these out.

What follows, then, is the most speculative and philosophical portion of this work. It represents an attempt to provide a critical sketch of or prolegomenon to the *positive* philosophy or ethic—or even "religion"—that could serve as the perceptual and moral "ground" for the unification of our many movements. In the framework I briefly develop here, the postmodern prince becomes the *form*, the political and phenomenal manifestation, of a *metahumanist* life philosophy. *Metahumanism* is the foundational ontology and ethical life-philosophy of the postmodern prince. It is the nascent, *historically immanent* philosophy of existing movements, as well as a "positive" normative framework that existing social movements *ought* to embrace and seek to universalize, a *Sittlichkeit* of the global civil society that must replace capitalist liberalism. In other words, it already "is" and *could become* (both at once) the *normative moral substratum* of all liberatory political action. Metahumanism provides us with the common philosophical (ontological) and spiritual (moral) basis for translating between "difference" and sameness, and for moving from what "is" to what "ought to be."

The neologism *metahumanism* intentionally conveys a contradiction or tension. By emphasizing metahumanism, I am suggesting that we must go "beyond" the anthropocentrism of the traditional liberal, humanist project. And this we can only do by incorporating the nonhuman other into our conception of "the human." This theme, which I develop through an outline of ethical practice grounded in attentiveness to *suffering*, is the main focus of this chapter. At the same time, by meta*humanism* I am also intentionally claiming a certain continuity with the Enlightenment, "progressive" tradition and ideal of a harmonious social order rooted in a positive account of our natural capacities and qualities as human beings.

Ontology has been in the news lately. Scientists have begun to arrogate to themselves godlike powers, creating entirely novel kinds of

species in the lab, inserting rogue DNA (taken from other plants or animals) directly into the ova of animals. New beings-in-the-world are being
summoned into existence by the cunning of Reason, "thrown" into an
alien and aseptic machine world where they typically arrive chronically
ill or disabled, disoriented, and utterly isolated from all other beings in
the universe. Still other scientists and entrepreneurs are reengineering
our own species being at the physical, genetic level, charting the human
genetic code in order to effect the ultimate reduction of the individual
human being—or "its" parts—to the status of a designer commodity.
Adorno once wrote: "In the midst of standardized, organized human
units the individual persists . . . . But he is in reality no more than the
mere function of his own uniqueness, an exhibition piece, like the fetus-
es that once drew the wonderment and laughter of children."[5] Now, even
the uniqueness of the human species has been put on display as an exhibition piece (the genome) and is threatened with extinction.

Meanwhile, in the Western academy, cultural studies theorists and
other academic intellectuals hold conferences celebrating our so-called
post-human times, singing the virtues of cyborgs, prosthetics, and bio-
engineering. Post-humanism is merely the latest in a string of commodity concepts spun off by academic industrialists to shore up the
crumbling appearance of use value in their work. Yet the significance
of the discourse, I think, is far greater than this alone would suggest.
With the arrival of post-humanism we may fast be approaching the
zero hour of the critical tradition. With the subject as such now placed
sous rature (under erasure), but this time not merely by clever critics but
by scientists who *literally* manipulate the stuff our dreams of ourselves
are made of, even the poststructuralist project self-destructs, as deconstruction is rendered irrelevant by the *fragmentation* of the ontological
unity of *Dasein*. This may seem a trivial point, but critical theory is
already dangerously in collusion with the final obliteration of all
things "human" by capital.

But no moral or political movement, it seems to me, that is unwill-
ing to declare itself to be in defense of *this being that we are—or that we
might become*, has any business calling itself liberationist. If critical
thought is to survive this implosion of theory, therefore, post-humanism will have to be met forthrightly—with a return to ontology and the
grounding of thought in a meaningful account of human being.

EMPATHY AND ATTENTIVENESS TO OTHERS

Ethical relations, broadly speaking, depend on what Daniel Brudney calls "attentiveness to the other."[6] Without this attentiveness, we risk mistaking a "who" for a "what"—that is, a being or subject for a thing—and so come to justify all manner of political violence. Without attentiveness to the other, neither the unity nor the moral purpose of the postmodern prince can be assured.

The basis of such an attentiveness to the other, I want to suggest, lies primarily in our ability to *empathize*. No theory of perception and totality would be complete without attending to the crucial *affective* dimensions of our existence as subjects and, in particular, to the ethical and political significance of *empathy*. This poses a certain problem for our analysis, however, since the role of sympathy in solidarity and the creation of the political community has in fact received little attention historically in modern political thought. Machiavelli set the tone for the tradition when he wrote that while few people know how to *feel* everyone knows how to *see*. In a way he was answering Plato's challenge in the early books of *The Republic*, where Socrates and his interlocutors spar over whether a man who merely *appears* to be just will be as likely to live as happily as the man who is *really* just. In Machiavelli's view, Plato's ideal of a convergence between politics and the good was just so much wishful thinking. What matters in political life, he argued, is *seeming*, not *being*—and not knowing the difference between the two will likely get a ruler, as well as all of us, his subjects, killed. To the extent that our praxis fails to take into account our nature as *perceiving* rather than inherently "reasonable" beings, in other words, we have no business constructing fancy theories of politics.

But though it is true that indifference to the phenomenal realm of appearances can be fatal to politics, the denigration of certain kinds of feeling in political life can also undermine the polity by legitimating ruthless state violence. In the masculinist, a.k.a. realist, tradition in political thought, two emotions above all others are ruled out of bounds by the theorist and strategist: empathy and love. While some radical theorists over the years have made *Mitgefühl* or "feeling with" others an integral part of their critical work—e.g., in Buddhist political thought, in the nonviolent philosophies of Gandhi and Martin Luther King, Jr., and in the contemporary theories of Marshall Rosenberg and feminist care ethics philosophers—it has been more characteristic of the radical tradition to view empathy with skepticism or outright hostility.[7]

Marxists have tended to view empathy as little more than a bourgeois convention—and a dangerous one at that. On the one hand, Marxism leaned rather heavily on "fellow feeling" among members of the working class as the practical basis of revolution. Yet despite the fact that he devoted his own life to working-class struggle, Marx apparently did not see the need to develop a theory of sympathy per se. Even the otherwise "soulful" Walter Benjamin could write of the "process of empathy whose origin is the indolence of the heart... which despairs of grasping and holding the genuine historical image as it flares up briefly."[8] Empathy—this powerful natural capacity of ours—must be held at bay, sublimated into the rationalist's passion for dispassion. Communists all over the world must therefore learn to "harden their hearts," like Pharoah, to the suffering of those who might interrupt the messianic time flow of revolution. But suppression of empathy, which arose historically out of the same masculinist ethos and instrumentalism as capitalism, is extremely dangerous. It is the same logic of control and violence that led Trotsky and Lenin to order the massacre of the striking Krondstadt sailors, that still allows nuclear war planners to prepare charts showing the efficient liquidation of hundreds of millions of human beings. Lenin's instrumental "hardness," the heroic "sacrifice" of his own emotional sensitivity on the altar of his revolution, led abruptly to the perversion of his humane dream of a world in which all people would realize freedom and happiness, and the eventual downfall of the very political and economic system he founded.[9]

But empathy, as a *mode of perception* in its own right, an "organ" enabling moral judgment, is a crucial missing link in existing social theories of praxis. As Johannes Vetlesen argues, in an important critique of Arendt's skepticism toward the intrusion of compassionate feeling in the political realm, empathy is a "sensuous-cognitive-emotional openness to the world" that "provides us with our principal mode of access to the domain of human experience."[10] For a subject to be capable of acting morally he or she must first be capable of *perceiving* a moral situation or dilemma.[11] And because attentiveness or "attunement" can be cultivated as well as thwarted, "the fostering of attentiveness and the creation of moral space is a social [and]... a political issue."[12]

Rumi, in his retelling of the tale of the men and the elephants, wrote: "Each of us touches one place / and understands the whole in that way." Rumi seems to be telling us that we gain ethical insight into the *true* nature of being, the condition of the world, only through feeling.

Perceiving the whole, it turns out, is not merely a matter of having or educating clear "sight." *Feeling* is the mystic's intuition; it is the "third eye" with which the initiate grasps the whole truth of divine Being. But only through an *affective* intersubjectivity, the sharing of "feeling" perspectives, does the whole reveal itself. Only from perception (as intentionality—as an apprehending, a temporal disposition toward) can moral judgment and action follow.

Some individuals come to the epiphany that injustice and oppression exist through personal acquaintance with oppression—i.e., personal suffering or embodied experience of unfreedom. However, there is only an indirect causal relationship between one's epistemology—and hence one's ability to perceive the whole—and one's social position. Not everyone who experiences oppression *understands* her own condition or situation in those terms (a condition of unfreedom). As feminist and critical race theorists now agree, one's "objective" location within a social hierarchy, or one's personal experience of oppression, is never, in itself, a sufficient condition for politicization.

But one's location in a subordinate position is in fact not even a *necessary* condition for critical insight; because solidarity, the phenomenological "glue" that holds together every movement, is constituted not only through "first-order" experiences of power, but also through "second-order" experiences—viz., through *empathy for those who suffer*. If to learn to "see" is to become "susceptible" to the world, to see morally means becoming susceptible to the *suffering* of others. Without this elemental and primordial capacity, "the phenomenon of 'suffering' would not be constituted as an object for moral judgment."[13] It is often by becoming susceptible to the suffering of others that our imaginative "sense" of or feeling for oppression develops: it is this that sets off the flash of cognitive and affective recognition that permits a wealthy individual (like Friederich Engels, say) to commit "class suicide" by advocating revolution, or a man to advocate the equality of women. There are many such cases of "sympathetic" political consciousness.[14]

Empathy appears to be essential in the constitution of every political identity, as well as a critical *moral* inhibition against violence. For although the ability to empathize with others is certainly no guarantee of solidarity, nor of ethical behavior, empathy can help us avoid some of the dangers inherent in political agonism. When we willfully deny empathy as a mode of access to human experience, we also blind ourselves to the outcomes and catastrophes of our own political judgments. Not only do we corrupt political life and cause needless suffering in the world, but we also subvert our ability to achieve our ends, whether those ends are "greatness" or universal social equality. Second, empathy must be highlighted in our theory of praxis because any *coalescence* of diverse movements—the core strategic concern of the postmodern prince—will be achieved only through the empathetic practice of listening to one another and working through the inevitable contradictions and prejudices that afflict every social movement. Empathy indeed proves to be the one emotion that makes the solidarity of the postmodern prince both *phenomenologically* and *politically* plausible.

As Santosh George observes, within the left one still finds "the all too evident baggage of racism, sexism, intolerance, dogmatism and obsolete thought and behavior patterns. What seems to persist is the inability of people to build and maintain consistent relationships and conversations [necessary] for ongoing strategic and tactical organizing." George writes:

> The task of the left in America is not just political or economical. It must be first and foremost psychological and social—i.e., it must start offering alternatives in practice and theory, to what is clearly the most insidious impediment to collective action—the fragmentation and atomization of society. As is clear from the experience of other left movements, the left displays within itself all the pathologies of larger society. While the left in America at least recognizes the need to be more democratic and inclusive. . . it needs to re-create the basis for social cohesion.[15]

Creating a practical basis for social cohesion within our movements will pose enormous personal and political challenges for all of us. What is essential in any process of "coalescence" is that everyone involved in such a process learn to be phenomenologically "attuned" to and respectful of the ontological reality of oppression, and to suffering, *as a totality*.

This last point is especially important. Empathy must be accepted and affirmed as part of our *modus vivendi* with the world. As such, it must not be manipulated or mobilized by a political directorate, nor subordinated to an ideology. That is, the object of our empathy must not be confined to concern *only* for other members in our own class, race, sex, or social group.[16] Empathy only approaches the transcendental and universal—that is, only approaches the power of a *faith*—when it is used to perceive the *totality* of suffering. Like political action itself, empathy must be boundless. This is because suffering "gestures" immanently toward universal moral significance. The significance of suffering, that is, is *primordial*. Suffering was the first *sign* indicating the first transcendental question—*Why?* The significance of my suffering transcends my self to implicate all other suffering beings. My suffering has an *ontological* significance that is prior to every *figurative* signification.

I take this to be the theological and ethical meaning behind Martin Luther King, Jr.'s famous phrase that "injustice anywhere is a threat to justice everywhere." Injustice, that is, is not morally objectionable because it "could happen to me" (i.e., that an injustice in one remote part of the world could spread to other places) but because at a profound, ontological level, *we are one* in our suffering as mortal, embodied beings. Subcommander Marcos, the charismatic spokesperson and unofficial poet of the Zapatista movement in Mexico, illuminated just this transcendental insight when he wrote, in what Marcos called a "majority-which-disguises-itself-as-untolerated-minority" postscript to one of his public communiqués:

> About this whole thing about whether Marcos is homosexual [an "allegation" the Mexican press had begun reporting]: Marcos is gay in San Francisco, black in South Africa, Asian in Europe, Chicano in San Isidro, Anarchist in Spain, Palestinian in Israel, an Indigenous in the streets of San Cristóbal . . . Jew in Germany, an ombudsman in the SEDNA [Department of Defense, Sedena], feminist in political parties, Communist in the post–Cold War era, prisoner in Cintalapa, pacifist in Bosnia, Mapuche in the Andes, teacher in CNTE [National Confederation of Educational Workers], artist without gallery or portfolio, housewife on any given Saturday night in any neighborhood of any city of any Mexico, *guerillero* in Mexico at the end of the twentieth century, striker in the [Mexican Workers' Confederation], sexist in the feminist movement, woman alone in the metro at 10 P.M., retired person in *plantón* in the Zócalo, campesino without land, fringe editor, unemployed worker, doctor without a practice, rebellious student, dissident in neoliberalism, writer without books or readers, and, to be sure, Zapatista in the Mexican Southeast. In sum, Marcos is a human being, any being, in this world. Marcos is all the minorities who are untolerated, oppressed, resisting, exploding, saying "Enough." All minorities at the moment they begin to speak and the majorities at the moment they fall silent and put up with it. All the untolerated people searching for a word, their word, which will return the majority to the eternally fragmented, us; all that makes power and good consciences uncomfortable, that is Marcos.[17]

With slight revisions, we might say that the floating signifier "Marcos" in this letter is also a sign for the political and *moral* unity of the post-modern prince. Like Walt Whitman's transcendental humanism in *Leaves of Grass*, which united the reader, the poet, and the suffering and joy of the world, Marcos's "poem" here moves us to answer globalization with the powerful "sight" given to us by our hearts: we "look out upon the world" and perceive the infinitely diverse face of human suffering and injustice.[18] It is out of the mutual recognition of this suffering that political unity is forged.

"Only sensuous beings affect one another," Feuerbach wrote. "I am an 'I' for myself and simultaneously a 'thou' for others. This I am, however, only as a sensuous being."[19] In such passages, Feuerbach prefigures existential phenomenologists like Husserl and Merleau-Ponty who, similarly breaking with the rationalism of Descartes, averred that we are not merely thinking beings but are also and even primarily "really existing beings."[20] Marx agreed with Feuerbach that our essence is a sensuous essence, but came to strikingly different conclusions, arguing that ideas and sentiments are *historically* constructed—that they arise out of material contradictions in society—and hence that our self-transformation and self-overcoming can only be achieved, and understood, in terms of actual historical struggle.

"To be sensuous is to *suffer*," Marx wrote. "Man as an objective, sensuous being is therefore a *suffering* being—and because he feels what he suffers, a *passionate* being. Passion is the essential force of man energetically bent on its object."[21] Man "as a natural corporeal, sensuous, objective being...is a *suffering*, conditioned and limited creature, like animals and plants."[22] As Marx wrote:

> Each of man's *human* relations to the world—seeing, hearing, smelling, tasting, feeling, thinking, being aware, sensing, wanting, acting, loving—in short, all the organs of his individual being, like those organs which are directly social in their form, are in their... *orientation to the object*, the appropriation of that object, the appropriation of the *human* world; their orientation is the *manifestation of the human world*; it is human *efficaciousness* and human *suffering*, for suffering, apprehended humanly, is an enjoyment of self in man.[23]

According to Marx, our bodies make us *natural* beings. On the other hand, our transcendence of this suffering, "animal" nature *makes us fully human.* Nature *is* our own body, hence our work upon nature effects the reconciliation of our own subject and object sides. To Marx, "nature"—and he includes in this category all other animal beings—is a *moment* within human species being.

While Feuerbach and Marx set out from real, sensuous existence in constructing their critical philosophies, however, both neglected to dwell on the significance of the fact that *we are not the only sensuous beings.* But if I am right, that empathy must seek the totality of suffering in order to approach the universal, then we must consistently attend the suffering of *all* others, *all* suffering beings.

HUMANISM, SUFFERING, AND LOVE

If I suffer, it is only because I am a creature capable of suffering—in other words, that I am "ensouled" and animal (from the Greek, *anima* or "soul"). Hence the *ethical* flaw in Marx's foundation—his reduction of *sensuous existence* to a *single* modality of sensuous being-in-the- world.

The problem with all previous iterations of humanism, including Marx's, is that they "see" only *human* suffering. Each, that is, assume the human subject as the sole, originary basis of meaning and value. This metaphysical conceit can be found, in crude form, in the thought of the ancient Greeks. But humanism as we conceive it today achieved its first full *philosophical* articulation in the thought of the Renaissance thinker, Pico della Mirandola. In his *Oratio de hominis dignitate* (On the Dignity of Man), Pico presented three ontological orders of being: the supercelestial, the human, and the animal. In this hierarchy, human beings are infinitely closer to the divine than to the animal. Although ostensibly we are the mediate being, the "metaphysical center," our animal nature is inessential to us. "As brutes are born, they bring with them . . .what they are going to possess," while "man" is "the molder and maker" of himself. "Who does not wonder at this chameleon that we are?" Pico asks. As God tells Adam, "'In conformity with thy free judgment. . . thou art confined by no bounds; and thou *wilt fix nature for thyself.*'"[24] This is not to say that we have no essence, however. Our essence lies in our ability to reason. And because divinity is immanent in reason, reason brings us into direct proximity with the divine.[25]

Pico's tripartite ontology, which dates in various forms at least as far back as ancient Judaic myth, would subtend much of the "critical" philosophy of the nineteenth and twentieth centuries. Subsequent versions of humanism all concur with Pico on one point, viz.. that the human being is unique and superior. Either because "he" is made in the image of God (his reason reflects divine essence), or because he alone possesses moral autonomy (Kant), or because he is an unfinished project and universal "species being" (Marx), or because he alone is a "nothingness," a being for whom existence precedes essence (Sartre).

Feuerbach argued that God was the inversion of humankind's true essence, a projection of our capacity for self-making onto an abstract concept of pure reason. Only in grounding "God" materially, thus, could theology be brought down to earth. The "new philosophy," he wrote, "declares that only the human is the rational; man is the measure of reason";[26] "whereas the old philosophy declared that only the rational is the true and real, the new philosophy... declares that only the human is true and real, for only the human is the rational; man is the measure of reason."[27] Marx subsequently took up Feuerbach's ontology of the "divine" nature of human reason—i.e., as self-originating, *sui generis*, essential—and transformed it radically but in ways that nonetheless preserved the humanist conceit of *Homo sapiens* as a being whose ontological significance lay in its *transcendent* essence, i.e., its *autonomy* from "mere" animal nature. According to Marx, the existing forces and conditions of production make it impossible for us to realize our *human* nature. We are stuck, as it were, with animal habits and ways of being. The significance of a world socialist revolution would therefore be to free our bodies and minds from their "animal" desires and qualities (biological needs) and, in effect, transform our animal senses into fully "human" ones. "But man is not merely a natural being: he is a *human* natural being. That is to say, he is a being for himself. Therefore he is a *species being*, and has to confirm and manifest himself as such both in his being and in his knowing."[28]

Marx's "species being" was in fact indistinguishable from what Mary Midgely terms "species solipsism," the metaphysical narcissistic disorder that causes us to forget that we are not alone on the earth. In this narcissism of literally cosmic proportions, we empty the universe of all nonhuman sentience and consciousness. While Marx rejected Feuerbach's grounding of "rational theology" of anthropology, claiming to have discovered a "scientific" basis in the dialectical conflict between classes throughout history, in presenting the human species as the only universal species being—i.e., the only being whose being allowed it to transcend itself—Marx nonetheless placed the human being at the center of a "theology" of his own. As Gramsci, who followed Marx uncritically in this regard, wrote in a letter to his wife, Giulia: "God is none other than a metaphor to indicate the ensemble of human beings organized for mutual aid."[29]

In many ways, this is a lovely sentiment. Certainly it represented an improvement over the liberal humanist ontology of the isolated, self-made individual. Yet it also indicates how trapped even "Western" Marxists like Gramsci were in the same solipsism that also lay at the foundation of bourgeois political economy. Marx accepted uncritically Feuerbach's assertion that, "the essence of man is contained only in the community and unity of man with man"; that "man for himself is man" and that "man with man ... is God."[30] In his conception, "species being" was to be realized in a conversation between the different selves of a *single* sovereign subject ("man"). By accepting Feuerbach's humanist notion that "man for himself is man," Marx effected the extermination in the realm of thought of the *sensuous existence, and experiences, of billions of other suffering beings-in-the-world* on earth.

What Marx failed to come to terms with was the *ontological* rather than the merely biological implications of Darwinism. According to Darwin, *Homo sapiens* was not *qualitatively* different, biologically and evolutionarily speaking, from other animal species. This assertion of biological continuity, however, could not but imply a firm refutation of Judeo-Christian ontotheology. The revolutionary historical significance of Darwin's *Descent of Man* lay here, in its systematic, empirically grounded delinking of human being from divine being. Although he was probably unaware of it, Darwin essentially confirmed what Pythagoras had believed several thousands of years before, namely that "we are all kin under the skin," that human beings and animal beings are *ontologically* similar, or similar in their essence. But Marx misplaced Darwin's insight that we evolved in a harmonious, dialectical dance with other natural beings, other beings-in-the-world.

If Marx—and most other commentators of Darwin at the time and since—misapprehended the true significance of Darwin's theory, however, he also failed to see how he might have corrected Feuerbach's "one-sided" humanism by clarifying Feuerbach's theory of *love*. In *Philosophy of the Future* Feuerbach wrote: "Being as an object of being—and only this being is being and deserves the name of being—is the being of the senses, feeling, and love. Being is thus a secret of perception, of feeling, and of love."[31] Love is what gives us our attachment to the world, but more than this, it is that which *gives us* "world" or "being" in the first place. "Love is passion, and only passion is the hallmark of existence. *Only that exists which is an object . . . of passion.*" And in loving ourselves, i.e., as "man," we truly become who we are, which is a being for which every object is an object of love *for ourselves.* In loving, we approach divinity. "Only in feeling and in love does 'this'—as in 'this person' or 'this object,' that is, the particular—have absolute value and is the finite the infinite; in this alone, and only in this, is the infinite depth, divinity, and truth of love constituted. Only in love is God . . . truth and reality. The Christian God is himself only an abstraction of human love and an image of it."[32] Only through *love*, by which Feuerbach meant realization of the intersubjective, *human* realm of "I" and "thou," could we realize our true potential.

Marx, however, disregarded Feuerbach's comments on the phenomenology of love and its relevance for human practice. Socialist theory consequently lost sight of the significance of the fact that we have *suffering*, and *the urge for companionship* (*eros*) in common with all other animal beings. Marx, like Nietzsche (who wrote with undisguised contempt of the "animal" instinct for the proximity and warmth of others—the stupid "herd," the lowly mice in a nest, etc.) at times seemed to denigrate *eros*. "The savage and the animal have at least the need to hunt, to roam, etc.—the need for companionship," he wrote. "Machine labor is simplified in order to make a worker out of the human being still in the making, the completely immature human being—the *child*."[33] Human culture goes through natural stages until it evolves (through dialectical conflict) from the "primitive" affect of companionship to the fully "human" panoply of senses that would take "man" himself, man "as a whole," as its final object.

The main consequence of this oversight was to distort the trajectory of collective action and social theory for the next century. Had Marx not rejected philosophy for empirical science, he might have perceived the possibility of a convergence between several different social movements in his century—socialism, abolitionism, feminism, and animal welfare. For, by the end of the nineteenth century, feminists like Charlotte Perkins Gilman and radicals like Henry Salt had begun to theorize, and practice, a synthesis of the many different forms of resistance. Alas, Marx and others were quick to see in such efforts only misguided, utopian, "bourgeois" efforts for reform.[34]

Only in the last quarter-century, in fact, with the emergence of the environmental, animal rights, and feminist movements, have philosophers, and activists at last begun to make progress in untangling the raft of ontological and hence *moral* errors that have marred the critical tradition. In decentering the human subject and exposing the collusion between "speciesism" and other ideologies of domination, social critics have begun to erode—at least in the realm of *thought*—the patriarchal ontotheological framework of millennia. For example, critics show empirically how the Holocaust and other modern catastrophes of cruelty were discursively, materially, and even technologically modeled on the human domination and killing of other animals.[35] Vegetarian ecofeminists, meanwhile, have made great strides toward the creation of a *new theoretical synthesis* to serve the twin goals of grounding critique in a new view of the whole while also presenting a positive ethical framework for guiding practice. Carol Adams, for example, has shown how ontologies of racism and sexism merge with, and emerge historically from, a "beastly theology" that has placed *male* human being closer to the divine than to the feminine and the animal.[36] Josephine Donovan, meanwhile, turns to Max Scheler's phenomenology of sympathy to develop a feminist care ethics grounded in attentiveness to nonhuman animal suffering.[37]

As these feminist critics have shown, what racism, patriarchy, and other systems of social domination have in common is an ideological metaphysic (or *episteme*, in Foucault's terms) rooted in the humiliation of *animal being*—renunciation of our own animal natures. In Marxist discourse much is made of the "reconciliation" of nature and culture once production is socialized. But true reconciliation cannot be found in Marx's philosophy, which instrumentally reduces nature to our own "body" as human beings. Reconciliation can only be found in the *re-enchantment* of the natural world—the discovery of the rich experiences, lifeworlds, and cultures of the nonhuman beings with whom we share the earth, and whose lifeworlds overlap with our own. Only in so transforming our relations with animal others can we have hope to effect a radical transformation in *human* social relations.[38]

NEW GNOSIS

Metahumanism represents the attempt to overcome the ontological category mistake at the heart of Western culture, viz., the reduction of other subjects, other modalities of being-in-the-world, to the status of things. Only by overcoming this category mistake, which has systematically rendered other species beings absent, *occluded* the "thickness" of nonhuman being-in-the-world, and depopulated the world of animal others in order to effect the designs of instrumental reason, can a qualitatively new *human* society, one founded on nonviolent and noncoercive institutions and norms, be envisioned.

One of the hallmarks of modernity is rationalization, the progressive reduction of the lifeworld to quantifiable procedures and methods. But in stripping nature of its mystery, Enlightenment disfigured the nonhuman. This, in turn, has led to our own disfigurement, as "disenchantment" as technological innovation and the scientific revolution yielded ever more powerful ways of controlling human beings, and not "only" other animals.39 Metahumanism, hence, is a dis-closing of actual Being—the education of our sensuous perceptions. This dis-closing is made available to us not only through reason, but also through feeling; through empirical science, but also through "myth." That is, it is a normative ethics, a leap through *immanence* to a *transcendental* faith and love, which "gives us" our empirical objects. I am not speaking of a return to superstition, but rather the recovery of what was true in the sacred all along, viz., the irreducible, *qualitative* manifold of being-in-the-world—that which can never be rendered homogeneous, or emptied of meaning, without unleashing a great violence against nature, and upon ourselves.

In *Love's Body*, Norman O. Brown called for a "return" to gnosis—that is, a return to an intuitive, mystical way of knowing, a fusion of nature and language, human and cosmos. But metahumanism is to be construed rather as the inversion of *gnosis*, the spiritualism of the early Christian mystics, insofar as it roots our being in our animal body, rather than in language. In this sense, metahumanism seeks to purge the divine from the human in order to rediscover *the divine in the animal*. In this *new* gnosis is the incipient form of a religion of immanence rather than transcendence, or rather, a transcendence through *consciousness* of immanence. The gnosis of metahumanism disoccludes, *reveals*, the language of nonhuman experience—the language in which the sufferings and pleasures of the body itself become the ground of all meaning. Its advent signifies the reversal of the Abrahamic religious conception of the human soul, and returns us to the ancient view of soul not as "mind" but as *anima* or "spirit": affirmation of "the soul," here understood as the irreducibly singular manifold of the living being-in-the-world, becomes the basis of defense of all "species beings" against oppression and domination. It is *love*, love for those who suffer in *this* world, that gives meaning to all metahumanist forms of practice. Love of embodied, sensuous being binds together the seemingly "different" movements and causes, e.g., bringing those seeking to democratize the means of production in harmony with those who would free animals from their cages and slaughterhouses, or those who would liberate themselves from the tyranny of the male gaze.

Such an embodied ethics is suggested in the pivotal scene in Toni Morrison's book *Beloved*, when the matriarch of a freed slave family, Baby Suggs, addresses her family in a clearing in the woods:

> "Here," she said, "in this here place, we flesh; flesh that weeps, laughs; flesh that dances on bare feet in grass. Love it. Love it hard. Yonder they do not love your flesh. They despise it. . . . And O my people they do not love your hands. Love your hands! Love them. Raise them up and kiss them. Touch others with them, pat them together, stroke them on your face 'cause they don't love that either. You got to love it, you! And no, they ain't in love with your mouth. . . . No, they don't love your mouth. You got to love it. This is flesh I'm talking about here. Flesh that needs to be loved. Feet that need to rest and to dance; backs that need support; shoulders that need arms, strong arms I'm telling you. . . . So love your neck; put a hand on it, grace it, stroke it and hold it up. And all your inside parts that they'd just as soon slop for hogs, you got to love them. The dark, dark liver—love it, love it, and the beat and beating heart, love that too. More than lungs that have yet to draw free air. More than your life-loving womb and your life-giving parts, hear me now, love your heart. For this is the prize." Saying no more, she stood up and danced with her twisted hip the rest of what her heart had to say.[40]

In this passage Morrison effectively ontologizes freedom. By "locating" freedom in the body and the heart, she implies that love and the simple pleasures of sensual embodiment, not only moral autonomy or reason, are constitutive of freedom. To speak of "ownership" of the freed self means not, as it does in slavery, economic ownership, but ownership in the phenomenological, embodied sense of "having" the world. There is no human freedom in separateness or aloneness; the free human being is not so much a social animal as an animal who is "loved thoroughly" by others. The meaning of the word *freedom* is thus revealed to be nothing more than the state of "being beloved." In Sanskrit, *freedom* in fact derives from the word *beloved*, the condition of being among one's loved ones. The escape from slavery depicted by Morrison in her novel is nothing other than the escape into freedom as *love*, that is, fierce attachment to the "this" of the world, to embodied being, through a community that enables love-of-self (sensuous existence). It is *love* of embodied, sensuous being, the "mere animal" love of affection, companionship, sexual ecstasy, the joy of being alive, that ultimately stands behind *every* emancipatory struggle, every social movement, every conscious action undertaken in the name of liberation.

But the grounding state of *Mitsein*, or being-with-others, is not limited to human-human relationships but pervades all human-nonhuman and nonhuman-nonhuman relations. Recent empirical research in cognitive ethology, comparative psychology, biology, neurology, and a variety of other scientific fields has confirmed what critics of human domination of animals have said for many centuries, which is that other animals are not qualitatively different from us in their emotional, genetic, or psychological makeup. Humans are not the only beings on earth capable of speaking, transmitting culture, using tools, thinking, or experiencing happiness, love, or trauma. The philosophical, political, and moral implications of this new research—research, it must be noted, which has only arisen because of the ecological and animal rights movements, which in turn only arose out of heightened "attunement" to animal suffering and modes of being-in-the-world—are truly staggering. If taken seriously, they would require an epochal shift in our conception of ourselves *ontologically*, to say nothing of overturning most existing forms of economic production, culture, and science.

As a "new" humanistic religion, or rather, a *meta*-religion, an *eco-ontology*, metahumanism must be rooted in the phenomenology of experience of *de anima* as such. Only in this way can praxis seek genuine (though always imperfect, incomplete) reconciliation between human and nonhuman, immanence and transcendence. We might compare such a praxis to a "song" of re-enchantment—a singing that is also a listening, through dis-closing of animal being-in-the-world.[41] In Kabbalist thought, the true mystic is a cantor of the cosmos, one whose song reaches out to embrace a wider and wider unity of self and other:

> There is one who sings the song of his soul, discovering in his soul everything— utter spiritual fulfillment.

There is one who sings the song of his people. Emerging from the private circle of his soul—not expansive enough, not yet tranquil—he strives for fierce heights, clinging to the entire community of Israel in tender love. . . .

Then there is one whose soul expands until it extends beyond the border of [nation and people], singing the song of humanity. In the glory of the human race, in the glory of the human form, his spirit spreads, aspiring to the goal of humankind, envisioning its consummation. From this spring of life, he draws all his deepest reflections, his searching, striving, and vision.

Then there is one who expands even further until he unites with all of existence, with all creatures, with all worlds, singing a song with them all.

There is one who ascends with all these songs in unison—the song of the soul, the song of the nation, the song of humanity, the song of the cosmos—resounding together, blending in harmony, circulating the sap of life, the sound of holy joy.[42]

We are divine, in the end, not because we are made in the image of a rational God, but because "God" exists at that moment when Being knows itself—touches itself—and hears its own "song." The realm of the *metahuman* is revealed not as the movement of World Spirit, but the movement of "body spirit" as it comes to "know" itself and the other through feeling and thought—i.e., empathetic attunement to and reflection on the manifold of sensory experience and consciousness. In replacing the ontotheological story of transcendence with this onto-poetic story of immanence and the reenchantment of nature, we would open ourselves to the divine within the *animal other*. "When somebody's presence does really make itself felt," Gabriel Marcel wrote, "it can refresh my inner being; it reveals me to myself."[43] Only by attending to animal *presence* might we awaken within ourselves a healthy form of self-love—a love for the kind of being we *could* become. Only by attending to the monsters we make of ourselves in inflicting ceaseless and unspeakable brutality and violence against the minds and bodies of other sensitive beings-in- the-world, might we begin to construct a new narrative about who and what we are. Reenchantment of nature in this way leads to the reenchantment of ourselves, which is the revelation that we ourselves are worthy of love, once we forsake the domination of other suffering beings.

THE FIGHT FOR EROS

Through metahumanism, the postmodern prince reveals that its basis is not just historical or "material," e.g., the expressive manifestation of contradictions in the structure of capitalism, but also ontological. Its basis, that is, lies in the telos of *all* living organisms toward freedom and love. Existentially and ontologically, the postmodern prince is the phenomenal form of the unconscious striving of being-in-the-world toward fullness of being, a striving manifested in the perpetual ethical dialectic between autonomy and solidarity, self and other. The frustration of this impulse, wrongly identified as "will to power" in Nietzsche's naturalistic ontology, but in reality nothing other than *eros*, is the source of all alienation and suffering. The ultimate spiritual or "religious" objective of a postmodern prince is to defend this *eros*, the life principle, from every social deformation rooted in *thanatos*, the death-drive. (For what are existing social movements but differing, partial manifestations of *eros*, the *will to life*?) It is in defense of being—"being," understood, however, not as Absolute but as *this* being-in-the-world, *this* suffering animal— that socialists struggle to vanquish capitalism, or that women join ranks to challenge the privileges and power of men. But metahumanism is not *merely* affirmation of the wonder of sensuous being. It is a vigorous ethic and a passionate *politics* to defend the lifeworld. "Today the fight for life, the fight for Eros, is the *political* fight."44

EPILOGUE

Although many things caused Antonio Gramsci anguish in prison, continual reflection on the left's costly mistakes in Italy must have brought him especially acute suffering. He had enough time on his hands to rue, especially, the so-called Livorno Split between socialists and communists, which had effectively reduced the Italian working class to its former status as "dispersed, isolated, a collection of individuals without any consciousness of class unity."[1] Throughout the late 1920s and early 1930s, as Mussolini's forces of reaction consolidated their hold, were rebuffed, then returned stronger than before, socialist theory and practice in Italy as elsewhere were increasingly distorted by the paranoid, authoritarian, and bureaucratic style of Stalin's Comintern. The Italian working class, bereft of an effective leadership that could help them express their needs and aspirations in a focused way, were eventually crushed by capital or incorporated into the fascist state. In Italy, Spain, Germany, and Japan—places where the left had failed to organize autonomous movements of their own, or to respond decisively to the rise of militarist nationalism by the colonial "have-nots"—the extreme right triumphed. The ensuing global catastrophe consumed many millions of lives and broke the back of the modern colonial world system.

Today, as in Gramsci's time, the most reactionary elements are emboldened and again on the move, while our own movements are dispersed, isolated, and agonizingly short of hope. Yet the dangers faced by socialists like Gramsci in the 1930s pale in comparison to those we face in the present. Ecological and economic emergencies of staggering proportions increasingly confound liberal remedy. Half of the world's human population barely subsist, while the greatest transfer of wealth from the poor to the rich in modern times accelerates. Tens of millions of people have become permanent refugees, forced by regional wars and economic depression into impoverished camps. Meanwhile, the warming of the earth's atmosphere, a gift bequeathed to humanity from the petrochemical industry, is shrinking the polar ice caps, a development that threatens a catastrophic rise in sea levels and regional droughts, inundating entire nations and destabilizing the world economic and political order (according to one report commissioned by the U.S. Department of Defense). Global warming has already led to mass plant and animal extinctions, and 2003 produced the hottest summer in five hundred years in Europe. The great coral reefs are dying. Commercial exploitation of the seas has removed whole chunks of the great oceanic food chain.

Faced with this apocalypse in the making, some critics in the industrialized world have cautioned prudence, and asked us to scale back our dreams. *El sueño de la razon produces monstruos*: the dreams, and slumber, of reason produces monsters. And no dream of reason produced such nightmares as the socialist dream of Babel. That dream, of a universal solidarity, led to catastrophe. Today's politics must therefore be a "struggle . . . against perfect communication, against the one code that translates all meaning perfectly."[2] And there is a grain of truth to this. It is true that human beings will never "again" speak in the same tongue. Translation is always an imperfect hermeneutics, and misunderstandings abound. No movement, no human society, can reconcile all conflicts, all antagonisms. Nor can any method or theory ever provide a complete and "apodictic" (logically necessary and certain) description of the whole, of the totality. Indeed, the desire to know the whole is an insatiable and destructive desire that derives from the illusion of the possibility of "certainty" fetishized by Descartes and by those who invented the modern scientific method. Late in his career, before his sudden and untimely death of a heart attack at the age of fifty-three, Merleau-Ponty wrote: "Politics is never able to see the whole directly. It is always aiming at the incomplete synthesis, a given cycle of time, or a group of actions. It is not a pure morality, nor is it a chapter in a universal history which has already been written. Rather it is an action in the process of self-invention."[3] Human knowledge, in other words, is at best asymptotic, approaching truth but never reaching it.

Yet this fact need not condemn us to relativism. Some viewpoints are more truthful than others, and in order to pursue ethical action in the world, a perspectival grasp of totality is entirely sufficient for the purposes of ethical and strategic action. Nor does abandoning the quest for a mythical "perfect" communication mean that we must abandon the search for *imperfect* unity and mutual comprehension. As Subcommandante Marcos declared in August 1994, addressing a massive international conference organized and hosted by the Zapatistas at Aguascalientes, in a rain forest in Chiapas, to discuss the crisis of democracy in Mexico and to chart the next strategies of the Mexican and global left:

> Aguascalientes, Chiapas: Noah's Ark, the Tower of Babel, Fitzcarraldo's jungle boat, neozapatista pipedream, a pirate ship; an anachronistic paradox, the tender madness of the faceless....

> One sits on the painful threshold of history to lament that which prudence now demands: the constant pain of doing nothing, of waiting, of despairing.... [But we] said that there was more than enough time, that what we lacked was shame at our own fear of trying to be better, that the problem of the Tower of Babel was not in the project itself, but rather the absence of a good system linking people up, and a team of translators.... The failure was the weak attempt itself, sitting by and watching how the Tower went up, how it was supported, how it fell down. The failure was in sitting by and waiting to see what history would say.... 4

> ... [Before] Aguascalientes, we said that the fear, the seductive terror that gushes from the sewers of power and has nourished us since birth, could be and should be put to one side.... That the fear of being just spectators should be greater than the fear of trying to find common ground, trying to find something that would unite us, something that would transform this comedy into history.

> [Before] Aguascalientes, we said that the differences that divide us and turn us against one another will not prevent us from uniting against a common enemy: the system of abuses so open and obvious that they make us impotent.

> ... That's why thousands of men and women, with their faces covered, the vast majority of them indigenous people, raised this tower, the tower of hope.

With his *Prison Notebooks*, Gramsci invited us to construct such a tower of hope—laboriously, patiently, but without any guarantees. He left us not with a blueprint showing us *what* to build, only some practical suggestions for *how* to build: how to translate between one "tongue" or mode of historical experience and another, how to break ground together, how to lay a foundation deep enough to support the "unbearable lightness" of a truly universal project. In the falling dusk of history it is hard to see what strategies we ought to pursue, and harder still to discern the shape of the tower we need, and perhaps ache, to build. Historical experience must be our lamp. But love must be our flame.

NOTES

INTRODUCTION

1 Tony Kushner, *Angels in America: A Gay Fantasia on National Themes, Part Two: Perestroika* (New York: Theatre Communications Group, 1994), pp. 13–14.

2 See also Jean-Marie Guéhanno, *The End of the Nation-State* (Minneapolis: University of Minnesota Press, 1995).

3 Leo Panitch and Colin Leys, eds., *The New Imperial Challenge*, Socialist Register 2004 (London: Merlin Press, 2003); Chalmers Johnson, *The Sorrows of Empire: Militarism, Secrecy, and the End of the Republic* (New York: Metropolitan Books, 2004).

4 Immanuel Wallerstein, *Utopistics* (New York: The New Press, 1998), p. 82.

5 Immanuel Wallerstein, *After Liberalism* (New York: The New Press, 1995), p. 44.

6 Ibid., p. 218.

7 G. W. F. Hegel, *Reason in History* (New York: Macmillan, 1953), p. 51.

8 Fyodor Dostoevsky, *The Brothers Karamazov* (New York: Modern Library, 1949), p. 26.

9 George Steiner, *After Babel: Aspects of Language and Translation* (New York: Oxford University Press, 1977), p. 60.

10 Daniel Brudney, *Marx's Attempt to Leave Philosophy* (Cambridge, Mass.: Harvard University Press, 1998).

11 Steiner, *After Babel*, p. 60 (original emphasis).

12 See Carl Boggs, *The End of Politics* (New York: Guilford Press, 2001).

13 Lydia Sargent, "The Big Picture," *Z Magazine* 2:4 (1993): 4, 6.

14 "It is now high time that the Movement bring together its many fragments in a single new national coalition powerful enough to stand up to the Machine.... While retaining its identity, each participating group must yield to the effectiveness of unity and single purpose and set aside divisive idiosyncrasies." ("Unite for Survival," Architects/Designers/Planners for Social Responsibility, *Nuclear Times*, mid-1980s). See also Andrea Ayvazian and Michael Klare, "The Choice: Decision Time for the American Peace Movement," *Fellowship*, Sept. 1986, and Bruce Birchard and Rob Leavitt, "A New Agenda," *Nuclear Times*, Nov./Dec. 1987, p. 12). "There must be room for focused issue activity, but

there must also be coordination and acceptance among all concerns in a multi-issue approach. We must be able to plan campaigns . . . that have clearly defined objectives." (Tom Wall, "Strategy and Tactics for the Grassroots Peace Movement," Nashua Peace Center, *The Drinking Gourd* 4, no. 11 [Nov. 1985]: 10). "Perhaps the term 'people of color' could be the basis of a new strategic unity" (Manning Marable, "A New Black Politics," *The Progressive*, August 1990, p. 23; in the same issue, see also Charlotte Bunch, "Against All Forms of Domination," p. 21). "Unless we can coalesce on something outside our own special interests, we in the gay community will remain an island unto ourselves" (Scott MacLarty, "Out There," *In These Times*, Nov. 14, 1994, p. 27). "[A] radical movement . . . needs an analysis broader than sexual orientation alone, and this analysis is one we have yet to define. We have yet to explain—beyond pronouncement—how or why race, gender, sexuality, economic inequality and oppression of all kinds are connected, and how movements based around them require a common strategy. Lesbians of color helped invent multiculturalism in an attempt to provide such an analysis. But the doctrine has come to be defined by its backlash. . . . We need clear-headed theorists and artists to articulate, in common people's language, our common vision" (Urvashi Vaid, "We Can Get There from Here," *The Nation*, July 5, 1993, p. 31).

15 Feliz Guattari and Daniel Cohn-Bendit, "Contribution pour le mouvement," in *Autogestion, l'Alternative* (November 1986), quoted in Luc Ferry, *The New Ecological Order* (Chicago: University of Chicago Press, 1995), pp. 112–13 (emphasis added).

16 Benedetto Fontana, *Hegemony and Power: On the Relation between Gramsci and Machiavelli* (Minneapolis: University of Minnesota Press, 1993), p. 13.

17 Antonio Gramsci, *Selections from the Prison Notebooks*, ed. Quentin Hoare (New York: International Publishers, 1971), p. 129. Hereafter, *SPN*.

18 Terry Eagleton, *The Illusions of Postmodernism* (Cambridge, UK: Basil Blackwell, 1996), p. 134.

19 David Harvey, *The Condition of Postmodernity* (Cambridge, MA: Blackwell, 1990).

20 Stephen Gill, *Power and Resistance in the New World Order* (New York: Palgrave, 2003), p. 221. The concluding chapter of Gill's book, "Toward a Post-Modern Prince," appeared first as "Toward a Postmodern Prince? The Battle in Seattle as a Moment in the New Politics of Globalisation," *Millennium: Journal of International Studies* 29:1 (2000), pp. 131–40.

21 Gill, *Power and Resistance in the New World Order*, p. 218.

22 Gramsci, *SPN*, p. 133.

CHAPTER 1

1 Sheldon Wolin, "Paradigms and Political Theories," in *Politics and Experience: Essays Presented to Michael Oakeshott*, ed. Preston King and B. C. Parekh (Cambridge: Cambridge University Press, 1968), p. 143.

2   Massimo Teodori, ed., *The New Left: A Documentary History* (Indianapolis, Ind.: Bobbs-Merrill, 1969), p. 37.

3   Ibid., pp. 36–37.

4   Ibid., p. 79.

5   Ibid., p. 80.

6   Raymond Williams, *Marxism and Literature* (Oxford: Oxford University Press, 1977), p. 132.

7   Nigel Young, *An Infantile Disorder? The Crisis and Decline of the New Left* (London: Routledge and Kegan Paul, 1977), p. 39.

8   Charles Taylor, *Hegel and Modern Society* (Cambridge: Cambridge University Press, 1979), pp. 1–2.

9   Charles Taylor, *Sources of the Self: The Making of the Modern Identity* (Cambridge, Mass.: Harvard University Press, 1989), p. 372.

10 J. G. Fichte, *The Science of Knowledge*, ed. Peter Heath and John Lachs (Cambridge: Cambridge University Press, 1982), p. 6. Quoted in Bob Fitch, *On Nietzsche: The First Philosopher of the Last Man* (ca. 1998), unpublished manuscript, p. 9.

11 Taylor, *Sources of the Self*, p. 374.

12 Taylor, *Hegel*, p. 2.

13 Taylor, *Sources of the Self*, pp. 496–97; see also p. 373.

14 Cf. Teodori, *The New Left*, p. 49.

15 Tom Hayden, quoted in *Participatory Democracy*, ed. T. E. Cook and P. N. Morgan, (New York: Harper and Row, 1971), cited by Young, *An Infantile Disorder?* p. 39.

16 See Young, *An Infantile Disorder?* pp. 44–46; cf. Josephine Donovan, *Feminist Theory: The Intellectual Traditions of American Feminism* (New York: Continuum, 1985), p. 152.

17 Daniel Guerin, *Anarchism* (New York: Monthly Review Press, 1970), p. 28.

18 Theodore Roszak, *The Making of a Counter-Culture: Reflections on the Technocratic Society and Its Youthful Opposition* (New York: Doubleday, 1969), p. 91.

19 Cf. Port Huron Statement (June 15, 1962), in James Miller, *"Democracy Is in the Streets": From Port Huron to the Siege of Chicago* (New York: Simon and Schuster, 1987), p. 332.

20 Mario Savio, "Free Speech," text of an address given during a sit-in held in Berkeley, 1964, reprinted in Teodori, *The New Left*, p. 161.

21 Daniel Cohn-Bendit, "Daniel Cohn-Bendit, Interviewed by Jean-Paul Sartre," in *The Student Revolt: The Activists Speak*, ed. Hervé Bourges (London: Panther Books, 1968).

22 Alain Touraine, *The May Movement: Revolt and Reform* (New York: Random House, 1971), p. 242.

23 Alfred Willener, *The Action-Image of Society: On Cultural Politicization* (New York: Pantheon Books, 1970), p. 195.

24 Ibid., p. 87.

25 Ibid., p. 90.

26 Cohn-Bendit, "Daniel Cohn-Bendit, Interviewed by Jean-Paul Sartre," p. 102.

27 Maurice Isserman, *If I Had a Hammer: The Death of the Old Left and the Birth of the New Left* (Urbana, Ill.: University of Illinois Press, 1987), p. 177.

28 Teodori, *The New Left*, p. 36.

29 Ibid., p. 79.

30 Bourges, *The Student Revolt*, p. 13.

31 Teodori, *The New Left*, p. 471.

32 Herbert Marcuse, "On the New Left," a talk given at the twentieth anniversary celebration of *The Guardian* newspaper, reprinted in Teodori, *The New Left*, p. 472 (emphasis added).

33 See David E. Apter and James Joll, eds., *Anarchism Today* (New York: Doubleday, 1971), especially Apter's "The Old Anarchism and the New—Some Comments," pp. 1–3.

34 Bourges, *The Student Revolt*, p. 11.

35 Cf. Paul Lyons, *New Left, New Right, and the Legacy of the Sixties* (Philadelphia: Temple University Press, 1996), pp. 196–97.

36 Paul Goodman, *New Reformation: Notes of a Neolithic Conservative* (New York: Random House, 1970), p. 61.

37 Ibid., pp. 61–62.

38 Quoted in E. P. Thompson, *Witness Against the Beast: William Blake and the Moral Law* (New York: The New Press, 1993), p. 18.

39 Ibid., pp. 108–9.

40 Ibid., p. 94.

41 Herbert Marcuse, *An Essay on Liberation* (New York: Pelican, 1969), p. 67 (original emphasis).

42 Guerin, *Anarchism*, p. 14.

43 Willener, *The Action-Image of Society*, p. 295.

44 Erich Fromm, *Escape from Freedom* (New York: Rinehart, 1941), p. 109.

45 Isaiah Berlin, *The Sense of Reality: Studies in Ideas and Their History* (New York: Farrar, Straus and Giroux, 1966), p. 185.

46 Fromm, *Escape from Freedom*, p. 107. See also Martin Luther, *The Bondage of the Will*, excerpted in *Martin Luther: Selections from His Writings*, ed. John Dillenberger (New York: Doubleday, 1961), p. 190.

47 Fromm, *Escape from Freedom*, p. 111.

48 Ibid., pp. 110–11 (original emphasis).

49 Ibid., p. 108.

50 See Gil Green, *The New Radicalism: Anarchist or Marxist?* (New York: International Publishers, 1971).

51 Teodori, *The New Left*, pp. 209–17.

52 Ibid., p. 47.

53 Ibid., p. 27.

54 Miller, *Democracy Is in the Streets*, p. 239.

55 Teodori, *The New Left*, p. 84.

56 Ibid., p. 85.

57 See Aldon Morris, *The Origins of the Civil Rights Movement* (New York: Free Press, 1984).

58 Quoted in Clayborne Carson, *In Struggle: SNCC and the Black Awakening of the 1960s* (Cambridge, Mass.: Harvard University Press, 1981), p. 216.

59 Ibid., p. 301.

60 Ella Baker interview (1967), in Emily Stoper, *The Student Nonviolent Coordinating Committee* (Brooklyn: Carlson, 1989), p. 272.

61 See Roszak, "The Dialectics of Liberation: Herbert Marcuse and Norman O. Brown, in *The Making of a Counter-Culture*, pp. 84−123.

62 "A Reply to Herbert Marcuse by Norman O. Brown," in Herbert Marcuse, *Negations: Essays in Critical Theory* (Boston: Beacon Press, 1968), p. 246.

63 Norman O. Brown, *Love's Body* (New York: Random House, 1966), p. 253.

64 Ibid., p. 258.

65 George Steiner, *After Babel: Aspects of Language and Translation* (New York: Oxford University Press, 1977), p. 62.

66 Roszak, *The Making of a Counter-Culture*, p. 115.

67 Marcuse, *Negations*, p. 229.

68 Cf. Brown, *Love's Body*, p. 255.

69 Marcuse, *Negations*, p. 238.

70 Marcuse, *An Essay on Liberation*, p. 67.

71 Ibid., pp. 69−70.

72 Ibid., p. 33 (Marcuse's emphasis).

73 Young, *An Infantile Disorder?* p. 326.

74 Herbert Marcuse, *Counter-Revolution and Revolt* (Boston: Beacon Press, 1972).

75 Ibid., p. 46.

76 Thompson, *Witness Against the Beast*, pp. 87, 90.

77 See Sale, *SDS*, also Young, *An Infantile Disorder?* pp. 314− 23; Weather Underground, *Prairie Fire: The Politics of Revolutionary Anti-Imperialism, The Political Statement of the Weather Underground* (Communications, Inc., 1974), p. 14.

78 Guerin, *Anarchism*, p. 13.

79 Herbert Marcuse, "On the New Left" (radio address, Radio Free People, December 1968), reprinted in Teodori, *The New Left*, p. 469.

80 Osha Neumann, "Motherfuckers Then and Now: My Sixties Problem," in *Cultural Politics and Social Movements*, ed. Marcy Darnovsky, Barbara Epstein, and Richard Flacks (Philadelphia: Temple University Press, 1995), p. 66.

81 "International Werewolf Conspiracy: A Little Treatise on Dying—Fight Foul, Life Is Real," leaflet distributed at the University of California at Berkeley, November 1968 (reprinted in Teodori, *The New Left*, pp. 370–71). Cf. Gary Snyder's poem, "'I hunt the white man down / in my heart" (quoted in Todd Gitlin, *The Sixties* [New York: Bantam Books, 1987], p. 228) and the similar refrain of Diane DiPrima's poem, "then you are still the enemy" ("Revolutionary Letters," in Teodori, *The New Left*, pp. 369–70).

82 Michel Foucault, "Preface," in Gilles Deleuze and Félix Guattari, *Anti-Oedipus: Capitalism and Schizophrenia* (Minneapolis: University of Minnesota Press, 1983), p. xiii.

83 Ron Chepesiuk, *Sixties Radicals, Then and Now* (Jefferson, N.C.: McFarland and Co., 1995), p. 129.

84 See Larry Neal, "Black Art and Black Liberation," 1969 issue of *Ebony*, p. 161; and Black Panthers, "The Black Panther Platform: 'What We Want, What We Believe,'" reprinted in *"Takin' It to the Streets": A Sixties Reader*, ed. Alexander Bloom and Wini Breines (New York: Oxford University Press, 1990), p. 166.

85 Armendo B. Rendon, "The Chicano Manifesto," reprinted in *"Takin' It to the Streets,"* ed. Bloom and Breines, pp. 177–78.

86 Radicalesbians, "The Woman Identified Woman" (1970), reprinted in *Radical Feminism*, ed. Anne Koedt, Ellen Levine, and Anita Rapone (New York: New York Times Book Co., 1973), p. 240. Cf. Ellen Willis, "Radical Feminism and Feminist Radicalism," in *The Sixties Without Apologies*, ed. Sohnya Sayres, Anders Stephanson, Stanley Aronowitz, and Fredric Jameson (Minneapolis: University of Minnesota Press, 1984), p. 108; Barbara Epstein, "'Political Correctness' and Collective Powerlessness," *Socialist Review* 19 (Spring 1991): 115–32.

87 That expressivism and capitalism indeed shared an "elective affinity" can be seen in the ease with which advertisers turned the libertarian and expressive culture of the Sixties structure of feeling to use in commodity aesthetics. W. F. Haug, *Critique of Commodity Aesthetics: Appearance, Sexuality and Advertising in Capitalist Society* (Minneapolis: University of Minnesota Press, 1986).

88 Todd Gitlin, *The Whole World Is Watching: Mass Media and the Making and Unmaking of the New Left* (Berkeley: University of California Press, 1980) , p. 234.

89 Harvey dates this sea change in the composition of global capitalist space-time to around 1972. David Harvey, *The Condition of Postmodernity* (Cambridge, Mass.: Basil Blackwell, 1990), p. vii.

90 Cf. Murray Bookchin, "Between the '30s and the '60s," in *Sixties Without Apologies*, ed. Sayres et al., p. 250; Young, *An Infantile Disorder?* p. 254.

91 Gitlin, *The Whole World Is Watching*, p. 234.

CHAPTER 2

1   Mary Daly, *Gyn/Ecology* (Boston: Beacon Press, 1978), p. 340.

2   Josephine Donovan, *Feminist Theory: The Intellectual Traditions of American Feminism* (New York: Continuum, 1985), p. 155.

3   Kathy Miriam, "Rethinking Radical Feminism: Opposition, Utopianism and the Moral Imagination of Feminist Theory," Ph.D. diss., University of California at Santa Cruz, March 1998.

4   J. G. Fichte, "Fourth Address," *Addresses to the German Nation* (New York: Harper and Row, 1968), p. 52 (emphasis added).

5   Donna Haraway, *Simians, Cyborgs, and Women: The Reinvention of Nature* (New York: Routledge, 1991), p. 78 (original emphasis).

6   See Isaiah Berlin, *The Sense of Reality: Studies in Ideas and Their History* (New York: Farrar, Straus and Giroux, 1966), p. 184; Norman O. Brown, *Love's Body* (New York: Random House, 1966), p. 262.

7   Daly, *Gyn/Ecology*, p. 34.

8   Gloria Anzuldua, "How to Tame a Wild Tongue," in *Borderlands/La Frontera* (San Francisco: Spinsters/Aunt Lute, 1987), p. 59.

9   Gloria Anzuldua, "Speaking in Tongues: A Letter," in *This Bridge Called My Back: Writings by Women of Color*, ed. Cherríe Moraga and Gloria Anzuldua (New York: Kitchen Table, Women of Color Press, 1983), p. 165.

10 For example, Anzuldua and Moraga, *This Bridge*, p. 195.

11 Ibid., p. 169.

12 Bob Fitch, "On Nietszche: The Last Philosopher on the First Man," unpublished manuscript, ca. 1998.

13 Berlin, *The Sense of Reality*, p. 178.

14 A version of the "Manifesto" originally appeared in *Socialist Review*; see Donna Haraway, "Manifesto for Cyborgs: Science, Technology, and Socialist Feminism in the 1980s," *Socialist Review* 80 (1985), pp. 65-108. The essay later appeared in Haraway's *Simians, Cyborgs, and Women: The Reinvention of Nature* (New York: Routledge, 1991).

15 Cf. Haraway, "Manifesto," *Simians, Cyborgs, and Women*, p. 158.

16 Haraway, *Simians, Cyborgs, and Women*, p. 9.

17 Donna Haraway, "Ecce Homo, Ain't (Ar'n't) I a Woman, and Inappropriate/d Others: The Human in a Post-Humanist Landscape," in *Feminists Theorize the Political*, ed. Judith Butler and Joan Scott (New York: Routledge, 1992), p. 86 (emphasis added).

18 Haraway, *Simians, Cyborgs, and Women*, p. 3 (emphasis added).

19 Ibid., p. 181.

20 Daly, *Gyn/Ecology*, p. 66; see Daly's section, "The Illusion of 'Dionysian' Freedom,"

pp. 64–69. "The pseudocreative power of boundary violation . . . is clearly an invasion of women's bodies/spirits and of all our own kind" (p. 71).

21 Ibid., p. 67.

22 Ibid.

23 Daly, *Gyn/Ecology*, p. 71.

24 Brown, *Love's Body*, pp. 247, 249.

25 Haraway, *Simians, Cyborgs, and Women*, p. 165.

26 Haraway, *Simians, Cyborgs, and Women*, p. 150.

27 Nicholas Negroponte, *Being Digital* (New York: Alfred Knopf, 1995), p. 218.

28 Theodore Roszak, *The Making of a Counter-Culture: Reflections on the Technocratic Society and Its Youthful Opposition* (New York: Doubleday, 1969), p. 276.

29 Haraway, *Modest-Witness@Second-Millennium*.

30 Haraway, *Simians, Cyborgs, and Women*, p. 82.

31 Haraway, *Modest Witness@Second-Millennium*, p. 82 (emphasis added).

32 Michael Hardt and Antonio Negri, *Empire* (Cambridge, MA: Harvard University Press, 2000), p. 367.

33 Ibid, p. 215.

34 But see Bob Fitch's "On Nietszche."

35 Mae Gwendolyn Henderson, "Speaking in Tongues," in *Feminists Theorize the Political*, ed. Judith Butler and Joan W. Scott (New York: Routledge, 1992), p. 161.

36 Audre Lorde, "The Transformation of Silence into Language and Action," reprinted in *Sister Outsider* (Freedom: The Cross Press, 1984).

37 bell hooks, *Talking Back* (Boston: South End Press, 1989), p. 18.

38 Ibid., p. 9 (emphasis added).

39 Ibid., p. 8 (emphasis added).

40 Ibid., p. 16.

41 Nadia Elia, "Affirming Life, Inscribing the *Intifada*: When the Subalterns Scream," *Radical Philosophy Review* 1, no. 1 (1998): 72–73.

42 Luc Ferry and Alain Renault, *French Philosophy of the Sixties: An Essay on Antihumanism* (Amherst, Mass.: University of Massachusetts Press, 1990), p. 18.

43 Trinh T. Minh-ha, *Woman, Native, Other* (Bloomington, Ind.: Indiana University Press, 1989), p. 20 (original emphasis).

44 Ibid., p. 94 (original emphasis).

45 Alluquere Rosanne Stone, *The War of Desire and Technology at the Close of the Mechanical Age* (Cambridge, Mass.: MIT Press, 1995), p. 17.

46 Brown, *Love's Body*, p. 160.

47 Ibid., p. 253.

48 Hardt and Negri, *Empire*, p. 363.

49 Ibid., p. 362.

50 See, for example, Shane Phelan, *Getting Specific: Postmodern Lesbian Politics* (Minneapolis: University of Minnesota Press, 1994), p. 139.

51 Teresa L. Ebert, *Ludic Feminism and After: Postmodernism, Desire, and Labor in Late Capitalism* (Ann Arbor, Mich.: University of Michigan Press, 1999), p. 119.

52 Ibid., p. 172.

53 F. T. Marinetti, "Destruction of Syntax—Imagination Without Strings—Words-in-Freedom 1913," in *The Futurist Manifestos*, ed. Umbro Apollonio (London: Thames and Hudson, 1973), p. 106 (original emphasis). Cf. Sue-Ellen Case, *The Domain-Matrix: Performing Lesbian at the End of Print Culture* (Bloomington, Ind.: Indiana University Press, 1996), pp. 7–8.

54 See Marjorie Perloff, "The Word Set Free: Text and Image in the Russian Futurist Book," in *The Futurist Moment: Avant-Garde, Avant Guerre, and the Language of Rupture* (Chicago: University of Illinois Press, 1986), pp. 117–60.

55 Marinetti, "Destruction of Syntax," p. 98.

56 Foucault, *The Order of Things*, p. xviii (original emphasis).

57 David Harvey, *The Condition of Postmodernity* (Cambridge, Mass.: Basil Blackwell, 1990), p. 36.

58 Fredric Jameson, *Postmodernism, or, the Cultural Logic of Late Capitalism* (Durham, N.C.: Duke University Press, 1991).

CHAPTER 3

1 Homi Bhabha, "Postcolonial Authority and Postmodern Guilt," in *Cultural Studies*, ed. Lawrence Grossberg, Cary Nelson, and Paula Treichler (New York: Routledge, 1992), p. 66.

2 Omar Calabrese, *Neo-Baroque: A Sign of the Times* (Princeton, N.J.: Princeton University Press, 1992).

3 That Bhabha may have been less concerned to communicate a thesis than to evoke a sublime experience seems confirmed by his reply to a respondent at the conference where he presented an early version of this paper. After hearing Bhabha's paper, a discussant (Fred Pfeil) said: "I confess that I found your paper of forbidding difficulty, as I think many people here did." To which Bhabha replied: "I can't apologize for the fact that you found my paper completely impenetrable. I did it quite consciously, I had a problem, I worked it out. And if a few people got what I was saying, I'm happy. If not, obviously it's a disaster." Bhabha, "Postcolonial Authority," in *Cultural Studies*, ed. Grossberg et al., p. 67.

4 John Rupert Martin, *Baroque* (New York: Harper, 1977), p. 268 (emphasis added).

5 Fredric Jameson, *Postmodernism, or the Cultural Logic of Late Capitalism* (Durham, N.C.: Duke University Press, 1984), p. 18.

6 See Georg Lukács, *History and Class Consciousness: Studies in Marxist Dialectics* (Cambridge, Mass.: MIT Press, 1971), p. 120.

7 Max Horkheimer, *The Eclipse of Reason* (New York: Continuum, 1994), p. 166.

8   See Peter Applebome, "Publishers' Squeeze Making Tenure Elusive," *New York Times*, November 18, 1996.

9   Mary Kaldor, *The Baroque Arsenal* (New York: Hill and Wang, 1981), p. 28.

10 Ibid., pp. 22–25.

11 Ibid., p. 25.

12 In the 1990s, a wave of mergers shrunk the number of prime contractors even further, causing weapons systems to exhibit even more grossly "baroque" characteristics. Cf. U.S. General Accounting Office, GAO/PEMD-96-10, Letter Report, 2 July 1996 (Washington, D.C.: GAO, 1996); Philip Shenon, "B-2 Gets a Bath to Prove It 'Does Not Melt,'" *New York Times*, September 13, 1997; James Dao, "16 of 21 B-2's Have Cracks Near Exhaust, Officials Say," *New York Times*, March 20, 2002.

13 Kaldor, *Baroque Arsenal*, p. 7.

14 Ibid., pp. 65–68.

15 Ibid., pp. 19–20.

16 Dante Germino, *Antonio Gramsci: Architect of a New Politics* (Baton Rouge, La.: Louisiana State University Press, 1990), p. 198.

17 See Mao Tse-tung, "On Practice," in *Selected Readings from the Works of Mao Tse-tung* (Peking: Foreign Languages Press, 1971), p. 67.

18 Ibid., pp. 77, 81.

19 Perry Anderson, *Considerations on Western Marxism* (London: New Left Books, 1976), p. 53.

20 See Clyde W. Barrow, *Universities and the Capitalist State: Corporate Liberalism and the Reconstruction of American Higher Education, 1894–1928* (Madison, Wis.: University of Wisconsin Press, 1990).

21 Sheila Slaughter and Larry L. Leslie, *Academic Capitalism: Politics, Policies, and the Entrepreneurial University* (Baltimore, Md.: Johns Hopkins University Press, 1997).

22 Ibid., p. 1.

23 See Richard Moser, "The New Academic Labor System (Part I)," in *Radical Philosophy Newsletter*, no. 52 (April 2001): 7.

24 Jean-François Lyotard, *The Postmodern Condition: A Report on Knowledge* (Minneapolis: University of Minnesota Press, 1984).

25 Ibid., p. 48.

26 Ibid., pp. 4–5.

27 See Paul J. DiMaggio and Walter W. Powell, "The Iron Cage Revisited: Institutional Isomorphism and Collective Rationality in Organizational Fields," *American Sociological Review* 48 (April 1983): 147–60.

28 Francisco E. Aguilera, "Is Anthropology Good for the Company?" *American Anthropologist* 98, no. 4 (December 1996): 735.

29 Ibid.

30 *The New York Times Magazine*, August 4, 2002.

31 Adrienne Rich, "Toward a Woman-Centered University," *On Lies, Secrets, and Silence* (New York: W. W. Norton, 1979).

32 Ibid., p. 134.

33 See Joanna de Groot, "After the Ivory Tower: Gender, Commodification and the 'Academic,'" *Feminist Review* 55 (Spring 1997): 130–42.

34 Patrice McDermott, *Politics and Scholarship: Feminist Academic Journals and the Production of Knowledge* (Urbana, Ill.: University of Illinois Press, 1994).

35 Ibid., p. 100.

36 Ibid., p. 181.

37 See Susan Bordo, *Unbearable Weight: Feminism, Western Culture, and the Body* (Berkeley: University of California Press, 1993), p. 218.

38 Rich, *On Lies, Secrets, and Silence*, p. 152.

39 Promotional brochure for the Xerox Palo Alto Research Center (Palo Alto, Calif.: Xerox Corporation, 1997).

40 Lucy Suchman, "Working Relations of Technology Production and Use," printed by the Xerox Palo Alto Research Center (Palo Alto, Calif., 1993), p. 1.

41 Ibid., p. 2.

42 Ibid., p. 3.

43 Wolfgang Fritz Haug, *Critique of Commodity Aesthetics: Appearance, Sexuality, and Advertising in Capitalist Society* (Minneapolis: University of Minnesota Press, 1986), p. 41.

44 Insofar as the principle of intellectual exchange here is aesthetic as well as monetary, it calls to mind nothing so much as the art manifestos of the Italian Futurists, which sought (decades before Andy Warhol) to erase the distinction between thought, art, and the commodity. Cf. Bruno Corradini and Emilio Settimelli, "Weights, Measures and Prices of Artistic Genius—Futurist Manifesto 1914," in *Futurist Manifestos*, ed. Umbro Apollonio (London: Thames and Hudson, 1973), p. 149.

45 See Pierre Bourdieu, "Universal Corporatism: The Role of Intellectuals in the Modern World," *Poetics Today* 12, no. 4 (Winter 1991): 664.

46 Niilo Kauppi, *French Intellectual Nobility: Institutional and Symbolic Transformation in the Post-Sartrian Era* (Albany, N.Y.: SUNY Press, 1996).

47 Ibid., p. 27; cf. Barbara Giudice, "An Era of Soul-Searching for France's Intellectuals," *Chronicle of Higher Education*, June 13, 1997.

48 Dana Polan, "The Spectacle of Intellect in the Media Age: Cultural Representations and the David Abraham, Paul de Man, and Victor Farías Cases," in *Intellectuals: Aesthetics, Politics, Academics*, ed. Bruce Robbins (Minneapolis: University of Minnesota Press, 1990), pp. 343–63.

49 Kauppi, *French Intellectual Nobility*, p. 127.

50 Ibid., p. 120.

51 Ibid., p. 128.

52 Michelle Lamont, "How to Become a Dominant French Philosopher," *American Journal of Sociology* 93, no. 3 (November 1987): 592.

53 Ibid., pp. 584–622.

54 Marx and Engels, *The Communist Manifesto,* ed. David McLellan (New York: Oxford University Press, 1992), p. 88.

55 On the rise of postmodernism in the United States, see Maria Ruegg, "The End(s) of French Style: Structuralism and Post-Structuralism in the American Context," *Criticism* 29, no. 3 (1979).

56 In the first few years of the twenty-first century, national and international poststructuralist stars like Spivak, Jacques Derrida, Michael Hardt, Homi Bhabha, and Julia Kristeva have been treated to celebrity-style profiles in the *New York Times* (replete with glamorous color photographs).

57 The casualization of academic labor, which has affected the humanities far more than other disciplines (e.g., nearly twice as many English instructors as engineering instructors are part-time—and they earn considerably less) have made lower-ranked faculty and graduate students the new beasts of burden of the university. Women, concentrated in lower-paying fields, earn less today than they did twenty years ago vis-à-vis their male colleagues. And the faculty pay spread between market-oriented fields and traditional disciplines, between community colleges and prestigious universities, between the lowest-ranked and highest-ranked faculty, has never been wider.

58 Scott Heller, "A Constellation of Recently Hired Professors Illuminate the English Department at Duke," *Chronicle of Higher Education,* May 27, 1987, quoted in Mary A. Burgan, "The Faculty and the Superstar Syndrome," *Academe* (May–June 1988): 10.

59 David R. Shumway, "The Star System in Literary Studies," *PMLA* 112, no. 1 (January 1997): 85–100.

60 Ibid., p. 87.

61 Dinitia Smith, "Creating a Stir Wherever She Goes," *New York Times,* February 9, 2002.

62 Clyde W. Barrow, "Beyond the Multiversity: Fiscal Crisis and the Changing Structure of Academic Labour," in *Academic Work: The Changing Labour Process in Higher Education,* ed. John Smyth (Buckingham, UK: Society for Research into Higher Education and Open University Press, 1995), p. 167.

63 Karl Marx, *Capital: A Critique of Political Economy,* vol. 2, ed. Ernest Mandel (New York: Penguin, 1978), pp. 200–6.

64 Roland Barthes, "Réponses," *Tel Quel* 47 (1971): 99, quoted in Kauppi, *French Intellectual Nobility,* p. 19; cf. Russell Jacoby, *Dialectic of Defeat* (Cambridge: Cambridge University Press, 1981), p. 15.

65 Jameson, *Postmodernism*, pp. 4–5.

66 Haug, *Critique of Commodity*, p. 44.

67 Jeffery P. Bieber and Robert T. Blackburn, "Faculty Research Productivity 1972–1988: Development and Application of Constant Units of Measure," *Research in Higher Education* 34, no. 5 (1993): 560.

68 Simon Marginson, "Markets in Higher Education: Australia," in *Academic Work*, pp. 32, 36.

69 We find a similar cluster of all things "cyber" in the same Routledge list: *The Cybercultures Reader, Cyberpower, Cyberborgs@Cyberspace?, The Cyborg Handbook, The Gendered Cyborg, Race in Cyberspace, Communities in Cyberspace, Cyborg Babies, The Politics of Cyberspace, Cyberspace Divide, The Governance of Cyberspace*, etc.

70 "Painters and sculptors produce sets, repeat and vary fixed patterns, and treat the decorative framework with the same care as the works of art themselves—if they feel the dividing-line between the work of art and the framework at all. The mechanized, factory-like method of manufacture leads to a standardization of production." Arnold Hauser, *The Social History of Art*, vol. 2 (New York: Vintage, 1951), pp. 196–97.

71 Kaldor, *Baroque Arsenal*, p. 83.

72 Title of an article by Bracha Lichtenberg-Ettinger in *Parallax 10* 1, no. 5 (Feb. 1995): 83–88. Cf. Marjorie Perloff, *The Futurist Movement: Avant-Garde, Avant Guerre, and the Language of Rupture* (Chicago: University of Chicago Press, 1986), p. 141.

73 Edward Tufte, "The Cognitive Style of PowerPoint," an essay published by Graphics Books (2003), p. 4.

74 Sue Ellen Case, *The Domain-Matrix: Performing Lesbian at the End of Print Culture* (Bloomington, Ind.: Indiana University Press, 1996).

75 Ibid.

76 Tufte, *Cognitive Style*, p. 4.

77 Ibid., p. 7.

78 Rey Chow, "Postmodern Automatons," in *Feminists Theorize the Political*, ed. Judith Butler and Joan W. Scott (New York: Routledge, 1992), p. 115.

79 Martin Jay, *Marxism and Totality* (Berkeley: University of California Press, 1984), p. 515.

80 Michel Foucault, *Language, Counter-Memory, Practice: Selected Essays and Interview*, ed. Donald F. Bouchard (Ithaca, N.Y.: Cornell University Press, 1977), p. 233.

81 Lukács, *History and Class Consciousness*, p. 103.

82 Antonio Gramsci, *Prison Notebooks*, ed. Joseph Buttigieg, vol. 1, (New York: Columbia University Press, 1992), §43, p. 128.

83 Tufte, *The Cognitive Style*.

84 Jürgen Habermas, *Theory and Practice* (Boston: Beacon Press, 1973), pp. 36–37.

85 Martin Jay, "For Theory," *Theory and Society* 2, no. 2 (April 1996): 174.

86 Foucault, *Language, Memory, Counter-Memory*, p. 207. See also Foucault's extensive

comments on intellectuals in *Power/Knowledge*, ed. Colin Gordon (New York: Pantheon Books, 1980). Also see Jean-François Lyotard, "Tomb of the Intellectual," *Political Writings*, trans. Bill Readings and Kevin Paul Geiman (Minneapolis: University of Minnesota Press, 1993), pp. 3-7.

87 To hold as Mao did that a theory is to be considered true only to the extent that it has been proven "useful" is in fact to subvert Marx's dialectic of praxis, which emphasized, rather, that *the truth is useful*—i.e., that truth is the purest expression of use value. Adolfo Sánchez Vázquez makes this point in *The Philosophy of Praxis* (London: Merlin Press, 1977).

88 R. W. Connell, *Which Way Is Up? Essays on Sex, Class and Culture* (Sydney, Australia: Allen & Unwin, 1983), p. 138.

89 Anarchists, for example, hold a similar belief in the tempering qualities of practice. "It is almost impossible to pass, so to speak, from abstract thought into life, from thought unaccompanied by life and lacking the driving power of life-necessity,"as Mikhail Bakunin put it. *The Political Philosophy of Bakunin,* ed. G. P. Maximoff (New York: The Free Press, 1953), p. 360. The paradigmatic strategic thinker, of course, was Sun Tzu. Ancient Chinese philosophy was blissfully unaware of the dualisms of Western culture and did not distinguish, as the Greeks did, between what the latter called practical wisdom (*phronesis*) and philosophical speculation (*theoria*).

90 Guy Debord, *Society of the Spectacle* (Cambridge, Mass.: MIT Press, 1995), p. 32.

91 Lyotard, "Tomb of the Intellectual," p. 7.

92 Emily Eakin, "The Latest Theory Is that Theory Doesn't Matter," *New York Times*, April 19, 2003.

93 Terry Eagleton, *The Illusions of Postmodernism* (Cambridge, Mass.: Basil Blackwell 1996), p. 13.

CHAPTER 4

1 Filippo Tommaso Marinetti, "Beyond Communism," in *Marinetti: Selected Writings,* ed. R.W. Flint (New York: Farrar, Straus and Giroux, 1972), p. 148.

2 Ibid.

3 Ernesto Laclau and Chantal Mouffe, "Post-Marxism without Apologies," *New Left Review* 166 (Nov.–Dec. 1987): 80.

4 Michael Hardt and Antonio Negri, *Empire* (Cambridge, Mass.: Harvard University Press, 2000), pp. xv, 218.

5 Ibid., p. 397.

6 Frederick Engels, *Anti-Düring: Herr Eugene Dühring's Revolution in Science* (Moscow: Progress Publishers, 1969), p. 57.

7 My account here follows David McClellan, *The Young Hegelians and Karl Marx* (London: Macmillan, 1969).

8   Marx and Engels, *The Communist Manifesto,* ed. David McLellan (New York: Oxford University Press, 1992), p. 51.

9   Marx and Engels, *German Ideology*, p. 47.

10 Ernst Bloch, *The Principle of Hope*, vol. 1 (Cambridge, Mass.: MIT Press, 1986), p. 255.

11 Marx and Engels, *German Ideology*, p. 109.

12 Marx and Engels, *Communist Manifesto*, p. 42.

13 Louis Althusser, *For Marx* (New York: Vintage, 1970), p. 227.

14 Ibid., p. 229.

15 Ibid., p. 229.

16 Ibid.

17 Ibid., p. 233.

18 E. P. Thompson, *The Poverty of Theory* (New York: Monthly Review Press, 1978), p. 122.

19 Ibid.

20 Ibid., p. 25.

21 Ibid., p. 98.

22 Althusser, *Essays*, p. 51, quoted in Thompson, *The Poverty of Theory*, p. 105.

23 R. W. Connell, *Which Way Is Up? Essays on Sex, Class and Culture* (Sydney, Australia: Allen & Unwin, 1983), p. 137. Cf. John O'Neill, *For Marx: Against Althusser and Other Essays* (Washington, D.C.: Center for Advanced Research in Phenomenology and University Press of America, 1982).

24 Connell, *Which Way Is Up?*, p. 137.

25 See Nancie E. Caraway, "The Challenge and Theory of Feminist Identity Politics: Working on Racism." *Frontier* 12, no. 2 (1991):126–27.

26 Didier Eribon, *Michel Foucault* (Cambridge, Mass.: Harvard University Press, 1991), p. 160.

27 Gérard Lebrun pointed out that *The Order of Things* "was haunted by Merleau-Ponty's negative presence," as Foucault's biographer, Didier Eribon, puts it (ibid., p. 157).

28 Cf. Michel Foucault, *The Order of Things: An Archaeology of the Human Sciences* (New York: Vintage, 1970), p. 159.

29 Ibid., p. xxi.

30 Cf. Michel Foucault, 1961 interview in *Le Monde*, quoted in Eribon, *Michel Foucault*, p. 75; *The History of Sexuality, The Uses of Pleasure,* vol. 2 (New York: Vintage, 1985), p. 4.

31 Peter Koestenbaum, Introduction, in Edmund Husserl, *The Paris Lectures* (The Hague: Martinus Nijhoff, 1975), p. xii.

32 Foucault, Foreword to the English edition, *The Order of Things*, p. xiv (my emphasis).

33 Michel Foucault, *The Archaeology of Knowledge* (New York: Pantheon, 1972), pp. 139–40.

34 Ibid., p. 138.

35 Susan Bordo, *Unbearable Weight: Feminism, Western Culture, and the Body* (Berkeley: University of California Press, 1993).

36 Maurice Merleau-Ponty, *The Phenomenology of Perception* (New York: Routledge, 1962), p. 304.

37 See Fredric Jameson, *Postmodernism, or the Cultural Logic of Late Capitalism* (Durham, N.C.: Duke University Press, 1991), p. 18.

38 Hubert Dreyfus and Paul Rabinow, *Michel Foucault: Beyond Structuralism and Hermeneutics* (Chicago: University of Illinois Press, 1983), p. 90.

39 Ibid., pp. 90-91.

40 Eribon, *Michel Foucault*, p. 161.

41 Michel Foucault, *Power/Knowledge: Selected Interviews and Other Writings*, ed. Colin Gordon (New York: Pantheon, 1980), p. 98; cf. p. 74.

42 Laclau and Mouffe, "Post-Marxism Without Apologies," p. 102.

43 Gayatri Chakravorty Spivak, *In Other Worlds: Essays in Cultural Politics* (New York: Routledge, 1988), p. 204 (my emphasis).

44 Marx and Engels, *Communist Manifesto*, p. 84.

45 Jacques Derrida, *Of Grammatology* (Baltimore: Johns Hopkins University Press, 1976), p. 60.

46 Joan W. Scott, "'Experience,'" in *Feminists Theorize the Political*, ed. Scott and Judith Butler (New York: Routledge, 1992), p. 26.

47 For example, Donna Haraway, *Simians, Cyborgs, and Women: The Reinvention of Nature* (New York: Routledge, 1991), p. 113 (Haraway's emphasis); Iris Marion Young, *Justice and the Politics of Difference* (Princeton, N.J.: Princeton University Press, 1990), p. 12.

48 Scott, "'Experience,'" p. 26.

49 Ibid., p. 32.

50 Ibid., p. 25 (my emphasis).

51 G. W. F. Hegel, Preface, "Philosophy of Right and Law," in *The Philosophy of Hegel*, ed. C. J. Friedrich, p. 225.

52 Ibid., p. 89.

53 Foucault, *Power/Knowledge*, p. 83.

54 Ibid., p. 81 (emphasis added).

55 Eribon, *Michel Foucault*, p. 282.

56 Hegel, *Reason in History*, p. 88 (emphasis added).

57 Jürgen Habermas, *The Philosophical Discourse of Modernity: Twelve Lectures* (Cambridge, Mass.: MIT Press, 1998), p. 277.

58 Eribon, *Michel Foucault*, p. 288 (Foucault's emphasis).

59 On Foucault's sympathy for Khomeini and Islamic fundamentalism, see Janet Afary and Kevin Anderson, *Seductions of Islam: Foucault, Feminism, and Iran* (Chicago: University of Chicago Press, 2004).

60 Hardt and Negri, *Empire*, p. 387.

61 Ibid., p. 61.

62 Habermas, *The Philosophical Discourse of Modernity*, p. 268.

63 Kirstie McClure, "The Issue of Foundations," in *Feminists Theorize*, ed. Butler and Scott, p. 364.

64 Bhabha, *Location of Culture*, pp. 192–93.

65 Margaret Thompson Drewal, "The Camp Trace in Corporate America," in *The Politics and Poetics of Camp*, ed. Moe Meyer (New York: Routledge, 1994), pp. 177–78.

66 Ibid.

67 Marx and Engels, *The German Ideology*, p. 530.

68 Michel Foucault, "Sex, Power, and the Politics of Identity," in *Ethics, Subjectivity, and Truth*, vol. 1, ed. Paul Rabinow (New York: The New Press, 1997), pp. 172–73.

69 See Frances Negrón-Muntaner, "Twenty Years of Puerto Rican Gay Activism: An Interview with Luis 'Popo' Santiago," *Radical America* 25, no. 1 (January–March 1991): 50.

70 Norman Rush, "What Was Socialism . . . and Why We Will All Miss It So Much," *The Nation*, January 24, 1994, p. 92.

71 Shirley R. Pike, *Marxism and Phenomenology: Theories of Crisis and Their Synthesis* (Totowa, N.J.: Barnes and Noble Books, 1986), p. 79.

72 Michel Foucault, "Preface," in Gilles Deleuze and Félix Guattari, *Anti-Oedipus: Capitalism and Schizophrenia* (Minneapolis: University of Minnesota Press, 1983), pp. xiii–xiv (my emphasis).

73 See Donna Haraway, "Ecce Homo, Ain't (Ar'n't) I a Woman, and Inappropriate/d Others: The Human in a Post-Humanist Landscape," in *Feminists Theorize the Political*, ed. Butler and Scott (New York: Routledge, 1992), p. 87; Young, *Justice and the Politics of Difference*, p. 235.

74 See Young, *Justice and the Politics of Difference*, p. 241; Wendy Brown, *States of Injury: Power and Freedom in Late Modernity* (Princeton, N.J.: Princeton University Press, 1995), p. 50.

75 See Foucault, "Two Lectures," *Power/Knowledge*, p. 81; *Language, Counter-Memory, Practice*, p. 233.

76 See Foucault, *Language, Counter-Memory, Practice*, p. 233.

77 See Jean-François Lyotard, *The Postmodern Condition: A Report on Knowledge* (Minneapolis: University of Minnesota Press, 1984), p. 66.

78 See Judith Butler, *Gender Trouble: Feminism and the Subversion of Identity* (New York: Routledge, 1990), p. 15; Haraway, *Simians, Cyborgs, and Women*, p. 3; Foucault, Introduction to Deleuze and Guattari, *Anti-Oedipus*, p. xiv.

79 See Young, *Justice and the Politics of Difference*, pp. 118, 235, 247; Butler, *Gender Trouble*, p. 15.

80 See Rey Chow, "Postmodern Automatons," in *Feminists Theorize*, ed. Butler and Scott, p. 115.

81 Brown, *States of Injury*, p. 50; Haraway, *Simians, Cyborgs, and Women*, p. 176; Young, *Justice and the Politics of Difference*, p. 234.

82 Cf. Michel Foucault, *Power/Knowledge*, p. 97; McClure, "The Issue of Foundations," in *Feminists Theorize*, ed. Butler and Scott, pp. 364–65.

83 Michel Foucault, "What Is Enlightenment?" *The Foucault Reader*, ed. Paul Rabinow (New York: Pantheon, 1984), p. 46.

84 Enzo, Paci, *The Functions of the Science and the Meaning of Man* (Evanston: Northwestern University Press, 1972), p. 331.

CHAPTER 5

1   For an analysis of some of the limitations of the anti-globalization movement, see Barbara Epstein, "Anarchism and Anti-Globalization," *Monthly Review* (September 2001): 1–14.

2   Alison M. Jagger, *Feminism and Human Nature* (New York: Rowman and Littlefield, 1983), p. 16.

3   See Didier Eribon, *Michel Foucault* (Cambridge, Mass.: Harvard University Press, 1991).

4   Foucault's politics and theories inspire gay and lesbian men and women on several continents. David Halperin goes so far as to describe Foucault "as an object of my worship," *Saint Foucault: Towards a Gay Hagiography* (New York: Oxford University Press, 1995), p. 7.

5   Ibid., p. 25.

6   There may have been other attempts, as well, and Foucault was placed under the care of a psychiatrist during the remainder of his studies. Ibid., p. 26.

7   John M. Cammett, *Antonio Gramsci and the Origins of Italian Communism* (Stanford, Calif.: Stanford University Press, 1967), p. 7.

8   Joan Cocks, *The Oppositional Imagination: Feminism, Critique and Political Theory* (London: Routledge, 1989), p. 74.

9   The notion that Foucault's view of the nexus between knowledge, intellectuals, and power represents the negation, *in toto*, of every particular of Gramsci's political thought flies in the face of much of the literature of cultural studies, where critics have been eager to portray Gramsci as a proto-postmodernist thinker. Some poststructuralist critics have appropriated Gramsci's thought, in an apparent effort to shore up the appearance of critical use value in their work. Homi Bhabha, for example, in a discussion of Gramsci, writes that "the work of hegemony is . . . the process of iteration and differentiation" (Homi Bhabha, *The Location of Culture* [New York: Routledge, 1994], p. 29). But Gramsci meant just the opposite.

10 Stanley Aronowitz, *The Crisis in Historical Materialism: Class, Politics, and Culture in Marxist Theory* (Minneapolis: University of Minnesota Press, 1990), p. 168 (emphasis added).

11 Giuseppe Fiori, *Antonio Gramsci: Life of a Revolutionary* (London: Verso, 1970), p. 127.

12 Antonio Gramsci, *Selections from the Prison Notebooks*, ed. Quentin Hoare (New York: International Publishers, 1971), p. 158 (emphasis added). Hereafter cited as *SPN*.

13 Gramsci, *SPN*, p. 130.

14 Quentin Hoare, Introduction to "The Modern Prince," in Gramsci, *SPN*, p. 123.

15 Niccolò Machiavelli, *The Portable Machiavelli*, ed. Peter Bondanella and Mark Musa (New York: Penguin Books, 1979), p. 159.

16 Benedetto Fontana, *Hegemony and Power: On the Relation between Gramsci and Machiavelli* (Minneapolis: University of Minnesota Press, 1993), p. 87.

17 "Nor can I express with what love he will be received in all those provinces that have suffered through these foreign floods; with what thirst for revenge, with what obstinate loyalty, with what compassion, with what tears! What doors will be closed to him? Which people will deny him obedience? What jealousy could oppose him?" Machiavelli, *The Portable Machiavelli*, p. 166.

18 Hence the title of Book I, Chapter LVII of Machiavelli's *Discourses*: "The People Are Strong When United but Weak as Individuals."

19 Later, Robespierre himself would write that "the plan of the French Revolution was written large in the books . . . of Machiavelli." Quoted in Hannah Arendt, *On Revolution* (New York: Viking Press, 1965), p. 30.

20 Fontana, *Hegemony and Power*.

21 Gramsci, *SPN*, p. 153. Cf. Machiavelli's reference to a story from Livy to demonstrate "the ineffectiveness of a multitude without a leader" (Book I, chap. 44, in *Discourses*, ed. Bondanella and Musa, p. 261). Machiavelli also observes that it is better to have a well-trained commander with a weak or unorganized army than a well-trained army headed by a poor commander (Book III, chap. 13).

22 Gramsci, "Political Struggle and Military Way," *Prison Notebooks*, ed. Joseph Buttigieg (New York: Columbia University Press, 1991), p. 219.

23 Carl von Clausewitz, from an unpublished Preface to *On War*, ed. Michael Howard and Peter Paret (Princeton, N.J.: Princeton University Press, 1984), p. 61.

24 Cf. Husserl: "Phenomenological experience as reflection must avoid any interpretive constructions. Its descriptions must reflect accurately the concrete contents of experience, precisely as these are experienced." Edmund Husserl, *The Paris Lectures* (The Hague: Martinus Nijhoff, 1975), p. 13.

25 Gramsci, "Political Struggle and Military Way," *SPN*, vol. 1, p. 219.

26 Kerry H. Whiteside, *Merleau-Ponty and the Foundation of an Existential Politics* (Princeton, N.J.: Princeton University Press, 1988), p. 44. Cf. Femia's observation of Gramsci: "Even in ostensibly consensual capitalist societies, the concrete behavior and responses of the masses provide intimations, however vague, of an alternative worldview." Joseph V. Femia, *Gramsci's Political Thought: Hegemony, Consciousness, and the Revolutionary Process* (Oxford, UK: Clarendon/Oxford University Press, 1981), p. 224.

27 Gramsci, *SPN*, p. 171. Margaret Leslie draws on Gramsci's active use of Machiavelli to make the case for contemporary theorists to be passionately involved in the world in "In Defense of Anachronism," *Political Studies* 18 (1970): 433–47.

28 Gramsci, *SPN*, p. 171.

29 Gramsci, *SPN*, pp. 170–71. Cf. Enzo Paci's interpellation of Husserl's phenomenology for a theory of historical action: "It is . . . possible to discover the occluded in the past in order to transform the present and proceed into the future. The unreachable past origin projects itself into the future, becomes telos. . . . It is while questioning the past . . . that I understand the present and the interest of the present for its own transformation." Paci, *The Function of the Sciences and the Meaning of Man* (Evanston, Ill.: Northwestern University Press, 1972), p. 23.

30 Gramsci, *SPN*, p. 171.

31 Ibid. For Gramsci, "the objective conditions for social transformations can be historically operative [only when] . . . subjectively perceived"; "the existence of objective conditions . . . is not yet sufficient: it is necessary to 'know' them and know how to use them. And to want to use them." Femia, *Gramsci's Political Thought*, p. 120.

32 Roger T. Ames, Introduction, *Sun-Tzu: The Art of Warfare* (New York: Ballantine Books, 1993), p. 59.

33 Ibid, pp. 39–41.

34 Barry Smart, for example, writes that Foucault's "principal objective" in his genealogical researches was "not the preparation or formulation of strategy" but the investigation of the ways in which the conditions of social existence are constituted. Barry Smart, "The Politics of Truth," in *The Foucault Reader*, ed. David Couzens Hoy (Cambridge, Mass.: Basil Blackwell, 1986), p. 171.

35 Michel Foucault, "Is It Useless to Revolt?" *Le Monde*, May 11, 1979, quoted in Eribon, *Michel Foucault*, pp. 291–92.

36 Michel Foucault, "Two Lectures," in *Power/Knowledge: Selected Interviews and Other Writings*, ed. Colin Gordon (New York: Pantheon, 1980), pp. 82, 85.

37 Michel Foucault, *Language, Memory, Counter-Memory, Discourse*, ed. Donald F. Bouchard (Ithaca, N.Y.: Cornell University Press, 1977), p. 207. See also Foucault's extensive comments on intellectuals in *Power/Knowledge*, cited above.

38 Michel Foucault, *Remarks on Marx: Conversations with Duccio Trombadori*, trans. James Goldstein and James Cascaito (New York: Semiotext(e), 1991), p. 159. First set of italics added, the rest are Foucault's.

39 Foucault, *Power/Knowledge*, p. 132.

40 Ibid.

41 Ibid., p. 133.

42 Ibid., p. 97.

43 Foucault, *Language, Counter-Memory, Practice*, p. 233.

44 Michel Foucault, "Preface," in Gilles Deleuze and Félix Guattari, *Anti-Oedipus: Capitalism and Schizophrenia* (Minneapolis: University of Minnesota Press, 1983), pp. xiii–xiv.

45 Useful military knowledge "cannot be forcibly produced by an apparatus of scientific formulas and mechanics." Clausewitz, *On War*, p. 146. "Knowledge must be so absorbed into the mind that it almost ceases to exist in a separate, objective way. In almost any art or profession a man can work with truths he has learned from musty books, but which have no life or meaning for him.... It is never like that in war. Continual change and the need to respond to it compels the commander to carry the whole intellectual apparatus of his knowledge within him" (p. 147).

46 Alex Honneth, *The Critique of Power: Reflective Stages in a Critical Social Theory* (Cambridge, Mass.: MIT Press, 1991), p. 195.

47 "Foucault gives only scant attention to the strategic considerations with which social groups seek to secure and widen their positions of social power." Honneth, *The Critique of Power*, p. 195.

48 Clausewitz, *On War*, p. 149.

49 Sun Tzu, *The Art of War* (Boston: Shambhala Books, 1988), p.113.

50 Foucault, *Remarks on Marx*, p. 172.

51 Interview with the *Quel Corps?* collective, reprinted in Eribon, *Michel Foucault*, p. 62 (emphasis added).

52 Marx and Engels, *The German Ideology*, ed. C. J. Arthur (New York: International Publishers, 1970), p. 64.

53 Gramsci, *SPN*, pp. 332–33.

54 Ibid., p. 144.

55 See Gramsci, *Prison Notebooks*, ed. Buttigieg, vol. 1, Notebook 2, § 75, p. 321.

56 See Gramsci's extensive remarks on "Spontaneity and Conscious Leadership," in *SPN*, pp. 196–200.

57 Cocks, *The Oppositional Imagination*, p. 75.

58 Cf. Maurice Merleau-Ponty, *The Phenomenology of Perception* (New York: Routledge, 1962), p. 38.

59 Fontana, *Hegemony and Power*, p. 32.

60 Ibid., p. 140 (emphasis added). See also pp. 24–25.

61 Ibid., p. 22.

62 The hegemonist is therefore one who seeks to become capable of "seeing whether what 'ought to be' is arbitrary or necessary; whether it is concrete will on the one hand or idle fancy, yearning, daydream on the other. . . . He bases himself on effective reality, but what is this effective reality? Is it something static and immobile, or is it not rather a relation of forces in continuous motion and shift of equilibrium?" Gramsci, *SPN*, p. 172.

63 "Hegemony is the formulation and elaboration of a conception of the world that has been transformed into the accepted and 'normal' ensemble of ideas and beliefs that interpret and define the world." Fontana, *Hegemony and Power*, p. 20.

64 Ibid., pp. 181–82 (emphasis added).

65 Gramsci, *SPN,* p. 129, passim.

66 Fontana, *Hegemony and Power,* p. 32.

67 Gramsci, *SPN,* p. 395.

68 Fontana, *Hegemony and Power,* p. 31.

69 Gramsci, *SPN,* p. 133.

70 Ibid., p. 350.

71 Antonio Gramsci to Piero Sraffa, January 2, 1927, in Antonio Gramsci, *Letters from Prison,* ed. Lynne Lawner (New York: Harper and Row, 1973), p. 66.

72 Gramsci, *SPN,* p. 158.

73 "The new type of intellectual uncovers and reveals the power and social bases of thought and knowledge, while at the same time this process of uncovering creates a critical type of knowledge." Fontana, *Hegemony and Power,* p. 28.

74 Ibid., p. 147.

75 See ibid., pp. 99–115.

76 Ibid., p. 102.

77 Jean-François Lyotard, "Nanterre, Here, Now," *Political Writings,* trans. Bill Readings and K. P. Geiman (Minneapolis: University of Minnesota Press, 1993), p. 59. Like Foucault, Lyotard argued that intellectuals ought not to try to educate, but rather should confine themselves only to "defensive and local interventions." Lyotard, "The Tomb of the Intellectual," in ibid., p. 7.

78 Laura Kipnis, "(Male) Desire and (Female) Disgust: Reading *Hustler,*" in *Cultural Studies,* ed. Lawrence Grossberg, Cary Nelson, and Paula Treichler (New York: Routledge, 1992), pp. 373–91.

79 Edward Said, *Culture and Imperialism* (New York: Random House, 1993), p. 303.

80 Foucault, *The Order of Things,* p. xviii (Foucault's emphasis).

81 See Fontana, *Hegemony and Power,* pp. 35–51.

82 Ibid., pp. 36–37.

83 Femia, *Gramsci's Political Thought,* p. 138.

84 "Political knowledge, therefore, is reduced to a technique and a means, which, by its very nature, does not contain within itself any ends or purposes: as instrument and technique it is ethically and morally neutral." Fontana, *Hegemony and Power,* p. 58.

85 Ibid., p. 57.

86 Benedetto Croce, *Philosophy of the Practical: Economic and Ethic* (New York: Biblo and Tannen, 1967; originally published in 1913), p. 304; see esp. pp. 293–305. See also Benedetto Croce, "In Praise of Individuality," *My Philosophy, and Other Essays on the Moral and Political Problems of Our Time* (London: George Allen and Unwin, 1949), pp. 180–207.

87 Fontana, *Hegemony and Power,* p. 60.

88 To an extent, the differences between Gramsci's and Foucault's conceptions of praxis can be mapped onto the tension between spontaneism and voluntarism in radical social and political thought. "Spontaneists" like Bukharin, Rosa Luxemburg, or Anton Pannekoeck held to some form either of determinism or radical populism or both, rejecting the need and desirability of strong leadership out of the belief that the inherent contradictions of capitalism can more or less be relied upon to "spontaneously" generate uprisings by the masses to unseat their masters. "Voluntarists," on the other hand—e.g., Karl Kautsky or Vladimir Lenin—argued that with the right strong political leadership, virtually any historical crisis can be resolved in favor of the oppressed. Socialists have tended toward voluntarism, while anarchists tend toward spontaneism. However, anarchists (e.g., Mikhail Bakunin) have at times smuggled some form of leadership or direction through the back door of their theories, while some socialist theorists (e.g., Cornelius Castoriadis) have sought to reconcile leadership with the self-autonomy of the proletariat. Chamsy Ojeili, "The 'Advance Without Authority': Postmodernism, Libertarian Socialism, and Intellectuals," in *Democracy and Nature* 7, no. 3 (Nov. 2001). Along this axis, Foucault falls closer to anarchism and spontaneism, and Gramsci (an avowed socialist) to voluntarism.

89 Brown, *States of Injury*, p. 42.

90 Benedetto Fontana, quoted in ibid., p. 42.

91 Wendy Brown, "The Time of the Political," *Theory and Event* 1, no. 1 (1997) (emphasis added).

92 Ibid.

93 Wendy Brown, *Politics Out of History* (Princeton, N.J.: Princeton University Press, 2001), pp. 42–43.

94 Clausewitz, *On War*, p. 142.

95 Marx's penetrating journalistic accounts of the Crimean War in the *New York Tribune* were well respected by that paper's readers. See Sigmund Neumann, "Engels and Marx: Military Concepts of the Social Revolutionaries," in *Makers of Modern Strategy*, ed. E. M. Earle (Princeton, N.J.: Princeton University Press, 1952), pp. 154–71.

96 See Raymond Aron's discussion of "Lenin as Interpreter of Clausewitz," in his *Clausewitz: Philosopher of War* (Englewood Cliffs, N.J.: Prentice-Hall, 1985), pp. 267–77. Also Edward Mead Earle, "Lenin, Trotsky, Stalin: Soviet Concepts of War," in *Makers of Modern Strategy*, pp. 322–64.

97 Michel Foucault, "Sex, Power, and the Politics of Identity," in *Ethics, Subjectivity, and Truth*, vol. 1, ed. Paul Rabinow (New York: The New Press, 1997), pp. 172–73.

98 Foucault, *Power/Knowledge*, p. 80.

99 See Stuart Hall, *The Hard Road to Renewal: Thatcherism and the Crisis of the Left* (London: Verso, 1988).

100 Chester Hartman, "Nineteen Perspectives for the Left," *The Progressive*, Nov. 1990, p. 18.

101 Kirstie McClure, "The Issue of Foundations," in *Feminists Theorize the Political*, ed. Joan Scott and Judith Butler (New York: Routledge, 1992), pp. 364–65.

CHAPTER 6

1   Niccolò Machiavelli, *The Prince*, in *The Portable Machiavelli*, ed. Peter Bondanella and Mark Musa (New York: Penguin, 1979), p. 135.

2   Hannah Arendt, *The Human Condition* (Chicago: University of Illinois Press, 1958), p. 51.

3   Ibid., p. 199 (emphasis added).

4   Gramsci, *Selections from the Prison Notebooks*, ed. Quentin Hoare (New York: International-al Publishers, 1971) p. 129 (emphasis added); cf. p. 194. Hereafter cited as *SPN*.

5   Ibid., p. 185.

6   Iris Marion Young, *Justice and the Politics of Difference* (Princeton, N.J.: Princeton University Press, 1990), p. 118.

7   Judith Butler, *Gender Trouble: Feminism and the Subversion of Identity* (New York: Routledge, 1990), p. 15.

8   Bruce Brown, *Marx, Freud, and the Critique of Everyday Life* (New York: Monthly Review, 1973), pp. 191, 195.

9   Henri Lefebvre, *The Production of Space* (Cambridge, Mass.: Basil Blackwell, 1991), p. 64.

10 Ibid., p. 64 (emphasis added).

11 Carl Boggs argued that "the constituent elements" of a new politics are at hand, "an emergent social bloc" that could "lead to an alternative ideological framework that subverts the dominant patterns of thought and action." Carl Boggs, *Social Movements and Political Power: Emerging Forms of Radicalism in the West* (Philadelphia: Temple University Press, 1986), pp. 5, 222. Feminist philosopher Sabina Lovibond called for a "global" political program whose "aims eventually converge with those of all other egalitarian or liberationist movements." Sabina Lovibond, "Feminism and Postmod-ernism," *New Left Review* 178 (1989): 22. James O'Connor made a similar case in his "Is Sustainable Capitalism Possible?" in *Is Capitalism Sustainable?*, ed. Martin O'Connor (New York: Guilford Press, 1994), p. 172.

12 Michael Albert, Leslie Cagan, Noam Chomsky, Robin Hamel, Mel King, Lydia Sargent, and Holly Sklar, *Liberating Theory* (Boston: South End Press, 1986).

13 Ibid., p. 144 (emphasis added).

14 C. D. C. Reeve, "Introduction," in Aristotle, *Politics* (Indianapolis, Ind.: Hackett, 1998), p. xxviii.

15 See Carole Pateman, *The Sexual Contract* (New York: Polity Press, 1988); and Charles W. Mills, *The Racial Contract* (Ithaca, N.Y.: Cornell University Press, 1998).

16 Immanuel Wallerstein, *After Liberalism* (New York: The New Press, 1995), p. 39.

17 Jules Michelet, "The People," in *The Varieties of History*, ed. Fritz Stern (New York: Meridian Books, 1956), p. 113.

18 Hannah Arendt, *On Revolution* (New York: Viking Press, 1965), p. 41.

19 Quoted in ibid., p. 30.

20 Fontana, *Hegemony and Power*, p. 13.

21 Hence the title of Book I, chap. 57 of Machiavelli's *Discourses*: "The People Are Strong When United but Weak as Individuals."

22 Gramsci, *SPN*, p. 125.

23 Machiavelli, *The Prince*, p. 164 (emphasis added).

24 Gramsci, *SPN*, p. 127 (emphasis added).

25 Ibid., p. 125.

26 G.W.F. Hegel, *Reason in History* (New York: Macmillan, 1953), pp. 40, 41.

27 Ibid., p. 32.

28 Ibid.

29 See Martin Jay, *Marxism and Totality: Adventures of a Concept from Lukács to Habermas* (Berkeley: University of California, 1984), p. 55; Charles Taylor, *Hegel and Modern Society* (Cambridge: Cambridge University Press, 1979), p. 10.

30 See Taylor, *Hegel and Modern Society*, p. 51.

31 Hegel, *Reason in History*, p. 49.

32 Ibid., p. 52.

33 Ibid., p. 66.

34 Ibid., p. 62.

35 Ibid., pp. 60–61.

36 Giuseppe Mazzini, leader of the Italian *risorgimento*, addressed Italian workers as follows: "But what can *each* of you, with his isolated powers, *do* for the moral improvement, for the progress of Humanity? . . . [D]ivided as you are in language, tendencies, habits, and capacities, you cannot attempt this common work. The *individual* is too weak, and Humanity too vast . . . . But God gave you [the] means when he gave you a Country, when . . . he divided Humanity into distinct groups upon the face of our globe, and thus planted the seeds of nations . . . . Your Country is the token of the mission which God has given you to fulfil in Humanity." Giuseppe Mazzini, "The Duties of Man," in Omar and Micheline R. Ishay, eds., *The Nationalism Reader* (Atlantic Highlands, N.J.: Humanities Press, 1995), p. 92.

37 Immanuel Wallerstein, *After Liberalism* (New York: W. W. Norton, 1995), p. 96.

38 Werner Marx, *Hegel's Phenomenology of Spirit: A Commentary Based on the Preface and Introduction* (Chicago: University of Illinois Press, 1975), p. 60.

39 Karl Marx, "The Eighteenth Brumaire of Louis Bonaparte," in *The Marx and Engels Reader*, ed. Robert C. Tucker (New York: W. W. Norton, 1978), p. 608.

40 Gramsci, *SPN*, p. 195.

41 Benedict Anderson, *Imagined Communities* (London: Verso, 1991).

42 V. I. Lenin, *What Is to Be Done? Burning Questions of Our Movement* (Peking: Foreign Languages Press, 1975), p. 36.

43 Lenin, *What Is to Be Done?* p. 135 (original emphasis).

44 Georg Lukács, *History and Class Consciousness: Studies in Marxist Dialectics* (Cambridge, Mass.: MIT Press, 1971), p. 306.

45 Ibid., p. 310.

46 Ibid., p. 142 (emphasis added).

47 Ibid., p. 339.

48 Ibid., p. 318 (original emphasis).

49 Ibid., p. 302.

50 Ibid., pp. 332–33; also p. 330.

51 Ibid., p. 326.

52 Georg Lukács, *Lenin: A Study on the Unity of His Thought* (Cambridge, Mass.: MIT Press, 1971), p. 59.

53 Lukács, *History and Class Consciousness*, p. 327.

54 V. I. Lenin, *"Left-Wing" Communism, an Infantile Disorder* (Peking: Foreign Languages Press, 1970), p. 7.

55 Ibid., p. 315.

56 Jean-Jacques Rousseau, *The Social Contract* (New York: Penguin, 1968), p. 141.

57 Ibid., p. 61.

58 Lukács, *History and Class Consciousness*, p. 337.

59 Ibid., p. 336.

60 Ernesto Laclau and Chantal Mouffe, *Hegemony and Socialist Strategy* (London: Verso, 1985), p. 2.

61 Giuseppe Fiori, *Antonio Gramsci: Life of a Revolutionary* (London: Verso, 1970), p. 241.

62 Gramsci, *SPN*, p. 147.

63 Ibid., p. 189.

64 Antonio Gramsci, *Prison Notebooks*, ed. Joseph Buttigieg, vol. 1, Notebook 1, §57 (New York: Columbia University Press, 1992), p. 165.

65 Ibid.

66 Ibid., p. 153 (emphasis added).

67 Anne Showstack Sassoon, *Gramsci's Politics* (Minneapolis: Minnesota University Press, 1987), p. 141.

68 Gramsci, *SPN*, p. 189.

69 Ibid., p. 189.

70 Ibid., pp. 146–47.

71 Ibid., pp. 146–47.

72 Ibid., pp. 181-82.

73 Mazzini, p. 96. Mazzini compared the country to a "Temple," with "God at the summit, [and] a People of equals at the base."

74 Gramsci, *SPN*, p. 133.

75 Lukács, *History and Class Consciousness*, p. 319.

76 Ibid., p. 336.

77 Richard Bellamy, *Modern Italian Social Theory* (Cambridge, UK: Polity, 1987), p. 139 (emphasis added).

78 Aristotle, *Politics*, p. 6.

79 Ibid., p. 51.

80 Ibid., p. 103.

81 Gramsci, *SPN*, p. 185.

82 Ibid.

83 Ibid, p. 161; cf. p. 182.

84 Ibid., p. 190.

85 Ibid., p. 181.

86 See Peter Ives, *Gramsci's Politics of Language* (Toronto: University of Toronto Press, 2004).

87 Antonio Gramsci, letter to Tatiana Schucht, November 17, 1930, in *Letters from Prison*, ed. Lynne Lawner (New York: Harper and Row, 1973), p. 184.

88 Gramsci quoted in Fontana, *Hegemony and Power*, p. 38.

89 Jay, *Marxism and Totality*, p. 159.

90 Antonio Gramsci, "A Single Language and Esperanto" (1918), in *Selections from the Cultural Writings*, ed. David Forgacs and Geoffrey Nowell-Smith (Cambridge, Mass.: Harvard University Press, 1985), p. 29. Gramsci's acute sensitivity to the cultural integrity of local linguistic tradition can be seen in the following letter to his sister, Teresina, concerning her son's schooling in Gramsci's native Sardinia: "I hope that you will let him speak Sardinian and will not make any trouble for him on that score. It was a mistake, in my opinion, not to allow Edmea to speak freely in Sardinian as a little girl. This harmed her intellectual development and put her imagination in a straitjacket. You musn't make this mistake with your children. For one thing Sardinian is not a dialect, but a language in itself, even though it does not have a great literature, and it is a good thing for children to learn several languages, if it is possible. Besides, the Italian that you will teach them will be a poor, mutilated language made up of only the few sentences and words of your conversations with him . . . he will not have any contact with a general environment and will end up learning two jargons and no language. . . . I beg you, from my heart, not to make this mistake and to allow your children to absorb all the Sardinian spirit they wish and to develop spontaneously in the natural environment in which they were born: this will not be an impediment for their future, just

the opposite." Antonio Gramsci, *Letters from Prison*, Volume I, ed. Frank Rosengarten (New York: Columbia University Press, 1994), p. 89. Letter dated March 26, 1927.

91   Gramsci (1920), *Selections from Cultural Writings*, ed. Forgacs and Nowell-Smith, p. 43.

92   Albert, Cagan et al., *Liberating Theory*, p. 145 (emphasis added).

93   "Pluralism is radical only to the extent that each term of this plurality. . . [i.e., each particular struggle] finds *within itself* the principle of its own validity, without this having to be sought in a transcendent or underlying positive ground for the hierarchy of meaning of them all and the source and guarantee of their legitimacy" (emphasis added). *Liberating Theory*, Ernesto Laclau and Mouffe, *Hegemony and Socialist Strategy*, p. 167. Here Laclau and Mouffe go beyond saying merely that *Marxism* should not be the "underlying positive ground" of all social movements to saying *every* "transcendent" principle must be rejected and that every movement find "within itself" its own validity. In their anti-Gramscian conception of hegemony, the multiple movements remain ontologically and even politically estranged from one another. Rather than a *common* project, "the project for a radical and plural democracy, *in a primary sense*, is nothing other than the struggle for a maximum autonomization of spheres on the basis of the generalization of the equivalential-egalitarian logic." Ibid.

94   Gramsci, *SPN*, p. 190.

95   Ibid.

96   Ibid.

97   Renate Holub, *Antonio Gramsci: Beyond Marxism and Postmodernism* (London: Routledge, 1992), pp. 125, 22.

98   Ibid., p. 141.

99   Maurice Merleau-Ponty, *The Structure of Behavior* (Boston: Beacon Press, 1963), p. 148.

100 Maurice Merleau-Ponty, *Sense and Non-Sense*, ed. Hubert L. Dreyfus and Patricia Allen Dreyfus (Evanston, Ill.: Northwestern University Press, 1964), p. 101.

101 Fontana, *Hegemony and Power*, p. 27.

102 Sun Tzu, *Sun-Tzu: The Art of Warfare*, trans. Thomas Cleary (Boston: Shambhala Books, 1988), p. 111.

103 Ibid., p. 113.

104 Ibid., p. 160.

105 Ibid., p. 148.

106 On patriarchal hegemony and the role of gender in the world system, see R. W. Connell, "The Big Picture: Masculinities in Recent World History," *Theory and Society* 22 (1993): 597–623. On gender in the American political process, see Kira Sanbonmatsu, *Democrats/Republicans and the Politics of Women's Place* (Ann Arbor, Mich.: University of Michigan Press, 2002).

107 Stuart Hall, *The Hard Road to Renewal* (London: Verso Books, 1988), p. 7.

108 Sun Tzu, *The Art of War,* p. 112.

109 Samir Amin, "Globalization and Capitalism's Second Belle Époque," *Radical Philosophy Review* 5, nos. 1 and 2 (2002): 92. Originally published in *Monthly Review* 52, no. 2 (2000).

110 Maurice Merleau-Ponty, *The Phenomenology of Perception* (New York: Routledge, 1962), pp. 52–53. In many ways, my remarks in this section build upon the earlier contributions of Marxist phenomenologists like Enzo Paci and Paul Piccone. See especially Paci's groundbreaking work, *The Function of the Sciences and the Meaning of Man.*

111 Ernst Bloch, *The Principle of Hope,* vol. 1 (Cambridge, Mass.: MIT Press, 1986), p. 255.

112 Merleau-Ponty, *The Phenomenology of Perception,* p. 4.

113 Praxis consists in "the re-presentation of the forgotten, the freeing of historical investigation from occlusion, the re-discovery of the occluded *Lebenswelt,* the renewal, as rediscovery, of the actual *Lebenswelt.* . . . Presence in time, in order to locate itself as the constituent, must disocclude itself and re-present the past, rediscover itself within the hidden or forgotten presence, and meaningfully constitute the future." Enzo Paci, *The Function of the Sciences and the Meaning of Man,* p. 37.

114 See ibid., p. 451; also Kerry H. Whiteside, *Merleau-Ponty and the Foundation of an Existential Politics* (Princeton, N.J.: Princeton University Press, 1988), p. 96.

115 "For knowledge to progress," writes Merleau-Ponty, "what was background must become figure. We must stop seeing as a fatum that which is a result of our own activity." Quoted in Whiteside, *Merleau-Ponty and the Foundation of an Existential Politics,* p. 96.

116 Gramsci, *SPN,* p. 158.

117 Gramsci's study habits in prison were truly extraordinary, especially in light of his circumstances. In a letter written during his imprisonment in Milan in 1927, where he was awaiting trial, Gramsci bragged that in the previous three months he had read eighty-two books—this in addition to reading five daily papers, some magazines, studying German and Russian, and memorizing a short story by Pushkin. Antonio Gramsci, *Letters from Prison,* vol. 1, ed. Frank Rosengarten, trans. Raymond Rosenthal (New York: Columbia University Press, 1994), pp. 109–10.

118 This "attention to phenomenological detail," as Renate Holub has described it, can be observed in the following remark by Gramsci, on the world economic crisis of the 1930s: "Whoever wants to give one sole definition of these events or, what is the same thing, find a single cause or origin, must be refuted. We are dealing with a process that shows itself in many ways, and in which causes and effects become intertwined and mutually entangled. To simplify means to misrepresent and falsify. Thus, a complex process, as in many other phenomena, and not a unique 'fact' repeated in various forms through a cause having one single origin." Antonio Gramsci, *Further Selections from the Prison Notebooks,* ed. Derek Boothman, Notebook 15, §5, (London: Lawrence and Wishart, 1995), p. 219.

119 Quoted in James Schmidt, *Maurice Merleau-Ponty: Between Phenomenology and Structuralism* (New York: Macmillan, 1985), p. 122.

120 Maurice Merleau-Ponty, "For the Sake of Truth" (1946), in *Sense and Non-Sense*, p. 165.

121 Thomas Kuhn, *The Structure of Scientific Revolutions* (Chicago: University of Illinois Press, 1970), pp. 60-61.

122 Barbara Taylor, *Eve and the New Jerusalem: Socialism and Feminism in the Nineteenth Century* (New York: Pantheon Books, 1983), pp. xv-xvi.

123 Ibid., p. 285.

124 In his *Political Economy of Racism* (Boulder, Colo.: Pluto Books, 1993), for example, Mel Leiman announces that his study will treat race "as intricately connected with but ultimately subordinate to the class question," because racism "is predominantly a form of class exploitation" (p. 4). "Although race, gender and class remain closely intertwined, and struggling against racism and chauvinism [i.e., sexism] is the core of class struggle against capitalism, an explanation of the inferior position of women and blacks rooted in race and gender differences recedes in explanatory power relative to class" (p. 343). Similarly, Teresa Ebert, in *Ludic Feminism* (Ann Arbor, Mich.: University of Michigan Press, 1996), her insightful critique of poststructuralist feminist theory, determines that all questions of gender power relations reduce to the "class question" (p. 27), that "the struggle over gender, race, and class inequalities. . . are finally situated in the contradictions of the social division of labor" (p. 13). Ebert relies on an economistic, reified base-superstructure argument, even going so far as to suggest that the rape of women by men is merely an effect of capitalism. Teresa Ebert notes that male sexual violence is often treated serially, as a datum, writing, "Rape is seen as a local accident." But Ebert then goes on to reduce the phenomenon of rape to "the effect of the global working of patriarchal capitalism" (p. 20).

125 For Gramsci, Fontana writes, "politics is the activity by which reality is continually created and re-created"—a conception he borrowed from Vico (Fontana, *Hegemony and Power,* pp. 23, 29).

126 Gramsci, *SPN,* p. 190.

127 Paci, *The Function of the Sciences and the Meaning of Man,* p. 335. See also Shirley R. Pike, *Marxism and Phenomenology: Theories of Crisis and Their Synthesis* (Totowa, N.J.: Barnes and Noble Books, 1986).

128 Whiteside, *Merleau-Ponty and the Foundation of an Existential Politics,* p. 94.

129 Leslie Cagan, "A More Coherent Movement," *The Progressive,* Nov. 1990, p. 21.

130 "There must be something in the historical field to which Marxism can appeal, just as there must be something—however ambiguous—on the horizon of the perceptual field which I try to make my friend see [by a gesture] when walking along together outdoors." Albert Rabil, Jr., *Merleau-Ponty: Existentialist of the Social World* (New York:

Columbia University Press, 1967), p. 123.

131 David Abram, *The Spell of the Sensuous* (New York: Vintage, 1996), p. 39.

132 Whiteside, *Merleau-Ponty and the Foundation of an Existential Politics*, p. 81.

133 Rumi, *The Essential Rumi*, ed. Coleman Barks (Edison, N.J.: Castle Books/Harper Collins, 1995), p. 252.

CHAPTER 7

1   Antonio Gramsci, *Selections from the Prison Notebooks*, ed. Quentin Hoare (New York: International Publishers, 1971), p. 132. Hereafter cited as *SPN*.

2   Ibid., p. 382.

3   G. W. F. Hegel, *Reason in History* (New York: Macmillan, 1953), p. 66.

4   Charles Taylor, *Hegel and Modern Society* (Cambridge: Cambridge University Press, 1979), pp. 124, 125.

5   Theodor Adorno, *Minima Moralia* (London: Verso, 1974), p. 135.

6   Daniel Brudney, "Marlow's Morality," *Philosophy and Literature* 27, no. 2 (October 2003): 318-40.

7   Marshall Rosenberg, *Nonviolent Communication: A Language of Life: Create Your Life, Your Relationships*, 2nd ed. (New York: PuddleDancer Press, 2003).

8   Walter Benjamin, *Illuminations* (New York: Schocken Books, 1968), p. 256.

9   Maxim Gorky recorded a conversation with Lenin, in which the latter initially waxed ecstatic about his appreciation for the beauty of Beethoven's music, before suppressing his feelings of love: "'I can't listen to music too often. It works on my nerves so that I would rather talk foolishness and stroke the heads of people who live in this filthy hell and can still create such beauty. But now is not the time to stroke heads—you might get your hand bitten off. We must hit people mercilessly on the head, even when we are ideally against any violence between men. Oh! our work is hellishly difficult.'" Quoted approvingly by Georg Lukács in *Lenin: A Study on the Unity of His Thought* (Cambridge, Mass.: 1971), p. 94.

10 Ibid., pp. 162, 13.

11 Arne Johan Vetlesen, *Perception, Empathy, and Judgment: An Inquiry into the Preconditions of Moral Performance* (University Park, Pa.: Pennsylvania University Press, 1994).

12 Ibid., p. 9.

13 Vetlesen, *Perception, Empathy, and Judgment*, p. 158.

14 See Sandra Lee Bartky, *"Sympathy and Solidarity" and Other Essays* (Lanham, Md.: Rowman and Littlefield, 2002).

15 Santosh George, "The Crisis of the American Left" (unpublished, 1992), pp. 1, 4.

16 Although this is only a thought, one could speculate that the sudden shift of political allegiances and affective attachments among socialists in the First World War—i.e.,

from the working class to the virulent forms of nationalism—was due to the ease with which a "one-sided" compassion, coupled with *ressentiment* (in Nietzsche's specific sense of that word), could be turned from socialist praxis to military aggression. In this regard, Hannah Arendt was on to something important when she noted, in her remarks on the French Revolution, the danger of admitting compassion into the political arena. However, as Vetlesen shows in his extensive critique of Arendt's Kantian skepticism toward the relevance of the emotions in moral judgment, it is even more dangerous to suppress or degrade empathy in political or moral action—as the case of the Nazis and death camps demonstrates all too well. See Vetlesen, *Perception, Empathy, and Judgment*, pp. 85–125.

17 Subcommandante Marcos, *Shadows of Tender Fury: The Letters and Communiqués of Subcommandante Marcos and the Zapatista Army of National Liberation* (New York: Monthly Review Press, 1995), pp. 214–15.

18 I am thinking in particular of Whitman's poem "I Sit and Look Out," which begins: "I sit and look upon all the sorrows of the world, and upon all oppression and shame, / I hear secret convulsive sobs from young men at anguish with themselves, remorseful after deeds done, / I see in low life the mother misused by her children, dying, neglected, gaunt, desperate." The poem continues on in this vein, of bearing witness, until the poet concludes, "All these—all the meanness and agony without end I sitting look out upon, / See, hear, and am silent." *Leaves of Grass* (New York: Boni and Liverite, 1921), pp. 234–35. Marcos in effect changes only the ending of Whitman's poem, challenging us to speak out—and to take strategic collective action.

19 Ludwig Feuerbach, *Principles of the Philosophy of the Future* (Indianapolis and New York: Bobbs-Merrill, 1966), p. 52.

20 Ibid., p. 52.

21 Marx, "Economic and Philosophical Manuscripts," in *The Marx and Engels Reader*, ed. Robert C. Tucker (New York: W. W. Norton, 1978), p. 116.

22 Ibid., p. 115.

23 Ibid., p. 87.

24 Pico della Mirandola, *On the Dignity of Man, On Being and the One, Heptaplus* (Indianapolis, Ind.: Bobbs-Merrill, 1965), p. 5.

25 Citing Pythagoras, Pico goes on to argue that the divine part of the human soul is reason. It is what brings us closest to God. Pico resolves the tension between Apollonian and Dionysian through a mystical dialectic in which we essentially *swoon with Reason*. "We shall be possessed. . . by these Socratic frenzies, which will so place us outside of our minds that they will place our mind and ourselves in God. . . . Then Bacchus the leader of the muses, in his own mysteries, that is, in the visible signs of nature, will show the invisible things of God to us as we philosophize, and will make us drunk

260   NOTES: PAGES 215-220

with the abundance of the house of God." Ibid., pp. 13-14.

26 Feuerbach, *Philosophy of the Future,* p. 67.

27 Ibid., p. 67.

28 Marx, "Economic and Philosophical Manuscripts," p. 116.

29 Antonio Gramsci, letter to Giulia Schucht of December 7, 1931, quoted in Dante Ger-
    mino, *Antonio Gramsci: Architect of a New Politics* (Baton Rouge, La.: Louisiana State Uni-
    versity Press, 1990), p. 215.

30 Feuerbach, *Philosophy of the Future,* p. 71.

31 Ibid.

32 Ibid.

33 Karl Marx, "Economic and Philosophical Manuscripts," p. 95.

34 As he and Engels scoffed in the "Manifesto": "A part of the bourgeoisie is desirous of
    redressing social grievances, in order to secure the continued existence of bourgeois
    society. . . . To this section belong economists, philanthropists, humanitarians,
    improvers of the social condition of the working class, organisers of charity, mem-
    bers of societies for the prevention of cruelty to animals, temperance fanatics, hole-
    and-corner reformers of every imaginable kind." Marx and Engels, "The Manifesto of
    the Communist Party," in *The Marx and Engels Reader,* ed. Tucker, p. 496.

35 For example, the Nazis owed many of their genocidal technologies and racial tropes
    to the practices of animal agriculture ("breeding"), and the mass industrial killing of
    animals pioneered in the Chicago stockyards. See William Patterson, *Eternal Treblinka:
    Our Treatment of Animals and the Holocaust* (New York: Lantern Books, 2002).

36 Carol Adams, "On Beastly Theology," in *Beyond Animal Rights: A Feminist Caring Ethic for
    the Treatment of Animals,* ed. Josephine Donovan and Carol J. Adams (New York: Contin-
    uum, 1996). Also see Carol Adams, *The Sexual Politics of Meat: A Feminist-Vegetarian Critical
    Theory* (New York: Continuum, 1990).

37 Josephine Donovan, "Attention to Suffering: Sympathy as a Basis for Ethical Treat-
    ment of Animals," in *Beyond Animal Rights,* pp. 147-69.

38 For a brilliant critique of the limits of Marx's conception of animals and nature, see
    Ted Benton, "Humanism = Specieism: Marx on Humans and Animals," *Radical Philoso-
    phy* 50 (1988): 4-18; also Benton's *Natural Relations: Ecology, Animal Rights and Social Justice*
    (London: Verso, 1993). Continental philosophers have recently begun to explore the
    phenomenology of human-nonhuman animal *Mitsein,* or intersubjectivity. See Peter
    H. Steeves's pathbreaking anthology, *Animal Others: On Ethics, Ontology, and Animal Life*
    (Albany, N.Y.: SUNY Press, 1999).

39 Theodor Adorno and Max Horkheimer, *Dialectic of Enlightenment* (New York:
    Continuum, 1993).

40 Toni Morrison, *Beloved* (New York: Random House, 1987), pp. 88-89.

41 Should it develop into a full-fledged movement, metahumanism could have the cultural power of a "second" Reformation (or a "second" Islam). To take Gramsci's references to socialism as a "church" and its revolutionaries as "priests" literally, for a moment: the postmodern prince might find the need to manifest through metahumanist "churches," replete with metahumanist prayer books, hymnals, and choirs. Existing social movement practice is ad hoc, ephemeral, fleeting—and increasingly ludic and libertarian. Establishing a meaningful spiritual and political presence at the grassroots level—meeting places for the community, a house of worship for a "congregation" to meet—would be a way to ensure continuity of the movement, a contemporary homologue to the radical union halls of old, but with a universalist rather than "corporatist" focus.

42 Daniel C. Matt, *The Essential Kabbalah* (Edison, N.J.: Castle Books, 1997), p. 154.

43 Gabriel Marcel, *The Mystery of Being: I. Reflection and Mystery* (Chicago: Henry Regnery Co., 1960), p. 252.

44 Herbert Marcuse, "Political Preface," *Eros and Civilization* (Boston: Beacon Press, 1966), p. xxv.

EPILOGUE

1 Antonio Gramsci, quoted in Giuseppe Fiori, *Antonio Gramsci: Life of a Revolutionary* (London: Verso, 1970) p. 147.

2 Donna Haraway, "A Cyborg Manifesto: Science, Technology, and Socialist-Feminism in the Late Twentieth Century," *Simians, Cyborgs, and Women: The Reinvention of Nature* (New York: Routledge, Chapman & Hall, 1991), p. 176.

3 Maurice Merleau-Ponty, *Adventures of the Dialectic* (Evanston, Ill.: Northwestern University Press, 1973), p. 4. For an excellent introduction to Merleau-Ponty's existential political thought, see especially Kerry H. Whiteside, *Merleau-Ponty and the Foundation of an Existential Politics* (Princeton: Princeton University Press, 1988). Martin Jay provides a succinct overview of Merleau-Ponty's shift toward an open-ended view of totality in his chapter on "Phenomenological Marxism: The Ambiguities of Maurice Merleau-Ponty's Holism," in *Marxism and Totality: Adventures of a Concept from Lukács to Habermas* (Berkeley: University of California Press, 1984), pp. 361–84.

4 Subcommandante Marcos, *Shadows of Tender Fury* (New York: Monthly Review Press, 1995), p. 245.

INDEX